INDIAN OCEAN

Mitsamiouli

GRANDE COMORE
(Ngazidja)

Itsandra
Beach

Moroni • Karthala

COMORO ISLANDS

Mutsamudu *ANJOUAN*
(Ndzouani)

• Domoni

Mamoudzou

Fomboni

MAYOTTE
(Maore)

MOHELI
(Mwali)

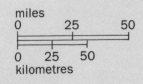

miles
0   25   50

0   25   50
kilometres

355.3

LAST OF THE PIRATES

The Search for Bob Denard

SAMANTHA WEINBERG

Pantheon Books ▥ New York

Library of Congress Cataloging-in-Publication Data

Weinberg, Samantha, 1966-
Last of the pirates: the search for Bob Denard / Samantha Weinberg.
p.   cm.
Includes bibliographical references.
ISBN: 0-679-42202-1
1. Denard, Bob, 1929-   . 2. Revolutionaries—Comoros—Biography.
3. Mercenary troops—Africa—Biography.
4. Comoros—Politics and government.   I. Title.
DT469.C7D468   1994
355.3'5—dc20   94-22427
[B]   CIP

Manufactured in the United States of America
First American Edition
9 8 7 6 5 4 3 2 1

To my grandparents, Lilian and
Harold Le Roith, whose
unbending confidence and
unqualified love has been a
constant support to me.

Contents

Murder most foul, as in the best it is,
But this most foul, strange, and unnatural.

Shakespeare, *Hamlet*
Act 1, Scene 5

Chronology

1843	Mayotte becomes a French Protectorate.
1884–6	Grande Comore, Anjouan and Moheli become French Protectorates.
1946	The Comoros are given 'Territoire d'Outre Mer' status.
1961	SAID MOHAMMED CHEIK becomes first President of the Comoros.
1970	Said Mohammed Cheik dies. PRINCE SAID IBRAHIM becomes President.
1972	SAID MOHAMMED DJAFFAR is president for two months until elections in December, won by AHMED ABDALLAH ABDEREMANE.
1975	Abdallah declares unilateral Independence on 6th July, but Mayotte refuses to secede. *First coup:* Abdallah is deposed on 3rd August SAID MOHAMMED DJAFFAR takes over as interim-president. Abdallah goes into exile in Paris.
1976	ALI SOILIH becomes President on 2nd January. France suspends aid. December: massacre of Comorians in Majunga.

1977   Ali Soilih disbands central government.
        Karthala erupts.

1978   Iconi massacre in March.
        Second coup: Ali Soilih deposed on 12th May by
        French mercenaries.
        ABDALLAH returns to become joint-president
        with MOHAMMED AHMED.
        Ali Soilih shot.
        December: ABDALLAH takes sole power.

1985   Attempted coups foiled, many imprisoned.

1987   Attempt to free prisoners fails.

1989   *Third coup:* 26th November, Abdallah is shot.
        27th November, the head of the Supreme Court,
        SAID MOHAMMED DJOHAR becomes
        interim-president.
        15th December, mercenaries leave for South
        Africa.

1990   SAID MOHAMMED DJOHAR wins
        presidential elections.
        Max Veillard shot.

1992   *Fourth coup:* Cheik and Abderemane Abdallah
        lead military coup attempt.

1993   24th April, ringleaders of the coup are sentenced
        to death. Sentences later commuted to life
        imprisonment.

LAST OF THE PIRATES

1

Pirates and Battling Sultans

I WATCHED THE PLANE ICON on the video screen above, silently tracking our route south from Nairobi, over Mount Kilimanjaro, then east, skirting the top of Zanzibar before heading into the vast, blue expanse of the Indian Ocean. Destination: the Comoros.

I had wanted to go to the Comoros since I first read about the islands five years earlier, in a book called *The Africans* by an American reporter, David Lamb. Buried in a chapter entitled 'Coups and Countercoups', between pages 111 and 120 – a disproportionately large section for the size and importance of the islands – lay the story of the Comoros:

> The Comoro Islands are only a speck in the Indian Ocean, four volcanic islands that, from the window of an airplane, look no bigger than icebergs, lost and adrift in the choppy seas . . . The islands are very beautiful and very poor and are known primarily, if at all, for their ilang ilang [sic], an exotic flower whose extract is widely used in French perfumes.

It seemed a romantic opening, but the story that followed was peculiar, even by African standards, where the bizarre and mystical are frequently accepted as normal. Lamb described a Cloud Coup-Coup Land filled with spice and intrigue where presidents were deposed as soon as they came to power, drugs were legalised, civil servants made to crawl through the streets in burlap sacks and teenagers were given guns in a sinister echo

3

of Mao's Cultural Revolution. He wrote of dreams and dogs and prostitutes and mercenaries.

Lamb gave me a name for one of these mercenaries: Bob Denard, a Frenchman, whose reputation was forged in the often bloody battles that accompanied the 'winds of change' which blew across Africa from the time decolonisation began in 1960. After working as a mercenary in the Congo, Katanga, the Yemen, Benin, Gabon, Angola, Biafra – the sight of these names sent a rush of adrenalin to my head – Denard had turned his attention to the tiny Comoro Islands and over-turned two presidents in three years. He was depicted as a *Boy's Own* hero, a romantic, modern knight, who fought on the side of good against corruption and brutality. It was perhaps Denard's love of adventure that attracted me most.

I had visited my grandparents in South Africa every year of my life and each time we had ventured slightly further north into 'the dark continent'. Those annual doses had served to feed my fascination with Africa and fuel a growing desire for adventure. As soon as I finished my studies, I went to live and work as a journalist in Johannesburg, scouring sub-equatorial Africa for material for articles. I travelled from Namibia and Angola in the west to Mozambique and Madagascar in the east, and the more countries I visited, the more remote my destination and the more bizarre my subject, the greater my enjoyment. I felt a different person out there; my cycle of highs and lows was magnified; I climbed the highest mountains of optimism and joy and fell into the lowest troughs of depression and pessimism. But I always felt alive.

In December 1989, I returned to the Namibian capital, Windhoek, after two weeks researching an article on dehorned rhinos in the desolate mountainous desert which comprises the far northwest of the country, to find the Comoros on the front of every paper. Banner headlines shrieked: MERCENARIES OUT! END OF AN ERA FOR THE DOGS OF WAR.

I read on. It appeared from the reports that there had been

another coup attempt on the tiny islands, in the course of which the President had been killed. The details were hazy; no one was sure exactly what had occurred and within days the story had faded out of the newspapers. All that seemed certain was that Denard was there at the time.

I determined that one day I would find a way to go to the islands and discover the real story of Denard, the perfume plants and the Comorian cultural revolution.

*

Thirty-seven thousand feet below, the apparently endless expanse of drought-dried, empty Africa turned briefly into a tangled mess of muddy delta. Then suddenly, the brown turned to an uninterrupted blue. The ocean seemed as infinite, as majestic, as overbearing as the land had been, and somehow more welcoming – yet at the same time treacherous, as if taunting the parched land with its volume of water.

I stared out of the window until the shimmering blue of the ocean seemed to be imprinted on my pupils, looking out for four small islands, described in an early travel book as: 'adorning the neck of the Mozambique Channel like a necklace of emeralds'.

The first sign of an interruption to the vast expanse of blue, was a heavy bank of grey cloud hanging over the island of Grande Comore. But as we circled lower I saw that the cloud did not cover the entire island, instead it hovered darkly over the mountainous centre, protecting the great Mount Karthala (the largest active volcano in the world) from prying eyes.

We shadowed the western coastline. From above, the mass of green vegetation, palm trees and rocks, seemed almost devoid of the white beaches I had thought were such a dominant feature of island life in the Indian Ocean. The runway came into focus, perched on a strip of land halfway up the west coast, as unnatural as an artificial limb. A fierce scar of black volcanic rock ran from the shrouded mountain and stretched into the sea, metamorphosing into a line of jagged rocks. As we made our descent, the deep, opaque blue of the sea became translucent turquoise crowned with flecks of white surf. We landed, passing over two small 'galawa' fishing boats just off the coast, which looked like halves of a scooped out banana, with arms on either side, afloat on the ocean.

As I disembarked from the jumbo jet, I was hit by a hot blast of air. My fellow passengers, a brightly-coloured crowd carrying bulging, cardboard boxes tied up with string, appeared unconcerned. They sauntered across the tarmac looking quite cool; the few women wrapped in patterned cloths, the men in long, thin white cotton robes or casual clothes, most sporting a smart embroidered white and cream Muslim hat known as a *koffia*. I lagged behind.

I was met by Papa Claude from the Galawa Hotel where I was to stay for the first few weeks.

'Welcome, welcome to the Comoros,' he said, ushering me into a small bus.

Papa Claude talked non-stop during the half-hour ride to the hotel.

'The Federal Islamic Republic of the Comoros consists of three islands; Grande Comore, Anjouan and Moheli. The fourth island making up the archipelago, Mayotte, elected to remain a French colony at the time of independence in 1975 . . .'

We were driving north towards Mitsamiouli, the second-largest town on the island of Grande Comore. The road was bordered by tall, verdant hills on the right and the clear turquoise sea on the left. Most of the coast was made of rough, black rocks of lava, which looked like lumps of charcoal and the few beaches we passed were full of Comorian children and fishermen, who turned to stare at the bus.

'. . . The total population of the three islands is close to 480,000, of which about half live on Grande Comore . . . Around 98 per cent of the people are practising Muslims. Islam is very important to our culture . . .'

I noticed that there was at least one white mosque in each of the tiny villages that straddled the coastal road and sitting around each of them, were flocks of men in *koffias* and white robes known locally as *bou-bous*.

'. . . Our major exports are vanilla, ylang-ylang – used as a base for perfumes – and cloves . . .'

It was very green and luxuriant. We drove past many brightly-coloured flowers and vines until we entered the outskirts of Mitsamiouli, which Papa Claude himself described as a village. A few faded Moorish buildings straggled along the edge of the wide, white, rubbish-strewn beach, while narrow streets reached inland. Most people seemed to be sitting around watching life pass lazily by, or wandering on the sand. The only sign of energy was a small group of yellow-shirted footballers running up and down one side of the beach.

'. . . The great majority of the population are tied to agriculture and fishing. But the economy depends on the outside world for the satisfaction of its most basic needs – rice represents an average of 50 per cent of the value of imports of basic products . . .' Papa Claude continued his litany in accented French.

Not far past Mitsamiouli, the bus turned left through the entrance of the hotel grounds. After the journey, it seemed like a piece of paradise; long, white and cool, situated on a promontory with the sea on either side.

That afternoon I joined Papa Claude at the pool bar. There were couples all around, lying by the pool, perched on stools by the bar inside the pool, and sipping coloured cocktails beside us. Most spoke with an unmistakable South African drawl, though there was a smattering of French accents as well. The hotel had been closed after the coup of 1989, but had reopened a year later.

I explained to Papa Claude why I was in the Comoros by myself and he pointed across the bay to a pretty, honey-coloured beach villa, covered in greenery, which stood on a tiny private beach.

'That was Bob's beach house,' he said. 'He often used to spend weekends there and would come to the hotel with his family on Sundays.'

'Does anyone live there now? Do you think I'd be able to look inside?' I asked.

'It's empty but I'm sure you could have a peer around. You'll have to ask Tony Kaye, who owns the boathouse. He was a good friend of Bob's. Unfortunately, he's away at the moment, but he'll be back next week. You know, we also have the wreck of the Masiwa here, the boat in which the mercenaries arrived in 1978. You could dive to see it.'

We both gazed at the house across the water as I tried to imagine the veteran mercenary amidst the palm trees. I failed.

'How many children have you got?' I asked Papa Claude.

He laughed. 'Me? None. I'm not married yet.'

'So why are you called Papa?'

'Ahh, it's because I look like my father. Everyone calls me Papa, it's quite a common name in the Comoros.'

'So why aren't you married?'

'I haven't enough money. You see, marriage is the most important event in a person's life in the Comoros and their standing in the village is affected by the kind of marriage they have. To be one of the elders or notables, you have first to make a "Grand Mariage" and that is very expensive. Sometimes it costs as much as twenty years' salary. But there is a grand mariage in M'Beni this weekend – would you like to come to it with me?'

Papa Claude explained that belief in the institution of the *grand mariage* was one of the main differences between the last two presidents (both eventually deposed by Denard); Abdallah, who was a traditionalist and wanted to preserve the old values – and the more radical 'Maoist', Ali Soilih, who believed it was a waste of money and wanted to abolish it in its present form.

'Were you a supporter of Ali Soilih?' I asked Papa Claude.

'No, no,' he chuckled wryly. 'You see I was interested in the

8

tourist trade even at that time. I had a lemur when I was seven and used to show it to all the tourists. Ali Soilih wasn't interested in tourism. He wanted to make this country into a socialist paradise. He was anti-capitalism – no one could own two houses – and he was anti-Islam, or at least, in its fundamental forms. He created a "Jeunesse Revolutionnaire", who were the real power in the country at that time. They were committees of young people, who ran every village – there were no police. They were violent, well paid and didn't go to school. Although if they had, they would have been your typical bully or teenage delinquent. They didn't respect the elders of the village and denigrated them. Everyone was scared of them and they thought up all sorts of horrible punishments.'

'Were you ever punished by the Jeunesse Revolutionnaire?'
'Yes, I was.' He grimaced.
'What for? What did they do to you?'
'I was fifteen years old at the time and one day I wore a pair of shorts. They grabbed me and said: "This is a Muslim country, you are not allowed to wear shorts," – that is how hypocritical they were – "you are sentenced to work without pay for twenty-five days in the 'modiria' ", which was a sort of village administrative centre. I had to leave school and work for that time. But mine was an easy punishment. Robbers had to do "rampart", which was when the JR put salt on the road and made the criminals crawl along on bare knees for 100 metres. And if anyone didn't keep to Ramadan, they were stripped to their pants, their faces were masked in white paint, shells were strung around their wrists and they were made to walk around the village while the youths sung out their faults and taunted them. "Are you going to do that again?" they were asked over and over. It was a form of public humiliation. We called it "mandamano".'

'So you must have been pleased when Bob Denard came to overthrow Ali Soilih?'
'Yes, all the people were very pleased,' Papa Claude said.

Then he added, 'Well, maybe not all. You had better talk to Ali Toihir, the hotel's public affairs attaché. He was in Ali Soilih's government. He'll be on duty tonight, just ask anyone for him.'

I went back to my room to change for dinner.

Each night the hotel had a theme connected with the islands' culture and Monday was 'Sultan's Night'. A group of hotel employees dressed up as the sultan and his hareem and moved around the tables joking with the guests. A good-looking, dark-skinned man in his early forties, with a neat moustache, came to sit beside me.

'Good evening, my name is Ali Toihir. Welcome to the Comoros.'

I asked him to tell me about the history of the islands.

'We have a long and colourful past. The Comoros were not always as you see them now,' he began. 'In the fifteenth and sixteenth century, they were a centre of maritime trade ruled over by powerful and power-hungry sultans – hence our nickname; "the archipelago of the battling sultans" and hence the performance tonight.' He glanced slightly ruefully at the sultan and his women.

The Comoros started to prosper as a stopping-off point for sailors, mainly because of their strategic position at the head of the Mozambique Channel. Ships carrying goods between the centre of Islamic trade, Kilwa, on what is now the Tanzanian coast, and the large and prosperous island of Madagascar, stopped on the way to take on board fresh water and replenish foodstuffs for the second leg of the journey across the often treacherous Mozambique Channel. Later, the archipelago was also a convenient staging post for European ships on their frequent trips to and from India.

The sixteenth century was a prosperous period for the Comoros; they traded with Portuguese settlers in Mozambique and Arabs in the Gulf. The island of Anjouan, for instance, was recorded as importing opium and cotton cloth from the Red Sea area and exporting rice, ambergris and slaves.

The first European challenges to the Portuguese stranglehold on trade in the Indian Ocean came in the early seventeenth century, with the founding of the British East India Company and its French and Dutch equivalents. They scoured the western Indian Ocean for bases, setting them up on the islands of St Helena, Mauritius and Madagascar and on the southern-most tip of the continent at the Cape of Good Hope. But the Comoros, with their ideal position, remained a favoured calling point. As a result of this, pirates moved into the western Indian Ocean. They based themselves on the northeast coast of Madagascar and waited for heavily-laden ships to come sailing up the Mozambique Channel. Frequently they set up ambushes around the Comoros, pouncing on the trading ships as they came in for fresh water and food. The pirates would wander through the islands' bazaars, picking up snippets of information about the movements of company trading ships and often selling their plundered property to the natives and sultans.

The ships from Europe would stop at a port and buy large quantities of foodstuffs, often whole herds of cattle and goats, which stimulated the economy and promoted trade. For a variety of reasons, they preferred certain ports – especially in Anjouan – and this initiated spates of inter-island rivalry. As these intensified into violent conflict, the different sultans sought protection and support from foreign powers, including the Europeans, Malagasy and East Africans. The inter-island raids also had a darker motive: the enforced recruitment of slaves, at that time by far the most lucrative trading commodity in the region. The sultans remained on good terms with the pirates, enjoying the benefits of increased trade and fearing the consequences of double-crossing them. But when the Dutch East India Company intensified its war on piracy, the islands became less secure as bases and the pirates began to view them as targets for attack and plunder.

'So you see Samantha, what happened here recently with the mercenaries, was only really a repetition of events that have occurred over and over in our islands' history.'

With that, Ali Toihir wished me goodnight.

2

Le Grand Mariage

P APA CLAUDE took me to see the old man of Mitsamiouli.
He led the way off the main road and deep into the maze of
alleys that snake into the hinterland. The deeper we went, the
simpler the houses were – stone turned to wood and grass. We
stopped on the way to visit his aunt. Her house was one dark
room dominated by a huge and ornate, carved wooden bed,
encrusted with enamel inlays. A couple of sepia photographs
hung on the wall, but apart from that there were few
ornaments. I was to find the same scene in almost all the
Comorian homes I visited; the bed was the most important
feature and frequently functioned as chairs and sofa. It
was normally large and beautiful and immaculately covered.
Papa Claude later told me that Comorians love sex.

We walked into the heart of the old town, passing the *place
publique* and the ablution pond. The *place* was an enclosed,
tumbledown square area fashioned out of stone and volcanic
rock. It was empty, as the centre of activity had moved out to
the main road.

The old men used to wash in the ablution place, a putrid,
green, square pond, down many steps, surrounded by high,
dark walls. Papa Claude said he would never use it, as he
suspected the water to be contaminated by men with infected
testicles. But some very old men still bathed there.

We sent a young boy to tell the old man we were coming,
while we went into a cramped, dark shop to buy him a present.
I gazed around in the gloom, trying to find something that
would make a suitable gift, but all I could see were stacks of

soap and tins of condensed milk. Papa Claude, however, found what he was looking for and plucked a plastic bag of disposable razors from the wall. 'This is what he would like.'

We followed the boy to the old man's home, a small dank room. He was sitting in a shaft of daylight on a rattan bench. We sat facing him on his narrow bed, covered by a yellow, foam mattress. He looked very old indeed. He was thin and shrunken and had lost all his teeth. When he spoke, it was with a pronounced lisp. He appeared to be delighted with the plastic razors and when – on Papa Claude's urging – he slipped off his white embroidered scull cap, it was to reveal a thick crop of brilliant white, closely-shorn hair.

I asked him about the legends of the islands. The old man started to speak with a quavering voice, fiddling with green plastic worry beads:

'Many many years ago, King Solomon came to these islands to celebrate his marriage to the Queen of Sheba. They were married inside the great volcano Karthala and when they left, they put her golden throne inside the crater, where it is guarded today by the jealous spirit, Bondé Souli.'

I encouraged the old man to continue, but he appeared lost in thought, gazing at a piece of sacking, printed with the words MADE IN POLAND, that was tacked on to the wall. Along with the sack were all manner of souvenirs tied with string to rusty nails that stuck out of the wall; some old legal dossiers, a cardboard packet, two pairs of old black shoes, old Arabic newspapers, a pair of black plastic sunglasses and sun-faded photos.

'A man as old as me has witnessed much and remembered much. I have many stories to tell,' he began again. 'The Portuguese came to the islands in the sixteenth century. They landed at a village called Bandamadji, but their boat was a wreck and they couldn't leave. They asked the villagers for help and the villagers replied that the stepladder – "ngazi" – was coming – "idja". The Portuguese thought they were telling them the name of the island, so they called it

"Ngazidja". We still call it that today, although the French name is Grande Comore.' The old man relapsed into private reverie.

I went back to Ali Toihir and asked him if it was true that King Solomon had married in the Comoros.

'That is the legend. But the earliest archaeological finds date back only to the fifth century, so nobody knows.'

During the latter part of the eighteenth century and first half of the nineteenth, the Comoros were engulfed in civil war. French plantation owners who had settled in Ile de France (now Mauritius) and the Seychelles, were eager for slaves and the sultans and chieftains of the Comoros and Madagascar fought each other to provide them and to find new sources of supply. The Comorians responded by building fortresses and citadels, and walls around the major towns, but still devastation was wreaked. The sultans looked to their European trading associates for protection, but they only sent arms and ammunition. Events in Madagascar eventually put an end to the raids, but not before the Comorian economy had suffered and the population declined. However, the rivalry between the battling sultans was undampened and in Anjouan, the feud between the towns of Domoni and Mutsamudu led the Sultan to invite the first mercenary, a Malagasy chief, Ramanataka, to settle on the island in 1828 – a move Abdallah essentially echoed a hundred and fifty years later, when he brought Bob Denard to the islands in 1978. Ramanataka went on to help the Sultan conquer the island of Moheli.

Victories in the Napoleonic Wars resulted in the British taking over Ile de France, the Cape of Good Hope and Ceylon and, in the peace that followed, extending their influence into the Sultanate of Oman. They forced anti-slavery treaties on to the coastal rulers and intensified their commercial activities. However, as the British started developing better communication networks and routes, annexing Aden in 1832, so the Comoros lost some of their importance as an international stopping-off point.

The French stepped in, occupying the islet of Nossi Be – off the northwest coast of Madagascar. But they still needed a naval base and so it was that in 1840, they struck a deal with the ruler of Mayotte, who signed a treaty ceding the island to France.

The British responded by establishing consulates on Zanzibar, off the Tanganikan coast, and on Anjouan. A period of relative political stability followed, although the Comoros were already in decline. Hard hit by the earlier pirate raids and particularly by the British crack-down on slave trading, the final blow came with the opening of the Suez Canal in 1869, which diverted the main shipping lines via Egypt. By the end of the decade only two or three ships stopped in the Comoros each year.

Around this time the islands started attracting the attention of colonial planters. The French developed sugar plantations on Mayotte and the British consul on Anjouan, William Sunley, started his own sugar factory, which proved to be very successful, thus encouraging Arab businessmen and the Sultan himself, to build their own. Sugar concessions on Grande Comore and Moheli were granted to foreign businessmen (in partnership with the local rulers), who prospered from the strong worldwide demand. In 1886, Grand Comore was made a French protectorate.

'That was really the end of our complete independence and the beginning of colonialism, which continues – whether officially or unofficially – to this day,' Ali Toihir told me. 'It wasn't a bad time for the Comoros: there was a certain amount of simple prosperity, work for our people and an end to the danger posed by raids from abroad. The focus of the violence shifted, as the rivalry between sultans intensified, until there was only one sultan on each island. The last Sultan of Grande Comore's grandson is a friend of mine, I will introduce you to him, Samantha. I think you will get on well.'

*

The next evening, Papa Claude picked me up after 'Tropical Night By The Pool', to take me to the 'harusi' – the *grand mariage* – in M'Beni.

We drove in the dark along the rutted, coastal road towards the north. Occasionally an open-sided bush taxi, sometimes without lights, would whoosh past us. The air was warm and I could make out the outlines of giant fruit bats as they swooped across the face of the moon. We stopped to pick up two women walking along the road, heading for the same wedding. They were from Mitsamiouli and had started out two hours previously. They knew Papa Claude and flirted and giggled with him. The larger one was wearing an extraordinary pink and silver ruffled dress. Papa Claude whispered to me that they were 'femmes de la rue', almost prostitutes.

'You see, for us it is very important for unmarried women to be virgins. Otherwise the marriage cannot go ahead. And Comorian men like women very much, sometimes they cannot wait until they are rich enough to get married, so they turn to the local women who are themselves too poor to attract a husband.'

'Do they pay them?'

'Yes, a little.'

'Is marriage just about money?'

'No, but many marriages are arranged by the parents. Often, the husband and wife do not meet until their wedding day. And because in the Comoros it is the women who own the homes, the poor ones tend to lose out.'

'How come the women own the homes?'

'That is the marriage bargain; a woman only gets married when her father has built her a house to live in. In return, the new husband pays the woman's family a dowry. You have seen all the half-finished houses around? They are normally started when a daughter is born and slowly finished as and when the father can afford it.'

'So where do these women live?' I asked, gesturing towards our giggling companions.

Papa Claude shrugged, maybe a little too casually: 'Probably with their families or together in makeshift houses.'

The village of M'Beni is the fourth largest in the Comoros, the stronghold of Said Mohammed Taki, one of the major opposition politicians and according to his opponents, a ruthless man. But to the villagers of M'Beni, he is a hero. The streets thronged with people in their party clothes – the men in smart, old-fashioned, baggy, dark suits and the women in *chirumanis*. It had started to rain softly and we parked the car at the house of a young friend of Papa Claude's sister. The friend had celebrated his *grand mariage* a year earlier. Although he was still young, his family were rich and had helped him to pay for it. His wife was pale-skinned, pretty and heavily pregnant. She swooped around fetching us thick sweet coffee, but only came to sit down when the men, a group of serious-faced elders in pressed suits and *koffias*, had left. Her young husband, by virtue of having had a *grand mariage*, is now among the village *notables*, a facet of the system that Ali Toihir had found particularly repugnant.

'Why should they be elevated to a respected position, regardless of their age and education, just because they wasted a lot of money on a four-day party?' he had said to me at the hotel earlier, explaining that he had preferred to have a civil wedding and use his money to give his daughters the best education available, at the French Lycée in Moroni.

But Papa Claude's friend's wife seemed happy with her new marital home. She kept it in a state of absolute neatness, decorated in the rather kitsch style – with varnished toffee-coloured ornaments and carved dark wood furniture with crimson *faux*-velvet cushions – that Comorians appear to favour. I asked why she hadn't gone to the ceremony with her husband and she explained that, as she has already celebrated her *grand mariage*, she is not allowed to go to another without her husband's permission.

'And he's made you stay at home tonight, when everyone in the village is outside at the celebrations?'

I was beginning to feel indignant, when she silenced me with a glance at her bulging stomach.

After saying goodbye, we went up a steep mud and stone track to the home of the bridegroom's family to view the bridal jewellery. This is one of the groom's major expenditures and the success of his wedding would be judged by the weight of gold he had bought, as well as by the lavishness of the ceremony. *Grand Mariages* can cost as much as 10 million Comorian francs (around £20,000). That night we guessed there was half a kilo of intricately-worked gold necklaces, rings, hair combs, bracelets, a gold watch and even a tiara, most made in the distinctively Comorian filigree style. The centrepiece was an ornate gold necklace, so heavy that I could not imagine anyone wearing it. Even Papa Claude looked impressed by its richness and whispered to me that it was a pretty good showing. The jewellery was displayed on a black velvet board, watched over by female relatives, who cooed and fussed, proudly collecting compliments as the guests walked by.

We then went to visit the bride in her new home, hidden up some stairs overlooking a cobbled, narrow alley in the old town. By the time we arrived it was raining quite heavily and an endless stream of people had tramped mud over her new green linoleum floors. Another bunch of women stood receiving the guests. We admired the new flock furniture and the bride's presents to the groom, laid out ceremoniously on the new carved double bed. They included the heavy black and gold robe he would wear for the betrothal the next day, a shirt wrapped in cellophane and a minutely embroidered new cream and white *koffia* which, Papa Claude informed me, would have taken three months to complete.

I was ushered through a hanging beaded door to see the bride, who was small, pale-skinned again, and pretty, her wrists decorated with intricate henna patterns.

Meanwhile the groom was having a ball. The dancing took place in what is, in the daytime, a food market. Fairy lights and paper decorations had been strung up for the occasion. A modern band was playing whining Arabian melodies on electric guitars and a synthesiser at one end, while the *notables* and honoured guests sat on wooden folding chairs in the middle. The rest of the men clustered around and the women stood on a ledge that ran along the inside edge of the building. When I went to stand with them, my *chirumani* merging in with theirs, an old lady came up to me and started chattering furiously in Comorian and pointing at something. I looked around for help and all the women started trying to enlighten me at the same time. During a slight lull, a young girl standing near me explained in French that the old woman was insisting I sashay up the aisle to put money in the box in front of the stage. This money would be given to the band and used to benefit the community – perhaps to paint the market walls.

I felt very conspicuous as I joined the line of elegantly clad men, some sporting a red fez above their dark suit, each carrying a walking stick, which they waved in the air in a hypnotic, graceful fashion. With about four hundred people watching, we waltzed up to the swaying melody and around the stage, brandishing our 1000 Comorian franc (about £2) notes, before ostentatiously putting them into the box. On the way back, I passed a man who rubbed his grimy notes all over my face. Here it was then, pure, unashamed, glorification of money. When I beat my red-faced retreat to my place on the ledge, the women smiled and congratulated me on my dancing.

We stood around for a long time, watching the men dance as if in slow motion. The French speaker, who had moved next to me, pointed out the young bridegroom, dressed in a tuxedo and bow-tie. She said, with awe in her voice, that he worked in Paris as a clerk, which was why he could afford to have a *grand mariage* at such a young age. I thought how sad it was that his future wife – who he may not yet have met – was missing out on such a stupendous party.

Papa Claude beckoned me out of the market, into the street, where the rain was still gently falling.

Le Grand Mariage

'What do you think?'

'It's wonderful. How long do they keep dancing like that? Do the women ever get to dance?'

'The women danced their dances earlier in the day. The men also danced different dances last night. Tonight they will continue until the early hours and tomorrow is the betrothal.'

'What happens there?' I asked.

'Well, they say their vows and afterwards they go back to their new house and spend their first night together. And, you'll like this, the grandmother spends the night under the bed.'

'What?'

'She's there really to make sure that everything goes off all right and for her granddaughter's protection. When they first get into bed, the grandmother knocks on the door three times, which is the signal for the groom to join her in the kitchen, where she watches him eat the aphrodisiac dinner she has prepared earlier . . .'

'What's the dinner made of?'

'Normally it's rice with chillies, garlic, nutmeg and cloves. They both then return to the bed and while he climbs in, the grandmother slips underneath. In the morning, he has to give her the blood-stained sheet attesting to the girl's virginity, which she then proudly displays in front of the village.'

'What if the girl has, you know, ridden too many bicycles?'

Papa Claude chuckled. 'Then the grandmother slaughters a chicken and uses its blood to stain the sheets. Nobody ever knows the difference.'

We searched for the two women we had given a lift to, to see if they wanted to come back with us. They were nowhere in sight – the pink and silver dress would have been hard to miss – and I suspect Papa Claude was maybe a bit disappointed when we gave up and wended our way back through the puddles to Mitsamiouli alone.

*

21

Ali Toihir was still up when we returned to the hotel after midnight. I told him we had been to a *grand mariage* celebration.

'What did you think of it?' he asked. 'It was impressive wasn't it? Did you go to see the bridal jewellery, did you see all the gifts? That is what Ali Soilih wanted to abolish; not our culture as he has been accused of doing, but the terrible waste of money. The Comoros have no chance to develop while the institution is in its present form. People save their whole lives for the occasion – often the men are in their fifties or sixties when they get formally married in this way – and then they squander all their hard-earned money in a cavalier fashion on something very ephemeral and most of it goes on imported goods. Afterwards they often give up working altogether and spend their time lolling around in the mosques. Still it's an important tradition, I just wish we could have the celebration without so much expense. But the elders hated Ali Soilih for trying to do this.

'Personally, although I agree with him about the grand mariage, I think he went about dismantling it in the wrong way. He didn't understand the importance of it in Comorian society. He was a very intelligent man and he believed in himself and in logic. The prophet, Mohammed, once said that custom and tradition are stronger than reason and intelligence. Ali wanted to change all that.

'There's the Prince I promised to introduce you to. Shall we go and say hello?'

I smoothed my hair and followed Ali as he threaded his way through the tables full of hotel guests. He stopped at the edge of the dance floor and pointed to a smallish middle-aged man who was dancing energetically to the pumping disco music. He was wearing white trousers, a black shirt with a huge monogrammed 'N' on the pocket, opened to show a white string vest, a zipped white waistcoat, white pop-socks and shoes and a belt with the same large 'N' on the buckle.

'That's Naçr-Ed-Dine,' Ali told me. 'He loves to dance. He

sometimes keeps the discotheques open all night while he dances. He's also President Djohar's cabinet chief.'

The Prince left his dancing partner and came to talk to us, although his hips didn't seem to notice and kept swivelling. He had a strong, honey-coloured Arab face; sloping forehead, large nose and intelligent eyes. His greying, thinning hair was brushed forward. He grabbed my hand and bent over to kiss it: 'Mademoiselle, enchanté. Welcome to the perfume islands.'

'Thank you. I think they are very beautiful.'

'Yes, you're right of course. I used to live in Paris, but whatever the comforts there, they don't compensate for the beauty of the Comoros. But have you seen the whole island? Yes? No? Well then you must come with me tomorrow – we're taking the President's helicopter to see Karthala.'

3

Karthala and the Prince

F EW CARS WERE ON THE ROAD at dawn, as I bumped
along in the first *taxi-brosse* of the day on my way to the
old airport. My fellow passengers were cheerful and sang
along to the Comorian music that was piped through from the
front of the truck. As we passed through the town of Itsandra,
my next door neighbour nudged me and said something about
mercenaries. I learnt that Denard and his crew had landed on
the beach when they came to depose Soilih in 1978. But there
was a different, more peaceful scene that morning; about forty
galawas, each with a lone fisherman inside, clustered around a
shoal of fish about 100 yards offshore. The small fishing
shacks clung to the arms of the bay and the rising sun just
caught the roughly-planed sides of the wooden canoes.

My neighbour smiled and introduced himself as Mahamoud
and said he was studying accountancy by correspondence. He
was neatly dressed and clutched a purple, plastic file to his
chest. He told me that he lived in a village above Moroni, near
Denard's old home and promised to show it to me later that
day. When we started talking, the other nine passengers, who
were crammed in the back together with baskets of mangoes
and bananas and cardboard boxes full of oddments like pans
and plastic plates, turned to listen.

'Why do you come in a taxi-brosse?' an old man asked.
'Normally the mzungus travel in green buses or cars.'

I told them that I didn't have the money to hire a car and that
the green buses of the tourist company didn't go anywhere at half-
past four in the morning. They laughed. 'You are a brave mzungu.'

We relapsed into companionable silence as we entered the outskirts of Moroni on what was my first visit to the capital. We had missed sunrise, hidden on the other side of Karthala, but a soft light diffused over the huddled shacks as we rounded the corner to the port, and was absorbed by the curved plaster walls of the great Friday mosque until they glowed a warm, muted pink. The lights inside caught the silhouettes of robed men against the delicate arches that defined the façades of the two-storied building.

The taxi swept along past a small shop. Barely more than a roadside shack, it announced its name in ragged painted letters over the crooked fading green door: 'Bon Chic Bon Genre'. The shop next door was simply named 'Chance'. There were more cars on the road now. Small, white, and often battered, Renault 4 taxis buzzed around, stopping to pick up extra passengers. These would squeeze in with whoever else was already in the car. Most people, however, were walking even at this early hour – throngs of them – clean against the scruffy streets and buildings, balancing fruit and vegetables in large palm-frond baskets on their heads.

I was dropped off at Iconi airport, which used to be the main airport before the new one was built at Hahaya with international aid money. The Prince was waiting there with his brother, Prince Kemal (who bore a remarkable resemblance to the young Haile Selasse) and Kemal's son, Jamil. Making up the party, was a technician from the Post and Telecommunications Ministry – for whose purpose the trip had been arranged – and two very lean and dignified French military pilots, their hair cut *en brosse*. They wore regulation gold-rimmed Rayban Aviators and khaki fatigues faded to exactly the right degree. They didn't say much, but occasionally turned to give a terse smile.

The helicopter – the President's own and the only one in the country – started warming up and we strapped ourselves in. We floated over the runway, before swooping across to Moroni and up Karthala's thickly-vegetated slopes. The

Prince sat beside me, smiling and patting my knee. He was wearing another extraordinary outfit; a matching bomber jacket and slacks, with a paisley cravat, trainers and mirrored shades. He looked like a hairdresser from the Sixties.

'In my capacity as cabinet chief, I am also commander-in-chief of the Comorian army,' he shouted into my ear. 'Do I not look like a soldier? We're going up to the mountain to see if Abbas', he gestured at the man from the post office, 'can work out a place to fix up our new satellite communications base.'

That sounded like a serious upgrade for the Comorian telephone system, which boasts only twelve international lines – eight routed through Paris and four for the rest of the world. Trying to reach anyone, even on the island, had often been more trouble than it was worth as the phones seemed to be permanently out of order and on the rare occasions I managed to get through to someone, the crackling was usually too intrusive for conversation.

We swooped on upwards, over more villages. The further up we went, the smaller and scraggier they got, until all signs of human habitation stopped and we hit the first strands of early morning cloud. The Prince grabbed my hand as we reached the crown of the volcano. We circled the crater and gazed down into its deep gaping mouth. The sides were steep and at the bottom there was a small, milky turquoise lake ringed with yellow froth. Sulphurous smoke was rising from the bubbles. Then we dropped below ground level into the crater and circled in the opposite direction in a wisp of soft cloud, gazing into the heart of the volcano, before landing. We could have been on the moon. The last small eruption, the Prince told me, had emanated from one of the secondary craters halfway up the main crater's walls. It had destroyed most of the bushy vegetation on one side, leaving a scab of dry mud.

The Prince and Jamil jumped into a small crater and Jamil gave me his disposable Kodak camera to take a picture of them. The co-pilot showed me some wild raspberry plants –

the berries shining as bright as brake lights – growing under rough, gorse-like bushes.

'Allons-y, we have to go, before the visibility gets too bad,' the pilot called to Abbas, who was strolling around from vantage point to vantage point, his *bou-bou* floating in the soft breeze. The Prince held out his hand to help me into the helicopter and then kept hold of it, as I tried to fix my seat-belt. By the time the engines had warmed up, the clouds were closing in. We took off and headed down the mountain.

'Look, there is Iconi, the village of my family,' said the Prince, pointing out a fort on top of a semi-circular hill. 'During the sixteenth century, the women of Iconi committed suicide by jumping off that hill – rather than be taken captive by marauding pirates. The wall you can see used to surround the family arsenal.' The pilot pointed out a school of dolphins, cavorting in pairs in the opalescent sea.

The Prince had said we could talk after the trip, but on our arrival we were greeted by the colonel-in-chief of the small French force in the Comoros, a Colonel Da Silva. Naçr-Ed-Dine looked torn between self-importance and regret as he beckoned me over. 'My dear, I am afraid I have some urgent affairs of state to attend to. But perhaps you would do me the honour of dining with me tonight. I will come and pick you up at seven.'

I wandered back towards town and into the tiny Café du Port. From a seat on the balcony, I gazed at the beautiful, old, big-bellied wooden boats, their ribs bleached and splintered, that rocked inside the simple marina.

When I finished my Coke I walked up the hill to the old market. Wherever I went, people stopped what they were doing and called out: 'Mzungu, mzungu. Edje [greetings]. Edje. Mzunguuuu.' I walked on. Men and women sat on the ground, lining the sides of the steep road, with their wares spread out on cloths in front of them: garlic and spices, peppercorns, tomatoes and mangoes, stinking fish and ageing meat, chickens – live and dead – cigarettes, detergent, blank tapes . . . The women were swathed in colourful *chirumanis*, the men in *bou-bous* and the food in flies.

Mahamoud lived in a small village a mile and a half above Moroni. He was sitting with a couple of friends on a whitened stone bench on the side of the road, still clutching his purple plastic file.

'Samantha, Karibu – welcome to my village, come and meet my mother.'

I followed him to a small cement-block house down a rutted track.

'Maman, may I present my mzungu friend, Samantha? Samantha, may I present my mother?'

'Edje!'

'Njema! [I'm fine]'

Mahamoud's mother was a small, neat-looking woman. She shyly beckoned me into her house; three tidy rooms, two with large beds and one with a table and a few chairs. She indicated that I should sit down and brought me a glass of sweet lemon juice, which I accepted gratefully. She sat smiling, watching us drink.

'My mother doesn't speak any French,' said Mahamoud. 'Many of the older generation never got that far with their schooling. Come with me and I'll show you my house.'

I said 'Lalaunono' [farewell] to his mother and followed Mahamoud into a tiny palm-frond hut. There was a small bed on the floor and a single chair and desk. His clothes were hung, neatly pressed, on hooks on the wall.

'When the young men reach puberty, they build their own houses, like mine,' explained Mahamoud. 'We eat with our families, but sleep on our own. Come, now we must go and look at Bob's house.'

Further up the road, the temperature was a little cooler and the vegetation more lush; ripe mangoes and giant speckled papayas weighed down the branches of the trees and there was a strong sweet smell of ylang-ylang. We passed many large white houses, part-hidden behind tall, padlocked gates, including one that Denard owned – but did not live in. Mahamoud said that most of the houses in this area – Daché – were owned by government ministers.

Denard's main residence was half a mile further, at the end of a short drive. It looked as though no one had lived there for some time. We snooped around and peered in the windows.

'The government wanted to claim his houses, but Bob said he would kill anyone who lived in them without his permission. He built them for his children,' said Mahamoud.

The large house was pleasant and honey-coloured with a big, dark, intricately-carved front door. French windows lined the front of the house, leading on to a veranda hemmed in by arches. We wandered round to look inside the numerous guest cottages. Many of the windows had been smashed and despite the bars on all of them, the inside of the house was empty. I asked Mahamoud where all the furniture was, but he just shrugged. We climbed up a little hill behind the house, to see Denard's small, perfectly symmetrical, private mosque, made of weathered plaster. Everything was still.

*

The Prince picked me up punctually and drove back to Moroni at tremendous speed, with scant regard for the state of the frayed and pot-holed road. He made charming small-talk and waved his hands around. By the time we parked, I had lost my appetite. He led me down a narrow alley into the heart of the old town, the Medina. Tall tenements on either side shut out the moon and starlight. We entered a small courtyard through a wooden door studded with brass horns, and climbed the steps to the second floor.

The Prince's apartment was elegant and understated. The window shutters were made of carved wood and the floor of white tiles. The furniture was minimalist and there were plants in the corners. A spotlight hidden under a small table threw intricate patterns on the walls. The paint was peeling off in places and the ceiling had started to subside, but everything was impeccably tasteful.

'This is lovely,' I said to my host, who was taking off his aggressively pin-striped jacket to reveal a matching waistcoat, and loosening his purple and green patterned tie.

'It is very humble for I don't have any money. But I was trained as an architect and practised architecture while I was in exile in Paris – during Abdallah's reign,' he explained. 'I don't do too much these days as politics keeps me busy but', he wagged his finger at me imperiously, 'I have only taken the post as cabinet chief as a strategy to improve the chances of my party, Chumma. It was the party of my father and now it is run by Kemal and myself. Chumma is known for having all the pretty girls.'

'Please tell me about your family.'

The Prince poured himself a large glass of whisky, put a classical compact disc on at low volume, dimmed the lights and settled down on a cushion on the floor.

'My great-grandfather, Samantha, was the sultan of Anjouan, Sultan Said Omar. He sent his son, Said Ali – my grandfather – to school in Cairo, where he became friends with the French ambassador and the King of Egypt. When his father died, my grandfather was given money by the King of Egypt to enable him to return to the Comoros. On reaching Grande Comore, he found it divided into small sultanates, constantly at war with one another. He was determined to unite these battling kingdoms into one peaceful country. But he could only do this by more war – this time he won with the support of the French and the aid of some rich Arab families based in Zanzibar. He proceeded to liberate the land and give it to the peasants. Sultan Said Ali died in Tamatave, on the east coast of Madagascar in 1916.'

The Prince appeared in no hurry to eat. A manservant he claimed to have borrowed for the evening from a local restaurant, hovered in the background waiting for a sign, but the Prince kept going with the whisky.

'When Sultan Said Ali died, his family came back to the Comoros, but they had no money. The sultan's wife was forced to sell her jewellery to pay for the children's schooling. Said Ibrahim stayed on at school in Tamatave, where he was consistently head of his class. He returned to the Comoros when he graduated and worked as a "petit functionnaire" for the French. He was a brilliant man and spoke the most beautiful French [as indeed did his son, Naçr-Ed-Dine]. He was very proper, very principled, a philosopher and conciliator, but not, in my opinion, a good politician. However, at the age of twenty-six, he became governor of Grande Comore.

'In 1940, at twenty-eight, he was one of the first to respond to De Gaulle's pleas for help and mobilised the Comorians to fight in the Second World War. De Gaulle never forgot and from that time onwards they were friends. As a reward, in 1946, De Gaulle suggested that the Comores could be "detached" from Madagascar and invited Prince Said Ibrahim to become a deputy in the French parliament. But around this time there was another brilliant Comorian student, Said Mohammed Cheik, studying medicine in Madagascar. He returned to the Comoros and joined forces with my father. Inevitably, however, after a time they became the heads of rival parties known as the Parti Blanc and the Parti Vert, and stood against each other at the next election. He had nowhere near the popular support of the Prince, but after huge electoral chicanery on Anjouan – where a young man called Ahmed Abdallah was in charge of arranging the voting and counting – he won. Abdallah made sure that Said Mohammed Cheik took every one of the 21,000 votes there. In return, he was nominated to the French Conseille Generale and later to the Senate.'

'Was that the same Abdallah who Denard worked for?'

'Yes, the old rogue. But he was just starting out in politics in those days. Do you like champagne? Myself I love champagne. Please join me for a glass before we eat.'

The Prince disappeared through rickety double doors and

returned with a bottle of Mumm Cordon Rouge in an ice bucket. For a Muslim, he had a well-stocked drinks' cabinet.

'When De Gaulle came to power he granted the Comoros the right to two deputies. So his old friend Ibrahim duly joined his rival, Said Mohammed Cheik, in the French parliament. When I was a student in Paris, I went to dinner with my parents and De Gaulle and his wife three times. He was a remarkable man,' said the Prince.

The food started arriving at last; small golden spicy samosas, spongy crumpets, meat, liver, bananas and two different fruit juices. We sat on the floor around low tables with beaten copper tops. The Prince, however, didn't stop his narrative, eating his dinner agonisingly slowly and occasionally stopping to leap to his feet and wave his hands around to emphasise a point, before sitting back down and pressing more food on me. The phone rang incessantly.

'My wife had a baby today,' he explained, somewhat apologetically. 'She's in Paris.'

'How exciting. What's the baby called?'

'Her name is Fatima Nawar – which means light – Naçr-Ed-Dine, keeper of the religion.'

In between phone calls, he continued his story.

'Said Mohammed Cheik died in 1970 and Said Ibrahim became president. He had to cope with a powerful French lobby trying to detach Mayotte from the Comoros so it could be used as a French naval base. The people in Mayotte were keen on the idea of autonomy from the other three islands, but my father had managed to cajole them into staying united. If he had been president during Independence in 1975, the four islands would have been together today. There followed a period of intense politicking and propaganda from all parties, after which he lost a vote of no confidence and was forced to step down.

'That was the time I decided to enter politics. Abdallah was gaining in power. He was, by this time, a French senator. He had come to our house before the no confidence vote to try to persuade my father to stand up to the pro-French lobby, but my father refused. Abdallah was reputedly the first person to put his hand up to vote against him. My father was very upset at this betrayal, and it was when I saw the expression on his face that I decided I had to fight to change this kind of behaviour.

'Prince Said Mohammed Djaffar was made the next president, as Abdallah was still a senator and thus banned from taking an official role in party politics. But he was very busy behind the scenes, working to change the electoral system so that the power was ready to fall into his hands when he was elected president in 1972.

'One of the few politicians not to switch their allegiance to Abdallah when my father fell from grace, was a clever young man who had been minister of works. His name was Ali Soilih. He had been a rigorously honest minister, never stealing a penny from the state coffers. He had a romantic and mysterious side. He was a mesmerising storyteller and loved reading cloak-and-dagger novels. We were at school together in Tananarive and after that he went on to study in Madagascar and Paris. When he returned to the Comoros, he started working at the Caisse Centrale, where he quickly climbed the hierarchy. When Abdallah came to power, Ali Soilih and I and some like-minded friends created a new political party, Umma – the father of Chumma – with my father at the head. It rapidly gained support as the reign of Abdallah started its downhill slide. Many of the parties which had originally supported Abdallah joined forces with Umma to form the United National Front, which campaigned on a pro-Independence ticket.

'By this time, there was a tide of public opinion in favour of Independence. Elections were scheduled to take place towards the end of 1975, but on 6th July – as a last ditch attempt to ensure he was the first president of the independent Comoros –Abdallah declared unilateral Independence. Mayotte, however, decided it wanted to stay a part of France and voted to refuse Abdallah's declaration. A state of emergency was declared.

'Ten days later, a large prayer meeting was held in Iconi, where Umma supporters prayed for their party. Sixty young men turned up, armed with rusty knives and pistols, saying they were off to overthrow Abdallah. But Ali Soilih spoke to them and appealed for patience, explaining that careful planning was needed if the operation was to be a success.

'A core team of ten Umma supporters with military experience was assembled and we were all allotted roles in the forthcoming coup attempt. I was put in charge of immobilising all the possible opposition's cars and getting together eighty strong men to take the guns after we raided the arsenal. It was very funny on the day. For the first job, I recruited thirty men from Iconi and, armed with umbrella spokes, we went around town, sticking them into car tyres. Three men went to the prefecture and while two talked to the men in charge – there weren't many on duty, as it was siesta time – the third surreptitiously punctured tyres.

'I joined Ali Soilih and his men and, armed with four rusty shotguns and five pistols, we drove to the military head-quarters in two old Renault 4s. Ali told the sentry that there had been a coup d'état and that Abdallah was finished. The guards weren't feeling too well; the previous night we had started a rumour that Umma was going to make trouble and the military were up all night patrolling and watching for us. They were very tired. Ali stuck a gun under the sentry's chin, while three of our men broke down the arsenal door and grabbed machine-guns from the racks. The military rushed towards us, but we sprayed automatic gunfire between the ranks and the soldiers turned and ran. The country had been taken and no one had been hurt in the entire operation. We drove back to Moroni, where we let off some grenades in the streets to let the people know there had been a coup, and the rest of our young men came and grabbed the arms we had liberated. Ali then went to the radio station and made an announcement: "In the name of the people, today is a great day. The government of Abdallah is no more." He was thirty-nine years old.'

By this stage the Prince was pacing the room, waving his arms around. He was keen to open another bottle of champagne, and continue the story. But we had already been talking for four hours and had only reached the 3rd of August 1975. I remembered the drive from the hotel and begged him to let me catch a taxi home.

'Certainly not. I cannot let you go back alone. But first we must visit my brother Kemal.'

It was a balmy night. We drove to Kemal's house, where despite the late hour there was a crowd of people sitting on benches in the garden, drinking whisky. Kemal insisted on showing me around his garden, a beautiful orchard planted with lemons, oranges, grapefruits, mangoes and papayas.

'Look at our rocky soil. Would you believe that fruit could grow like this? Why don't our people start growing more fruit? We could be rich from fruit, but instead they prefer to import rice from China. Look at this garden; is this not beautiful?'

He reminded me of the Last Emperor of China, retired from the world to become a gardener. Kemal was similarly passionate about his orchard.

Fortunately, one of the other people at Kemal's was heading towards the hotel and offered me a lift home. I left as Naçr-Ed-Dine was getting stuck into another large whisky and muttering about nightclubs.

*

Ali Soilih was content to control everything from behind the scenes after the coup and Prince Said Djaffar was once again elected interim-president. Prince Said Ibrahim declined to take office himself until democratic elections had been held, but gave his support to the interim government. However there was a problem: the French Ambassador had warned Abdallah of the planned coup and he had managed to flee to his home island of Anjouan on an old Air Comores DC4, where he holed up and threatened to secede from the Comoros or organise a countercoup. Ali Soilih knew he had to be stopped, but his young army had no experience, and Abdallah had seventy trained men with him on Anjouan.

Soilih turned for help to his friend Yves LeBret. A French hero from the Second World War, who had settled in the Comoros and created Air Comores and the Maloudja Hotel (now the staff quarters of the Galawa Beach), LeBret had connections in Paris and was rumoured to be close to the government. He contacted a friend of his, an Algerian ex-senator called Claude Dumont, and explained the problem. Dumont said he knew a man who could help and phoned an old friend of his, the most famous of French mercenaries, 'Colonel' Bob Denard.

LeBret, Dumont and Denard met in Paris. LeBret explained the situation to Denard – that Abdallah's conservatism and corruption had made him increasingly unpopular with the people and his inflexible stance towards Mayotte had led to its separation from the other three islands of the Comoros. Denard had been going through a bad stage; since the end of the Congo wars, the demand for the services of professional mercenary soldiers had waned and he had been existing for some time on more peripheral work. He thought that Ali Soilih – an ally of the noble Prince Said Ibrahim and a professed moderate – represented the hope of the future.

Forty-eight hours later, on 19th August, Denard agreed to help Soilih and immediately dispatched two men to the islands: a pilot from the Gabonaise Presidential Guard (which Denard had helped to set up), and a former French Secret Service officer. Denard flew straight to Gabon to raise troops and with the $15,000 he had been advanced, bought 300 automatic weapons and hired a plane from the veteran campaigner based in Rhodesia, Jock Malloch. He touched down in Moroni on 5th September 1975, dressed in the uniform of a French army colonel, complete with a row of decorations and the insignia of a paratrooper on his chest. He brought with him 10.4 tonnes of 'special freight'.

The weapons were stored at Yves LeBret's villa and the next day, Denard's five officers arrived on the Air France scheduled flight.

Denard's first meeting with Ali Soilih went well. 'Ali is intelligent and speaks well. He has theories which seem good. One could not have predicted what he would have become,' Denard wrote later. Soilih thanked Denard for coming and acknowledged he was in need of assistance.

The next fifteen days were frantically active. Denard and his men recruited an army of Comorian youngsters and embarked upon an intensive training programme. His deputy, Rene Dulac, another old brother at arms, arrived.

D-day: midnight 20th September 1975. The troops assembled at the airport. At 4 am, the first plane, a Cessna carrying four people, took off, followed by the remaining planes at that time in the Air Comores fleet, a DC3 and DC4 carrying a total of a hundred and twenty men. Dulac and LeBret landed in the Cessna and took the control tower. Abdallah, hearing the shots, fled to Domoni on the other side of Anjouan. The rest of the men disembarked and started heading across the island, the newly-trained Comorians brandishing their empty firearms – only the mercenaries' guns were loaded. They made rapid progress and there was only one incident; a young relative of Soilih's called Moissi, was surprised by a guard at a crossroads and was decapitated with a machete. He was later made a hero of the revolution and Ali Soilih named his élite unit of guards after him.

Denard and his men laid siege to Abdallah in Domoni and after forty-eight hours, he surrendered. To his great surprise he was given a send-off at the airport with full military honours due to a head of state. On his arrival in Moroni, he was put under house arrest in his Daché mansion, guarded by three attractive young women.

That evening, the governing committee held a meeting to try

to decide what to do with Abdallah. Ali Soilih urged the others not to kill him. 'Are you crazy? We have just achieved a near bloodless revolution – do you want to spoil it?'

At the end of the year, Abdallah was allowed to slip out of the country with a diplomatic passport, having been made to swear on the Koran that he would never re-enter politics. He left for Paris with a cheque from Ali Soilih for 300 million Comorian francs (about £600,000).

The Comoros were ripe for the ideas of the young Ali Soilih.

4

The Madman of Moroni

I WAS INVITED to a party at Denard's beach house. Tony Kaye, the owner of the boathouse, had opened up the small house at Trou de Prophete for his staff to celebrate the last Thursday before Ramadan. They would have a blow-out night of drinking, smoking and dancing before the strictures of the fast began.

I walked along the beach, lit by the last sliver of the waning moon to a soft, shimmering silver. The waves crashed against the reef and the smell of salt mingled with the wafting scent of ylang-ylang. The party was in its early, mellow stages. Tony's son, Graham, showed me around the house. It sat at the end of a bumpy road on a grassy lawn, just above a private beach. Ahead lay the bay, with the lights of the hotel sparkling on the far side and to the left was the Trou de Prophete – a deep water 'hole'. The house was small, surrounded on three sides by a wide veranda covered in palm thatching. The outside walls of the veranda were made of scalloped stone, supported by dark wooden poles, which the men from the boathouse had decorated with crispy, pink bougainvillaea and banana palm leaves. They had put wooden chairs outside and on the veranda. The man in charge of the food stood guard over a barbeque, cooking bananas and manioc – a bread-like vegetable.

The house had been completely gutted by the locals. There was no furniture, no windows or doors. Only the basic structure remained: one large bedroom, a smaller one and a bathroom. The kitchen was in a small outhouse to one side.

But the heart of the house must have been on the terrace, under a big, fragrant frangipani tree (now in full bloom) that sat at the edge of the small, grassy garden.

'That's where I first met Denard,' said Graham. 'He was sitting in a large armchair under the tree having a cup of tea. His wife and kids were with him. He seemed like a very nice, regular guy.'

'How come he's given your father this house?'

'Well, he hasn't exactly been given it, but Bob told him we could use it. Dad's considering moving in, but he doesn't want the local guys or the present government to associate him with Bob. There's still a lot of bad feeling about.'

A wiry man with rheumy eyes came up and offered me a samosa and meat with pancakes. He introduced himself as Ahmed – 'but you can call me Ed' – and said he had organised the party, paying a woman to clean up the house and delegating the cooking and decorating amongst his colleagues at the boathouse. What was I doing in the Comoros, he asked?

'I'm trying to find out more about the islands' history and about Bob Denard,' I told him.

Ahmed's face stiffened into a sneer that was half fearful, half derisory: 'The mercenaries! They treated us badly. They put me in a water tank filled up to my neck and made me stay there for six hours. Then they threw me into jail where I nearly starved.'

'Why? What had you done?'

Ahmed was called away, but gestured for me to wait, that he would be back soon.

The music started. First they put on the waka-waka – which means chatter-chatter in Comorian – to which catchy beat each new batch of tourists at the Galawa were taught a special dance. It was not unlike the Birdy Song: 'Na-mana-mana – ooh-ooh, waka-waka – ayaaee. Numanamanamanaa-aa oooh-oooh wayaaayee.' The men from the boathouse were laughing as they imitated the 'entertainments manager' and the tourists. Then they put on genuine Comorian 'Volcanique' music and starting moving their bodies in fluid and rhythmic gyrations. The beat was more African than Arabian and it was impossible to keep still. The music was turned up and everyone was soon saga-ing and dancing up a sweat together. Bruce Lee, a small guy from the boathouse, greeted guests at the door in a falsetto South African accent: 'Hi guys, I'm Bob Denard, welcome to my house.'

'Don't they mind that it's his house?' I asked Ahmed.

'No, tonight it is a Comorian house. Tonight it is a party house.'

The atmosphere reflected well on Denard. The men had never been to the house before. Denard had very much kept to himself in the Comoros, no one really knew what he had got up to in his private life, but there were no ghosts floating around, just the shell of a simple beach house.

Ahmed's words, however, had cast a shadow over Denard. I wandered down to the boathouse the next morning to find him. His eyes looked more bloodshot than ever.

'It looks as if you had a good night. How're you feeling today?'

He winced. 'Ramadan starts in a couple of days. I'm not going to be able to drink or smoke for six weeks. It was worth it.'

We sat under a palm tree with some fresh mango juice and Ahmed chain-smoked as he told me his story. But first he made me promise I would not write his real name.

'Why, who are you scared of?' I asked.

He just shivered and shrugged. 'It is not good to talk too much in the Comoros. You never know when the mercenaries might be back.'

Ahmed came from Moroni. He was seventeen when the Comoros declared themselves an independent state. At Soilih's accession to power he became one of the committee members of his local branch of the Jeunesse Revolutionnaire. There were sixty branches around the islands and each was run by a committee of young people – all under eighteen – twelve senior delegates and ten juniors. Their job was to police the area and keep the streets quiet and clean. One of Soilih's first acts when he was voted in as president on 2nd January, 1976, was to break all ties with France, which involved among other things, expelling the French expatriates and dissolving the gendarmerie. If someone was caught doing wrong, they would be hauled in front of the committee and lectured on the aims and rules of the revolution.

'But why were all the committee members young?' I asked Ahmed.

'The old people were very set in their ways. The young people could understand the new situation. Ali Soilih made many broadcasts on the radio explaining how the country was going to change its rhythm from colonial to independent. His main aim was to educate the people; everyone was taught to read and write in Comorian, schools were built and the young were encouraged to extend their education. We built a "modiria" in each region to house the administrators who would help to sort out the problems of people living in their villages. The youth were paid CF 6,000 – the maximum salary – to work on these houses. It was a good idea, because if anyone had a problem, they didn't need to travel all the way to Moroni to sort it out.

'But the old people didn't like Soilih. They said he was destroying our traditions, because he banned women from wearing black veils, legalised marijuana and wanted to abolish the grand mariage as it was a waste of time and money. He thought the marriage ceremony should only last for one day. And he wanted to reform the notables, who spend most of their time in the mosques. Soilih tried to persuade them that after saying their prayers they should go to work. They didn't like that, but if they kept disobeying orders, they were sent to jail for three days and made to do "rampart".'

'Don't you think that old people should be respected, instead of being ordered about by teenagers?'

'Yes . . . well no . . . I don't know. Ali Soilih had to teach them the new ways. The Jeunesse Revolutionnaire were his mouthpiece. We had sworn against violence and fighting. He told us that we had to explain to an offender the right route before resorting to punishment. He was a good man. He wanted to uplift the country – now people would like him back.'

'But was Ali Soilih all good? If so, why was he known as the Madman of Moroni?'

Ahmed just shrugged and went to help some tourists rig up a boat.

*

I went to find Ali Toihir and explained I wanted to talk to someone who would give me a balanced view of Ali Soilih.

'Maybe you should go and see Mouzawar Abdallah. He was Ali Soilih's foreign minister, but I think he would give you a fair impression. Be careful though, he is a very clever man. People call him "the Snake" because he always somehow manages to keep out of trouble.'

Mouzawar's telephone was not working, so I caught a *taxi-brosse* into town and dropped a note through his door. It was approaching midday on a Friday and most of the town were preparing themselves for the week's most important prayers. I walked down to the port and settled inconspicuously on a high wall outside a small mosque facing the great Friday mosque. In the light of day, its walls had lost their pink glow and looked as if they could do with a lick of Dulux, but its curves were still gentle and its proportions near perfect.

'Allah akbar ashad ala ilaha ilallah ashad ana Mohammed rasul-lah'

The mwadhini's call to the faithful echoed through the crescent-shaped Place Badjani. Men started to trickle into the square, gravitating towards the mosque. All were wearing white *bou-bous* and *koffias*, the *notables* were distinguishable by their flowing coloured coats and embroidered scarves. They carried small prayer-mats and some also held the *tasbih*, prayer beads, to help them count their thousand prayers to God.

From my vantage point, I could clearly see the diverse origins of the Comorian people; Arabian like the Prince, Malayo-Polynesian and African. Above their uniform white *bou-bous*, their facial characteristics were emphasised. A few looked up and shouted 'Edje! Are you going to pray with us?'

'Njema! How can I? I am a woman,' I joked back.

Cars pushed into the square as the mwadhini's call was broadcast from loudspeakers at the top of the tower. The trickle turned into a steady flow and then into a torrent as the calls became more urgent. The Friday mosque quickly filled up. Hundreds of pairs of shoes on the steps testified to the number of people squashed inside. The two smaller mosques were also full and the overflow milled around the great tree in the middle of the *place*, or crammed on to the balconies of nearby shops and offices (including the aptly-named Royal Transit). Everyone was chattering.

As one o'clock drew nearer, latecomers hurried towards the mosques and jammed the square with parked cars, paying no attention to a gendarme who waved his arms around and tried to prevent vehicles from entering. An army truck rumbled up and two soldiers got out, their uniforms clearly visible through the semi-transparent *bou-bous*.

Just before one o'clock, a soft wailing came from the speakers. There was absolute silence. Facing north, everyone knelt on their mats, prostrated themselves, sat up again, down, up, stood. Not completely synchronised, it looked like a complex Mexican wave. Four small boys, squashed in the back of a Renault 4 truck parked in the centre of the square, were about twenty seconds behind the main body of people, but concentrating hard, their eyes closed, they held their rhythm. After a short period of stillness, the young boy standing on his mat on the wall just behind me started whispering his prayers. The whole square filled with whispers.

Then, as quickly as it began, it was over. There was a palpable release of tension and the area once again filled with chattering. Everyone looked happy and I felt myself echoing their smiles. People burst out of the mosques, all talking at the same time. They jumped in cars and started hooting or ambled away to a large lunch and siesta.

*

I woke the next morning to discover the students were on strike and had barricaded the roads. They, the teachers, hospital workers and civil servants had been striking on and off for three months over pay: they hadn't received any. The President, Said Mohammed Djohar – Ali Soilih's half-brother – had left the previous day for France to try to beg an advance on next year's aid money, in order that the people could be paid before the beginning of Ramadan. Radio Comores announced that his trip had been successful and that he was returning the next day with FF 8 million which he had promised to distribute immediately. So the strike was bound to be short-lived.

I decided to avoid the barricades by catching a galawa to Mitsamiouli. After some haggling, one of the galawa captains based on the hotel's beaches, agreed to take me there for CF 4000. He wore a grubby Total hat, white-rimmed plastic sunglasses, a pair of baggy, pin-striped trousers and jelly sandals. He introduced himself as Zebaba. I sat behind him on a little bench at the back of the boat. It was about the same size as a two-man canoe and there was barely enough room to fit my feet in the bottom of the boat. Zebaba paddled from the front, using a rough oar on one side. He told me that his galawa had been carved from the trunk of one mango tree. It had taken four men a day to make it.

Our progress was slow; partly because it was low tide and we kept getting stuck on sandbanks, but also because Zebaba's boat had a few holes in it, so we had to keep stopping to bail out.

He told me he had been one of the 'Jeunesse Revolution-naire' under Ali Soilih, whom he insisted was 'very sweet'. Abdallah was 'part-good, part-bad', while Bob Denard was 'un criminel'.

We rounded the headland to Mitsamiouli and came upon dozens of women wading in the shallows. They were wearing long dresses or *chirumanis* that dragged in the water and hats or cloth turbans on their heads. Each woman carried a branch of leaves to beat the water to attract the fish, which they caught in their cloth shawls and slipped into crude, basket-weave bags that they slung over their backs. They chattered constantly, laughing and calling out to each other across the water. But they fell silent when I approached and turned their backs.

'The Comorian women are very shy of mzungus,' Zebaba told me.

I clambered out of the boat not far from the shore and waded through deep, sticky sand until I reached the black rocks of lava. Once, when I fell over, I heard the women laugh.

I had landed at the north end of town and started walking, slowly in the muggy heat, towards the centre. Everyone I passed shouted 'Edje!' One young man walked alongside me and started talking in rapid unintelligible French about 'showbiz'. He said I could call him 'Madg – after Imagination, my favourite band.'

Students and teachers were milling around the centre of town.

A young man in a red T-shirt pounced on me: 'We, the teachers and professors, have been on strike for three months now. Don't believe anyone who says we have been off for five.'

'I'll take your word for it. Why are you on strike?'

'We haven't been paid since last year and we've had no pay rises since 1984. Our working conditions are terrible. We want to draw up a protocol with the government to improve our conditions.'

A student butted in: 'We, the students, are on strike in sympathy with our teachers [as if they had much choice].

Exams are coming up and because of the interruptions to the school year, we fear it will be another "année blanche".'

'We've set up road blocks around the island and on Anjouan and Moheli too, for an indeterminate length of time,' said another in a yellow surfing shirt.

'We won't stop the strike until the minister of finance is sacked,' said a teacher.

'Why?' I asked.

'Because he's a Mossad agent,' another replied.

When I asked some more students, they appeared to have different aims: 'We want books!' 'We want pay!' 'We want a new government!' 'Djohar must resign!'

I could see how Ali Soilih had managed to arouse the passions of the youth and to use them as the driving force of a revolution directed against the traditions of the lethargic elders.

An English teacher from the Lycée in Mitsamiouli was more eloquent: 'We are fighting for our rights; for the right to have reasonable living conditions. We are tired of not receiving our salaries every month and we can't feel motivated if we don't have the money to eat. If we aren't paid by Monday, there will be a tragic situation,' he added mysteriously, refusing to elaborate. But since the radio had said that Djohar had promised to pay them on Sunday and I knew he now had the money, I wasn't too worried.

I walked back along the road, skirting the barricades. The first were only a short way out of town; a felled palm tree followed by a wall of black lava rocks which some younger boys were decorating with coconut husks. Further on I climbed over another small wall, followed by a barrier made of bushes, the skeleton of a burnt-out car that had been dragged into the middle of the road and another palm.

A few tired-looking kids sat by the barricades, but they said they didn't know who had built the road blocks – nor why there had to be so many in a row on the only road around the island.

'These are good barricades,' they told me. 'No one could get past them.'

I reflected that an army truck filled with ten men would be able to take them down in no time. It exemplified the isolation of the independent Comoros – three small forgotten islands adrift in the Indian Ocean, with virtually no links to the rest of the world. While Eastern Europe was in turmoil and the Persian Gulf in uproar, the Comorian students were trying to overturn the government with decorated palm tree barricades. It was hard to appreciate the extent of the Comoros' isolation, until I was asked whether England was in Paris or heard Reunion Island referred to as 'the metropolis'. But it must have been different in the period before Independence, when France still exerted a strong influence over the islands; when the Comorian students had mirrored the French students in staging their own revolt in 1968. Ali Soilih and Ali Toihir had played an active part in that movement. Some people say that the slogan, '*l'imagination prend le pouvoir*', had stuck in the mind of the future president. However, while much had changed in the rest of the world since the heady days of 1968, the Comoros had stayed suspended in a time capsule.

*

Ali Toihir looked frantic when I arrived back at the hotel.

'We're trying to reorganise all the staff rotas for Ramadan. It causes enormous problems. No one's allowed to eat or drink anything at all during daylight hours and we have to pray five times a day. This means we get up at about half-past four in the morning for breakfast and can't have any food – or even water – until half past six in the evening. By the afternoon, everyone's wilting and short-tempered – especially the kitchen and dining-room staff.'

'When exactly does Ramadan begin?'

'It is signalled by the new moon. The moon is very important to us, not only is it the symbol of Islam – for that reason we have it on our flag – but it is thought that the Comoros were named after the moon. When the early sea-faring Arabs first came to the islands, they called them "El Kamar" – the Islands of the Moon and that is probably where "Les Comores" came from. The moon also dictates many of our actions; it tells us whether the time is propitious to marry or start a business – and it marks the start of Ramadan. Everyone gathers on the beaches in the evening the new moon is meant to appear and the first one who sees it cries out and rushes to tell the Qadi [religious leader], who is the only person allowed to announce the beginning of Ramadan.'

'But what if it's a cloudy night?' I asked.

'Well, then it's OK to hear the news on the radio. Ramadan starts on the same evening across the Islamic world and if, for example, they see the moon in Iran but not here, we can take that as the official start of Ramadan.'

I decided to walk down to Mitsamiouli to look out for the new moon. It was a warm evening, the setting sun cast a blue glow on some children who were playing volley-ball on the littered beach. Several men in immaculate *bou-bous* were promenading along the coastal road.

I stopped by the open area at the side of the road where a small knot of people had gathered to watch a game of dominoes. Six old men hunched around a wobbly plastic-topped table, jealously guarding their small pile of pieces. In turn each man would lift one up and, from a great height, slap it down on the table with a loud *thwok*. The game was fast and furious. If anyone laid down a dodgy piece, the others would shout 'Haa!' whereupon the offender would throw his hands into the air. There would be a heated post mortem, which the onlookers would join in, before the winner with obvious glee on his face gathered all the pieces and dealt them out for the next game.

Across the square, another small crowd had formed around two men playing Mraha, a game I had seen played in East Africa. They sat opposite each other with a wooden carved board between them. Above, flies were dying on a large, blue strip-light strung between two trees that lit the faces of the players as they frowned in concentration. They were very serious, seemingly oblivious to the noise generated by the domino players. Each player started with thirty-two dried beans which they scattered with dexterous, fluttering hand movements around the rows of shallow carved holes on either side of the board. Their supporters would nod sagely as a move was completed. A man tried to explain the rules of the game to me, but it was too complicated.

The light was failing but still there was no sign of anyone looking for the moon. At around half past six, the men started packing up their games and drifted towards the mosque where the mwadhini was calling them to evening prayers. Ramadan had begun.

I walked along the back streets, passing small doorways and rooms packed with people watching videos, their faces illuminated by the flickering glare from the television set. Children in ragged dusty clothes hung around the shadows, latching on and following me as I passed.

*

The army had indeed cleared away the barricades in the night, and the teachers and civil servants were paid one month's salary the next day. This enabled them to buy the ingredients needed for the elaborate nightly Ramadan dinners. During the fast, Comorians spend more than double what is normal on their food. Mouzawar Abdallah had invited me to his house that night. I should arrive at 6.30 pm when he would have finished his early evening prayer.

I found his house on a bend in the road up to Daché, very near the centre of town. It had a view of the comings and goings of the police station and prison. His office was in a small room on the ground floor and I walked up the outside steps to the living quarters on the first floor. Mouzawar greeted me on a vine-decked balcony. He looked exactly as I imagined a Comorian politician should look. He had an intelligent wizened face, thick glasses, a receding hairline, and just the right amount of facial hair to give the impression of being wise without being too obtrusive. He wore an immaculate, fern-coloured safari suit and polished shoes that clacked when he walked. He spoke in an impassioned manner, his voice rising and falling, in varying timbres, with well-judged dramatic pauses. I liked and respected him immediately.

'Hello Samantha, may I present my son, Kamil, and daughter, Jasmine. Do you mind if we sit down straightaway – it's been a long day,' he said apologetically. Kamil, meanwhile, was looking at the table and positively drooling.

At first we just concentrated on eating. Mouzawar's wife kept bringing more and more plates of delicious food through, but didn't join us herself.

'She's shy because she only speaks Comorian,' said Mouzawar. His children ate in silence, answering my questions in monosyllables, their eyes fixed on their plates.

Mouzawar, however, was the consummate host and kept me entertained with a stream of erudite small talk throughout the meal. 'We will talk business when we have finished,' he said.

More plates of food continued to arrive.

'Do you always eat like this?' I asked.

'No, this is for Ramadan. We don't eat all day, so we make up for it many times over in the evenings.'

After dinner we went outside, sank into the comfortable chairs on the veranda and drank spicy, ginger tea. Mouzawar, though still in his fifties I guessed, was one of the old men of Comorian politics. He had been a founding member of the Parti Blanc and was president of the Comorian National Assembly in 1975, before he came to loggerheads with Abdallah over the issue of Independence, and resigned. Mouzawar believed there should have been a constituent assembly in the run-up to Independence, so as to keep Mayotte with the other three islands. Abdallah refused, fearing that he would lose the balance of power.

'Abdallah was autocratic, even then. He was ambitious. He was a patriarch. He wanted to be a dictator because he believed that power was the source of riches and vice versa. He wasn't a man of dialogue, he wanted sovereign power. His ideas were straight from the school of the Fourth Republic – like Houphouët-Boigny's of the Ivory Coast. He wanted to be a feudal chief or lord and wasn't prepared to accept political confrontation.'

However Abdallah pre-empted the planned constituent conference and declared unilateral Independence.

'After I resigned I was on stand-by. I knew Abdallah could not last long, but I took no partisan position, waiting instead for someone to emerge who would be good for the country. Straight after the coup, Ali Soilih came to me and asked if I would join the revolution. I said I would, although I am not by nature a revolutionary. He put me in charge of co-ordinating the two new governing bodies; the Conseil de la Révolution and the Conseil Executive Nationale.'

'If you were not a revolutionary, why did you agree to work with Soilih. Did you believe in him?'

'Ali Soilih's socialism was not doctrinaire; it was more an instrument, a means to an end. Despite what everyone says, he was not a Marxist-Leninist. I was his foreign minister for two and a half years. I led the Comorian delegation to the United Nations General Assembly on 12th November 1975, when we were formally admitted as its 143rd member. Not once in that time did I visit an eastern bloc country . . .'

'Not even China?'

'China was different. No, we were not doctrinaire communists. It was more of a case of DIY socialism. Ali believed in systems of co-operative agriculture and regroupment. He had many ideas and did a great amount of good for the agriculture of the country. Very sincerely, I was proud to be his minister of foreign affairs, to undertake this responsibility for my country.'

'Prince Naçr-Ed-Dine told me that Ali Soilih studied

agriculture in France with Pol Pot and that they influenced each other. Is it true?'

Mouzawar snorted. 'I very much doubt it. Soon after Ali Soilih came to power, he dismissed Bob Denard and his band of men and came to blows with France over the Mayotte question. The people had voted overwhelmingly for independence from Moroni, and the French – perhaps seeing Mayotte as an ideal base for their navy – backed them. On 21st November, Ali Soilih launched a "surprise" invasion of Mayotte, only informing the then-President Said Djaffar of his plans by telephone just before he left. He had, apparently, been assured by the French that the small force of gendarmes based on the island would have departed to Reunion and the resident warships would be out on exercise. However, he was greeted by a mob of angry locals, who threw stones at him and his accompanying "force" of fifty men, and spat on them. Some of the women raised their skirts and bared their bottoms at him. They flooded the airstrip and blocked it with oil drums to prevent any other planes from landing. Soilih had to be rescued by the French forces and left humiliated. He blamed France for allowing this to take place and cut all ties with them. France immediately stopped aid money and technical assistance, leaving Ali Soilih to go it alone.'

'So what went wrong?'

'To understand that, you must first understand the nature of Ali Soilih. He had an impassioned sentiment for his country. He was a mystical character and saw himself as the saviour. He believed that politics was a business of friends – he called all his fellow politicians "brother". But the first turning point, I believe, was in March 1976, the date of the first plot to overthrow him, masterminded by Said Mohammed Taki. That is when his basic premise of trust failed. He became more introverted.

'Then, in December 1976, there was the massacre of Majunga. At least, 1,400 Comorians living in Majunga on the west coast of Madagascar were killed by the local Malagasy tribe. The evacuation and relief programme exhausted the state finances, already hard hit by the withdrawal of French aid money. Ali's agricultural schemes had little hope of great success in these conditions.

'He was also becoming exhausted, trying to run everything himself. Inevitably, he was losing control of the monster he had created. The fifteen- and sixteen-year-olds in the revolutionary youth had the weapons, the money and the political power to do what they wanted. And they started abusing this power to inflict psychological torture on the elders. Only the Moissi [his élite commando] were really dangerous, but the behaviour of the revolutionary youth was unsustainable. Youth cannot remain indefinitely in power.'

The new American Ambassador arrived at the airport in 1977, to find that he had to present his credentials to a teenager with a gun. A West German diplomat turned up on a chartered flight from Madagascar to discuss a proposed large agricultural grant. He found a procession of prisoners being marched past the airport. They were dressed in burlap sacks, their heads were shaved and their faces painted with white stripes. A member of the revolutionary youth walked behind them with a megaphone, announcing each prisoner's alleged crimes to the people who lined the streets. The West German hitched a lift into Moroni on an old truck and arrived at the agricultural ministry to find it was manned by two illiterate seventeen-year-olds. He caught the next plane out. The Comoros failed to get their grant.

In April 1977, Ali Soilih took the extreme step of disbanding the government and sacking all the civil servants. He followed this up by burning the government archives. It was a final V-sign to tradition and the past. Under the new 'Fundamental Law' the state was declared to be a 'democratic, lay and socialist republic' and was run by an eleven-man state council. Most power was devolved to the 'modiria'.

'The third turning point was in 1977,' Mouzawar continued, 'when Karthala erupted, causing widespread devastation. This was the final straw. Ali felt he was being battered by a coalition of political forces – both internal and external – and natural forces. It was a psychological shock that was too much for a man already under enormous strain. And this, I think, marked the final transformation of the régime, into a violent and anarchic one – as demonstrated by the massacre in Iconi, in March 1978, in which the Moissi killed at least ten people, after the villagers had attacked members of the local revolutionary youth.'

Mouzawar had a look of distant regret in his eyes as he finished: 'Ali Soilih was an extraordinary man. He was the most intelligent man of his generation. He lost power because he was ambitious and because he felt he couldn't trust anyone enough to share it. His régime had collapsed by the time he was overthrown. But it was better than Abdallah's reign and that, in turn, was better than what we have now.

'Please excuse me, I have to pray. I hope you will come back and see me again, perhaps one morning. We Muslims get very exhausted in the evenings during Ramadan.'

5

Dog of War

THE KASH KAZI began in earnest. I awoke early to the sound of claps of thunder and flashes of lightning. The wet season, which was meant to start in December, but which like the weather in the rest of the world, was obviously a few months out of synch, had reached the Comoros at last. The rain beat down. Large drops fell thick and fast to stain the beach an earthy brown. The palm trees creaked and swayed in the wind.

By mid-morning it was still not fully light. I drove into Moroni. Huge puddles had formed in the holes in the road. People were walking along the edge, their sodden robes – which normally floated with a life of their own – clung to their bodies. The luckier ones huddled under droopy, ineffective umbrellas. The cloud draping Karthala was heavy, dark and menacing.

In town, the streets were almost free of pedestrians. Everyone seemed to be sheltering in doorways, trying to dry off while waiting for a slight respite from the storm. But the rain just kept on coming. Nobody looked too unhappy; the rain was vital for farmers and domestic users alike. As Papa Claude had explained to me, the island is volcanic, the soil porous, so when the water falls, it sinks straight into the ground. There is, therefore, no permanent water on the island – no rivers, lakes or ponds. The Grande Comorians have to collect and store water in cisterns at the back of their homes for use during the seven months in the year when there is virtually no rain at all.

I went to the Banque Internationale des Comores in the main square. An imposing white building with a castellated roof, it was mercifully dry inside. Apart from a small branch in Mitsamiouli, it is the only bank on the island. Across the road lay the post office, also large and white, but not so handsome. I went around the back to the Poste Restante, one cubbyhole in the midst of the large receiving room. Letters were spilling off wooden tables into piles on the floor. It looked absolute chaos, but the letter I had been expecting was there, on the top of the pile.

I took it to the Café du Port to read. The café was closed due to Ramadan, but I sat down at a small blue plastic-topped table on the veranda. The letter was from a friend, Giles. He and three other friends were coming out for a holiday in three weeks – which I realised was only four days away.

I looked at the rain battering down on the slate-coloured water and at the grey, dismal buildings and panicked. The hotel was out of the question, so I decided to go that afternoon to ask Mahamoud if he knew of a house to rent – he seemed to know everyone.

In the meantime, I was hungry and thirsty, but as it was Ramadan, most places were closed. I asked for directions to a local restaurant, Choidjou, that Papa Claude had recommended. It was authentically Comorian. I sat at a large table in a low-ceilinged, open-sided hut made of plaited palm leaves, split in half by a large, knotted tree. Coloured fairy lights were strung around the edge, decorated by small strands of balding tinsel. The tables were covered by Malagasy white cotton cloths, embroidered with coloured flowers. There were matching napkins and the plates were made of white china, edged with delicate brown patterns. It was empty, but appeared to be open.

A large man ambled across the courtyard and introduced himself as 'Djedje', the owner. He wore a brown safari suit and his whiskered face seemed to be permanently creased into a gap-toothed smile. He took my order for fresh mango juice and disappeared back into the kitchen for a quarter of an hour, before I had a chance to order some food. I could see that I was going to be there for some time. So I got out my folder of cuttings and copious notes on Bob Denard.

*

Robert-Pierre Denard was born on the 7th April 1929 in Bordeaux. His early life was spent in the small village of Grayan (population, 500), wedged between the vineyards of the Medoc and a forest of pines. His parents, Léonce and Marguerite, had lived the six years since their marriage in China – where Léonce was a warrant-officer (first class) in the colonial service. He loved the adventure of serving abroad and Marguerite enjoyed the colonial way of life. She was a graceful, languid, elegant, pale and dreamy woman. But when she returned home for the birth of her son – followed a year later by Léonce – her dreams faded and she was never really happy living the simple life in a small village.

The family – Léonce, Marguerite, young Robert and his elder sister, Georgette (known as Nenette) – lived in a modest, comfortable house in the village, surrounded by the houses of Léonce's extended family. The Denards were one of the larger and more important families in tiny Grayan.

Robert was a normal child according to his teacher: 'Not good, not bad; average, peaceable; not aggressive or a fighter.' His best friend was Roger Voluzan, who today runs the village café. In the summer, Roger and Robert used to cycle to the nearest beach at Le Gurp, between Soulac and Montalivet, or paddle in the streams that run through the pine forest.

The first event that was to have a profound impression on the hitherto quiet, pastoral life of the young Denard, occurred on 29th June 1940, when the German troops marched into Bordeaux and thence to Grayan. Eleven-year-old Robert watched the columns of tarpaulin-covered Opel-Blitz lorries and motorcyclists in green oilskin, snake into the village. He was fascinated by the quantity of impressive equipment; the jeeps, the guns, the uniforms and by the military bearing and assurance of the proud young conquerors.

'They appeared magnificent to our kids' eyes: beautiful, sporting, merry, with their marvellous machines, tents, side-cars, guns. We looked on enviously as they played war games in the dunes and we followed their tracks to collect their spent cartridges, which we filled with powder, so that we too could play at war. Those boys weren't much older than us; running, singing, smart in their uniforms with red armbands . . . and they had guns!' he is quoted as saying in Pierre Lunel's book, *Le Roi de Fortune*. He vowed to himself that he would, one day, become a military leader.

By the time liberation came, Léonce had joined the local cell of the Communist Party and fifteen-year-old Robert had acquired a German submachine-gun, added a year to his age and enrolled in the 'École de Méchanicians de la Marine'. He stayed in the navy for eight years, attending a training course in the United States, before being promoted to quartermaster (the equivalent of corporal in the army) and sent to Indo-China. There he served under General Pontchardier, though his ship was mainly involved in routine patrol work around the Mekong delta.

This period was to have a great effect on Denard. He learnt about the rigour of military life and also of the superiority of the officers and the hierarchical barriers that make it very difficult for a poor boy with a strong regional accent to climb to the top of the ladder. He resented the injustices of the French system and in 1953 – still a quartermaster and still dreaming of the command he believed to be his destiny – he quit the army and joined the police in Morocco.

Based in Casablanca, he was assigned to a right-wing section of the anti-terrorist brigade. He cut a dashing figure; a large, physically powerful, colourfully dressed, moustached man. His flamboyance was bound to bring him to the attention of all sorts of people and it was probably in those days that he made his first contacts with the French secret services.

In 1954, he was allegedly involved in a plot to assassinate Pierre Mendes-France, the left-wing Jewish intellectual and French prime minister, while on a visit to Rabat. Denard and two other men, Serrou and Bertrand, drove up to Mendes-France's lodgings in the French residence and fired through the window. The politician, however, had gone out hours before. Despite an alibi from his new wife, a Moroccan Jewess, Giselle Rebot, Denard was found guilty and sentenced to a term of imprisonment. After serving fourteen months, however, he was cleared of the crime and with Giselle and their son, Philippe, he returned to Paris.

This was the low point in Denard's career. He found work as a representative for a firm selling heating and bathroom appliances. On meeting some friends in a bar five years later in December 1960, he described himself as 'bored shitless'. One of his friends, another veteran of Morocco called Manu, showed Denard an advert in a classified section: 'A mining company in Katanga is recruiting security officers, preferably ex-military . . .' There followed an address in Brussels and a telex number.

Denard disappeared into the night and the next Manu heard of him was six months later when he saw a picture of him in a newspaper – dressed as a dashing officer of the Katanganese gendarmes and sporting the beret of the paracommandos.

The attempt by the Katanganese leader, Moise Tshombe, to secede from the newly-independent Belgian Congo (later to become known as Zaire), marked the revival of the mercenary profession. It was also the beginning of Denard's career.

*

Sir Walter Raleigh described mercenaries as: 'Seditious unfaithful disobedient destroyers of all places and countries whither they are drawn as being held by no other bond than their own commodity.' And such is the prevailing attitude now towards the 'Dogs of War' and 'Soldiers of Fortune'. But they were not always held in such low esteem.

Dog of War

Governments around the world have used mercenary soldiers since time immemorial. The Greek, Xenophon, who in his book, *Anabasis*, describes his antics as one of an army of 10,000 hired to take part in a civil war in Persia in 401 BC, was then – and still remains – a hero. In the fourteenth and fifteenth centuries, the balance of power between rival states within middle Europe and later France, was frequently controlled by 'Free Companies'. These were armies comprised of professional soldiers who sought a new way of life after their former living had been destroyed with the dismantling of the feudal system. They were hired by states who wanted to attack another state – or defend their own. Sometimes different free companies would find themselves fighting against each other. The successful company chiefs were lauded, knighted, given property – and paid. It made more sense for wealthy powers to hire foreign soldiers to do their dirty work, rather than risk the lives of their own subjects.

During the Renaissance, the wealthy rival states in Italy used mercenaries – both foreign and Italian – to fight against each other. While in the succeeding centuries, the Swiss established themselves as the most efficient, fiercest mercenaries in Europe. It was the Swiss who – indirectly – led to the fall from grace of the mercenary profession. After the massacre of the Swiss Guard at the Tuilleries in Paris, the French people rose in their millions to fight for their Revolution – and the idea that a man should fight for his country's honour became accepted. It was no longer enough to be able to rely upon the – often questionable – loyalties of paid foreign soldiers. Sovereign nations had to find another way to raise their forces; their rallying cry was that of patriotism. And if patriotism was to work, then the opposite had to be unacceptable. As this patriotism gripped the hearts of loyal subjects around the world – so the mercenary profession suffered: it became morally repugnant.

The British government had had frequent recourse to the armies of foreign governments or feudal chiefs over the preceding centuries. During the American Revolution, after both Catherine the Great and the Dutch government had turned down their requests to hire 20,000 mercenaries, the British managed to secure the services of private German armies, by paying large sums of money to their patrons; their Serene Highnesses the Hereditary Count of Hanau, the Duke of Brunswick and the Landgrave of Hesse Cassel. In the event, the Germans surrendered, as Pitt the elder had predicted in a speech to parliament:

> My Lords, you cannot conquer America. In three campaigns we have done nothing and suffered much. You may swell every expense, accumulate every assistance you can buy or borrow, traffic and barter with every pitiful German prince that sells and sends his subjects to the shambles of a foreign power. Your efforts are forever vain and impotent, double so from the mercenary aid on which you rely: for it irritates to an incurable resentment.

Still, it was only with the aid of Prussian troops that the British managed to defeat Napoleon in the battle of Waterloo. And to this day, we maintain Nepalese Gurkha regiments. For, if one uses as the strict definition of the term 'mercenary': 'a soldier who is paid to serve a foreign government' (Larousse), the Gurkhas – as indeed the French Foreign Legion – meet the criteria.

It is only the rather dubious moral superiority conferred by 'patriotism' that theoretically separates professional soldiers in national armies from mercenaries paid by the governments of countries other than their own. But in practice, they are often very different animals. For if you take away patriotism, what is there apart from money (and mercenaries were not often well paid) that makes a man risk his life? The spirit of adventure? A love of fighting? A desire to escape from everyday life?

Once the motives for being there have changed, so too, inevitably, do the methods and codes of practice.

*

Djedje duly brought the most exquisite, sweet mango juice and sat down to tell me the arrangements for his *grand mariage* later in the year.

'I need five cows and twenty foulés to feed the guests,' he said proudly.

'What's a foulé?' I asked.

'You don't know what a foulé is? Come with me, I have one around the back.'

He led me to a rubbish garden, in which stood the biggest, fattest brown goat I had ever seen. Djedje went up to him and scratched his horns. The goat, far too fat to run away, arched his neck in apparent pleasure.

'What's his name?'

'Foulé.'

Foulé looked as if he was ready to give birth to triplets.

'He eats all the leftovers from the restaurant,' Djedje informed me. 'In the evenings, he comes into the kitchen and sits in the corner, eating the scraps from people's plates. I have to bring him in otherwise someone will steal him.'

'Did Bob Denard ever eat here?'

'Yes, often. All the mercenaries came here to eat and the French co-operants too. They all knew me because I am the best cook on the island. I used to be Ali Soilih's chef and then Abdallah's for a short while – but he didn't like me because I had worked for Soilih.'

'What was Denard like?' I asked.

'*Vraiment gentil*, very nice.'

'And Ali Soilih?'

'Vraiment gentil.'

'What did he like to eat?' Djedje looked a bit puzzled at this, as if wondering why on earth I would want to know.

'Well, you know, rice and poulet au coco, manioc . . . Comorian food.'

I went back to sit down. The rain had eased off, but it was still gloomy. Djedje went back into the kitchen.

*

In Katanga, Bob Denard quickly climbed the ranks of the hotchpotch mercenary force comprised of a – mainly European and Southern African – smattering of former legionnaires, army drop-outs and social misfits. The total number of white mercenaries in Katanga and the Congo at any one time over the succeeding eight years never exceeded five hundred, but their profile, importance and military success was always far greater than their physical presence would have suggested. This was in part due to their fighting tactics – they relied on short, sharp, brutal attacks by small forces of men in heavily armed jeeps. In what was in essence a guerrilla war in the African bush, the elements of surprise, shock and noise turned out to be remarkably successful. The mercenaries lived rough, fought hard and suffered from a reputation for brutality and looting. In the context of Katanga, and later the Congo, however, their behaviour was probably no worse than that of their range of opponents.

Denard's section, commanded by the veteran legionnaire, Capitaine Robert Faulques, fought for Tshombe against the UN-led troops – described by the mercenaries as *supermercenaires*, since they too were being paid to fight for a country that was not their own – who were trying to hold the country together. In the second battle of Katanga in December 1961, Denard, in charge of the heavy mortar, made a name for himself for bravery.

By the time of the third battle a year later, Faulques had gone, leaving Denard in charge of the thirty-odd mercenaries based at Kolwezi – the last bastion of Katanganese resistance against the UN troops. Denard was again noted for bravery and loyalty to his men (he forced their payment arrears out of

Tshombe) and became respected in the mercenary world, where these attributes are placed above all others, as a fighter and a leader. Unlike regular armies, mercenary soldiers choose their own leader, who is only powerful for as long as they choose to follow him.

It was in Katanga that the French mercenaries, with some pride, coined the name *les affreux*, the terrors. Denard was later to describe himself as *le plus affreux des affreux*.

When the Katanganese revolt failed, Denard joined a group of French officer-mercenaries training Royalist soldiers in the Yemen. He resurfaced in the Congo in November 1965, as Colonel 'Mad' Mike Hoare was leaving with some fanfare, after he had 'swept the country clean of savages'.

Lieutenant-Colonel Denard became the leader of Six Commando, under the presidency of Tshombe's former rival, Mobutu Sese Seko.

Within two years, Mobutu had shown himself to be a violent and bloodthirsty leader. He became paranoid that the mercenaries he hired – particularly those led by the Belgian planter, 'Black' Jacques Schramme – would rise up against him. He started making plans to dismantle their units, giving Denard orders to disarm Schramme. But instead, Denard made a secret visit to Schramme's headquarters to warn him of the plans. Together they plotted to overthrow Mobutu.

On 5th July 1967, Schramme and his men marched into Stanleyville and Bukavu, in what would become known as the mercenaries' revolt. But the promised back-up from Denard's forces failed to materialise. One of his officers was turned back by an ambush while trying to reach Bukavu to relieve Schramme. Denard himself was shot by a stray bullet which lodged in his skull during a rearguard action in Stanleyville airport. He stayed, however, half-paralysed for two more days, commanding his men and being nursed in the meantime by a Greco-Zairian, Marie-Elisa, who treated his wound with ice and a concoction of plants. He was air-lifted out to Rhodesia on 12th July in a stolen DC3, and soon after made Marie-Elisa his second wife.

Denard was discharged from hospital with a limp (which he still has), and a cane and made his way to Angola. He re-established contact with Schramme, who still just held Bukavu. A plan was hatched whereby Denard would bring a force over the border into Katanga, creating a 'second front' which would relieve some of the pressure from Schramme. He assembled a strike force of 110 white mercenaries and 50 Katanganese, but once again he failed to provide the kind of assistance the Belgian by this time desperately needed.

On 1st November, two hours before dawn, Denard and his men crossed the border on bicycles in what would become known in the annals of mercenary history as 'the bicycle invasion'. They captured some vehicles and made a base in the town of Kasagi, not far from the border. Thousands of Katanganese flocked to help, but Denard had only 20 rusty Mauser rifles to share between them. Attempts at capturing an armoury at Dilolo failed and they fell back hurriedly, abandoning Schramme to his uncertain fate. Three men were killed by their own rearguard ambush on the way back.

It was a bitter disappointment to Schramme, who could no longer expect to hold on to Bukavu in the face of a violent onslaught by the Congolese National Army. Feeling betrayed by his fellow mercenary leader, he sent this radio message to Denard:

'*Ici Schramme en personne. Situation sans issue. N'avons plus de munitions. Ne savons pas encore comment çela va finir. Reglerons compte plus tard.*'

('This is Schramme himself. Situation hopeless. No more ammunition. Don't know how it will finish. I'll deal with you later.')

Denard and his men retreated back into Angola, while the remaining mercenaries and Schramme were fortunate to escape alive, thanks to the International Committee of the Red Cross who oversaw their evacuation into Rwanda.

Denard failed to warn the thirty-odd French mercenaries working in the capital, Leopoldville, that the revolt was going ahead. There must have been a reason why he didn't alert them, but the results were horrific. Only one of the mercenaries, Mobutu's Algerian-born former bodyguard, lived to tell the tale of how the unsuspecting mercenaries were rounded up and executed.

From Katanga, Denard worked briefly in Biafra and was involved in operations in Angola and Kurdistan, before spending some time working for the right-wing President Bongo of Gabon, where he was a member of the 'Club Gabonnais', a group of ex-legionnaires and mercenaries living in Gabon.

However, after the flop of the bicycle invasion, his reputation was on the wane. He needed another big operation to revive it. The chance came with Benin.

Benin, formerly Dahomey, is an impoverished strip of land on the west coast of Africa between Nigeria and Togo. It was taken over on 26th October 1972 by a left-wing military group led by Major Mathieu Kerekou. He proceeded to kill or imprison his opponents and to nationalise the major French companies – both of which acts angered the old guard. A 'Dahomey National Liberation Movement' aiming to restore to the presidency Dr Emile Zinzou, was formed. It was backed by the rulers of Gabon, Togo (who felt threatened by Benin's military régime) and Morocco. (Denard was later to say that the leaders of four countries were behind the coup attempt – the fourth probably being Giscard d'Estaing of France.) On 5th November 1976, the Movement signed a contract with a 'Colonel Gilbert Bourgeaud' (one of Denard's better-known pseudonyms – he was also known at different times in his life as Jean Maurin, Antoine Thomas, Remy Destrieux and Mustapha M'hadjou) for the hire of 90 technicians – 60 white and 30 black – to overthrow Kerekou's régime. The total budget agreed upon was in excess of US $1 million.

On Saturday, 15th January 1977, the strike force, code-named Force Omega, flew into Gabon from their training base in Morocco in a DC8 leased from another Africa veteran, Jock Malloch (whose charter company Denard allegedly part-owned). They transferred to the DC8 Denard had bought from Malloch and took off at 1 am for Cotonou, the capital of Benin.

They landed just after dawn and took control of the airport with little trouble. Denard and the 'control group' stayed in the tower, guarded by nearly half the men. The others – nearly all white – split into two groups and set off on foot to town. One group occupied an apartment block and started shelling the presidential palace from one side, while the other group shelled it from their base in the palace of congress on the other side.

However, there were two vital circumstances that Denard's meticulous planning had not bargained on: the presence of a detachment of highly-trained North Korean soldiers, who had accompanied their visiting vice-president and who were quick to take up arms to back the local forces; and secondly, that by some quirk of fate, the president had spent the night in a house three miles away. So while the reinforced Beninois Presidential Guard replied to the mercenaries' attack, starting a fierce fire fight in the centre of Cotonou, President Kerekou had made his way to the radio station where he broadcast messages on the 'Voice of the Revolution', exhorting his people to defend their country against 'a group of mercenaries in the pay of international imperialism'.

Denard, in charge in the control tower, realised his attack had failed and a safe retreat became his primary objective. He called his men back to the airport and they took off less than three hours after they had landed. But in the rush of the departure, they left behind them on the tarmac an assortment of weapons and equipment, ammunition crates (including one labelled 'Colonel Maurin' – the pseudonym Denard had used for the mission) six dead and over fifty wounded Beninois. Two mercenaries were dead and one live one, Ba Alpha Umaru, was forgotten on top of the control tower.

Inside the crate bearing the name 'Maurin', a special investigating mission from the United Nations found documents setting out, in immaculate detail, the plans for the coup. The papers also named every one of the people who had taken part in it and even the identification number of the guns each man had carried. This enabled the families of three of the Beninois, who had been shot down in the course of the mercenaries' escape, and all of whom had dual nationality, to open a civil case in France against Denard and, somewhat surprisingly, only one of his men, Philippe Boyer.

Denard and Boyer were originally charged with murder, but after ten years of legal battles the charge was changed to that of criminal association. Denard was tried *in absentia* in France and given a five-year prison sentence. In Benin, they gave him the death sentence.

*

The rain had finally stopped and the sun came out. Leaves and petals glittered with raindrops and Moroni was turned, briefly, into a city of diamonds. People thronged back on to the streets, chattering loudly and laughing as they were sprayed by taxis careering along the muddy roads. I walked up to Mahamoud's village.

I found him, once again, sitting on the bench by the side of the road talking to his friends, still accompanied by the purple plastic file.

'Mahamoud, I have an urgent problem and I don't know if you can help me. Some friends are coming here for a holiday in a few days' time and I need to find a house to rent. Do you by any chance know of one?'

Mahamoud's face lit up. 'I do, I do. It's close to here.'

Mahamoud dragged me a short way back down the road. We turned left to be confronted by large red metal gates. Mahamoud shouted for the *gardien*, who came running towards us with an enormous smile on his face.

'Samantha, this is Abdou, the gardien. He has worked here for twenty years.'

The *gardien* smiled some more, and gabbled something I took to be a welcome in Comorian. He was wearing an old and frayed thin cotton *bou-bou*, through which I could see a holey T-shirt and some battered, pin-striped trousers. He was very thin, with a walnut-brown, creased face and few remaining teeth. But his eyes were bright, friendly and mischievous. He led us to the house.

I was enchanted. The garden was filled with ylang-ylang vines, whose aroma was almost overpoweringly sweet after the storm. Unusual varieties of palm tree sprouted from every corner and bushes of red hibiscus flowers blazed everywhere. The house was large and white. Its vast covered terrace was edged with graceful arches, covered by sprawling vanilla vines, which added to the heady, olefactory cocktail. Spiral steps led up to an open room on the second floor, housing a three-quarter-sized billiard table. The inside of the house was spacious, light and tasteful, furnished with hand-woven wicker chairs and simple, carved wood tables.

Happy, I returned to the hotel. Ali Toihir was waiting for me with a message from the Prince saying that my interview with President Djohar had, once again, been postponed. I decided to spend the next day diving to the wreck of the *Masiwa*, the boat that Denard and his men arrived on to overthrow Ali Soilih in May 1978.

*

The last year of Ali Soilih's reign had quickly turned into a farce. The coffers were empty and the country was bankrupt. The president knew he had lost control of the system and it was only a matter of time before he himself would be deposed. In a last desperate gesture, he called a referendum asking for his people's support. Fifty-five per cent voted in his favour. (A figure remarkable for its apparent honesty – rarely in Africa do you see a one party state being returned by less than 98 per cent.) He embarked on an ambitious plan to bring the country to a state of self-sufficiency in food by reducing rice imports and increasing maize production. But with no money to invest and what appeared to be a breakdown in the country's social system, the project was doomed to failure. The president knew that a majority of popular support was not enough. He increasingly resorted to drink and drugs and spent more and more time consulting his witch-doctor. One day – so legend has it – the witch-doctor told Soilih that he would be killed by a white man with a black dog. The next morning he sent the Moissi to kill all the dogs on the island.

Abdallah, meanwhile, had been keeping a close watch over the situation from his sumptuous apartment in Paris's 16th arrondissement. Always politically astute, he judged that the time was ripe to reverse the coup that had put Ali Soilih into power. He got together with the heads of the two other great fortunes in the Comoros, Mohammed Ahmed and Kalfane, the latter an Indian wholesaler, and they decided to contact the man who had overthrown Abdallah two years earlier.

In February 1977, through a mutual contact, a meeting was arranged between Abdallah and his two henchmen and Denard, Rene Dulac and Saint-Hubert, who had been involved in the coup of 1975. Abdallah was frank: he wanted to be back in power in the Comoros. If Denard could help him and the coup succeeded, he would assure him a fat fee and a longer-term contract reorganising and training the Comorian armed forces.

It did not take Denard long to agree. He was already sore with Ali Soilih for throwing him off the islands after he had helped him back to power. At the time he had envisaged the sort of contract Abdallah was now offering. And there were perhaps two other reasons for accepting the contract: Denard felt he had been tricked by Soilih into thinking that the coup of 1975 was the right thing for the country, when in fact Soilih had – in Denard's eyes – abandoned his pragmatic stance and implemented a communist system shortly after taking power.

(Denard has always claimed to be a committed anti-communist crusader.) And secondly, it is not unreasonable to conjecture that the old dog of war, still limping from the episode at Stanleyville airport, was fed up with chasing around Africa, risking his life for other people's countries, and was now ready to settle down to a more peaceful existence. He had decided that the beautiful, simple Comoros was the place in which to do this.

The islands were teetering on the edge of madness, but it was a benign madness compared with the brutalities and bloodletting that were sweeping over much of Africa. And for Denard and his *troupe* of battle-hardened mercenaries, after what they had been through in the preceding decade, it would be like a playground.

Denard started to plan the attack with meticulous attention to detail. The last decade of his career had been dogged by failure. He was determined to make this work. His first plan was to fly in at night and storm the presidential palace in an operation similar to Benin. The Comoros should be much easier, with its small population and amateurish, undisciplined army. By April he had assembled a force of eighty-two men, when the bad news came through that South Africa had refused them transit visas. The men were released from their contracts and Denard went back to the drawing board.

By September, Abdallah was losing hope. He spent most of his time in his apartment, speaking little and praying often. Denard went to ask for more money, which Abdallah was unable to supply. Three million French francs had already been invested by the co-conspirators. So Denard took the major step of deciding to help finance the operation himself – something he hadn't done in twenty years of mercenary action. He mortgaged his Citroën garage in Grayan and raised an additional FF 2 million. He drew up a new, ambitious and daring plan: the coup would rely almost entirely on the element of surprise. A small group of men, armed only with light hunting guns, would arrive at night by sea. They would land silently in rubber dinghies, swiftly take the presidential palace, and neutralise the main military base. Their primary objective would be to capture Ali Soilih, giving him no opportunity to rally the people to his side – the key factor that had gone wrong in Benin. The operation would be over in minutes and the Comoros would be under their control before anyone was awake.

Denard had a trump card which he hoped would ensure that the Benin débâcle was not repeated. Years before, when he still only had half an idea of returning to the islands, he had installed a fellow mercenary in place. This man, Christian Olhagary, had set up a profitable shipping business in Moroni and had won the trust of Ali Soilih. Olhagary would be the vital inside link to ensure that Soilih was inside his palace when the mercenaries struck.

Others had been sounded out as well. The military commander was in the know and was to make sure that the effective, Tanzanian-trained troops, were safely on manoeuvres on the island of Anjouan. Mouzawar, then foreign minister, made sure he was abroad. A few others had been taken into Abdallah's confidence, but no one, not even the wily old ex-president, knew the exact day the coup would take place.

Satisfied with the plan, Denard went to Abdallah and told him it would go ahead. He stressed the need for absolute secrecy.

Denard moved to Geneva and opened a bank account under the name of Henri-Antoine Thomas. He bought an apartment and started looking for a boat for the phantom company he had set up, 'Le Société de Navigation pour le Développement des Travaux Maritimes', based in Panama. In the port of Lorient, he found the vessel he was looking for – a reasonably-priced 75-metre trawler called the *Cap Fagnet*.

He set a small group to work on refitting the boat, creating hiding places for men and weapons. By the end of February, work was nearly completed. 'Monsieur Thomas' re-registered it as the *Antinéa*, for use in geological surveys. The weapons and equipment were bought. Fifty men were selected from thousands of applicants who had replied to adverts placed in the European press, and put on stand-by in France. Denard told them they were headed for South America, but those who had served with him before knew better than to ask the real destination.

In the middle of March, Denard held a final meeting with Abdallah in Mohammed Ahmed's apartment in Paris.

'We are leaving on 22nd March, Mr President,' he told him. 'D-day will be at the end of April or beginning of May.'

Abdallah wrote down a list of people Denard could count on to help once he arrived. They included the manager of the airport, Ahmed Cassin; Salim Ben Ali, the religious leader; Abbas Djoussouf, a one-time minister of Soilih's – and my new friend, Mouzawar Abdallah, 'the Snake'. Some of them were in prison, others were playing a double game. Olhagary, meanwhile, was awaiting Denard's signal.

The boat docked at Las Palmas on 27th March. Denard sent the captain, Blanchard, back to France and assumed command himself. The remaining mercenaries were boarded along with the equipment, which included three Zodiac inflatable boats, three 50-hp engines, black combat uniforms and green berets, camouflaged wire netting, waders, flares, binoculars, walkie-talkies and a first-aid kit. The weapons – 20 Remington bushmaster 12-calibre rifles, 20 light submachine-guns and 4 Winchester rifles – were stored in a secret compartment in the belly of the ship. Plenty of food and drink was taken aboard, supervised by the Katanganese chef, Noël, who had brought along his German Shepherd, Raqui.

Discipline was strict at sea. Alcohol was forbidden and the men were made to work out and train every day. Denard, normally taciturn and aloof, joined in and ate with the men. A team spirit was created. Only days before the operation was scheduled to take place, Denard unveiled the plan to the men, telling them he had received a telegram saying that the contract in Puntas Arenas had been cancelled and that they had a new contract in the Indian Ocean. He explained the situation in the Comoros and outlined the role each man would take.

On the night of 12th May 1978, the forty-six men in the commando put on their boots, black uniforms and navy woollen caps. They blackened their faces and checked their weapons. They packed small black rucksacks with the equipment and food each would need, including a green beret, a pair of epaulettes, and nylon garottes for those detailed to take out the guards. It was a windy night and there was a strong swell.

The men were ready.

*

The sun was hiding behind a cloud when I dived down to the *Antinéa* – formerly the *Cap Fagnet*, now renamed the *Masiwa* – which the hotel had sunk just outside the bay only months earlier. The limited visibility added to the unease I felt on first seeing the watery grave of the ship I had been thinking and hearing so much about. I was unprepared for its size; it was a giant rusting red carcass. We swam around the outside, peering into the dark interior. There were brightly coloured fish everywhere, buzzing about busily, unconcerned by the boat's history. A giant turtle crawled along the sea-bed and an octopus waved his tentacles through a porthole. It was very peaceful. The eerie feeling quickly vanished, a product of the weather and my imagination. When we resurfaced, the sun was shining once again.

6

The Landing

THE HOUSE WORKED OUT extremely well. Mahamoud assigned himself to us on a semi-permanent basis, disappearing only at meal and prayer times. We were lucky to have him.

Everyday, just before lunch, we would drive in a rented Peugeot 205 to the tiny beach below the old Itsandra Hotel (now closed) for a swim. There we would leave our clothes in piles under an old coconut tree, its delicate trunk bent gracefully like a swan's neck, and run into the calm, turquoise sea. I would swim fast, with strong strokes, far out, until I could see beyond the reefs of black volcanic rock that almost encircled our small perfect patch of white sand, to the larger, longer beach at Itsandra village.

*

Two nautical miles off the beach, shortly after midnight on 13th May 1978, Bob Denard ordered the *Antinéa* to drop anchor, its prow facing Itsandra.

The men were given their final instructions. Each knew exactly what he had to do. They lowered the three Zodiacs into the water. Denard got into the leading boat. He had made it clear that he wanted to be the first to set foot on the island. The swell had still not died down, but at 2 am he gave the sign to go. By the light of the stars, they navigated towards the beach. On the shore, a light shone inside Itsandra's mosque. Using it as a guide, they motored gently through the black rocks and on to the pale sand.

76

The Landing

They were divided into three groups: the first headed directly off to the military camp at Voidjou, a few miles to the north; the second acted as a rearguard, protecting the boats and equipment, while Noël the cook covered the crossroads between the beach and the presidency. Denard led the third team through the dark to the president's palace, three miles away at M'roudjou.

As Olhagary had said, there were only four bodyguards on duty. They were quickly and quietly disarmed. One of the mercenaries, Gerard, destroyed the door of the palace and followed by another, Marquès, they burst into the president's bedroom. They found Soilih in bed with two young girls. He was in a deep, alcohol-enhanced sleep. The girls started screaming hysterically and he awoke with a fright. 'Don't shoot!' he begged. Revolver to his head, they threw him on the floor and snapped handcuffs on his wrists.

By three o'clock, the news had come through on the walkie-talkie that the army had surrendered and the Tanzanian instructors had been taken prisoner. There were only four casualties: three policemen in civilian clothes who, alerted by shots at the army camp, had driven up in a Renault 4, only to be shot by the mercenaries – and one guard. A mercenary had also been wounded.

Offering no resistance, Ali Soilih dressed and moved into his sitting-room. Denard walked in.

'Here I am,' he said. 'So Mr President, this is the price one pays for failing to keep one's word with one's friends.'

'I should have known it would be you. Only you could do something like this,' Ali replied.

He was taken away and put under close guard in a locked room.

Moroni was still asleep at 5 am. The radio station, under mercenary control, was broadcasting martial music. Denard started to make phone calls, trying to reach the people on his list. He used the name Abdallah had bestowed on him in Paris before his departure.

'Hello, the liberation army has landed. This is Colonel Said Mustapha M'hadjou. The President Ali Soilih has been overthrown. Voidjou and the radio station are in our hands.'

An hour later, as the townspeople started to leave their homes, they were surprised to see armed white men in black uniforms positioned around Moroni. They crept back into their houses, turned on their radios and waited for instructions as to what to do. Meanwhile, the rest of the mercenaries quickly rounded up members of the Moissi.

By eight o'clock, the men in black had secured all the important points, including the two airports, and quelled the pockets of resistance. There were scenes of jubilation on the streets of the capital. The many people who had suffered towards the end of Soilih's régime, danced and sang the praises of the liberators. Even the president's supporters realised it was in their best interests to join in. Many recognised Denard from his previous time on the islands.

Denard went to the prison where, amongst many other opponents of the last régime, he found Abbas Djoussouf, whose name was on Abdallah's list. He freed him and said he would be needing his help.

As Noël, dressed in white, walked through the town with the black dog Raqui, the people stopped to point. They whispered the words of the sorcerer's prediction.

*

Ali Toihir had suggested that I meet Abbas Djoussouf. 'That man is involved in everything, Samantha,' he had said. 'He was a minister under Ali Soilih and Abdallah. He knows exactly what is going on.'

I found Abbas eventually in front of the Friday mosque, where he was directing the building of a new, EC-funded roundabout, only the second in the country. We went back to his house, which was near the Choidjou restaurant.

He lived in a simple, one-storey, white house next-door to his engineering company. It was moderately proportioned, but filled with large, powerful modern paintings in bold oranges and greys. There was a satellite dish on the roof and all the most up-to-date gadgets inside. We sat on deep sofas on the terrace, while rain drummed down on the corrugated iron roof. I studied Abbas's face. It was gaunt and deeply lined. His eyes were large and tired and he had a thick moustache and glasses.

I asked what had happened between him and Soilih.

'I was close to Ali before he came to power. When Djaffar was made president, I was his minister of foreign affairs. But when Ali formed his new government, I said I wanted to concentrate on my business.'

'Why was that? What did you think of Ali?'

Abbas yawned. 'He had both positive and negative sides. He was good at the start of his régime, but he soon started going off the rails. People close to him said that he took drugs. I don't know but I think there is a good chance that could be true. In terms of politics too, he was part-good, part-bad. He had some good ideas, but he was naïve with regards to the French and he tried to go too fast for the Comorian people. We aren't suited to rapid change. The best way to teach our people something is to go slowly, not to force them to put their head in a noose, cosh them on the head or put them in prison. And he wanted to go too far: not only did he force the population to work, but he took their religion away and tried to dismantle the bourgeoisie – such as it is in the Comoros. He wanted to do everything at the same time.'

'But why did he put you in prison?'

'Well, one of his plans was to set all the big families to work in the modirias. He sent his militia to fetch me and I told them that I, my wife and my mother, refused to work in the modiria. I knew it would provoke him. In the end he tried to frame me. He sent men around to my house, to try to talk me into joining a plot to kill him. Later he sent the militia to arrest me on suspicion of planning a coup. I was never interrogated. There was a farcical trial and afterwards I was led around the streets.

My feet were bare and the people threw grass on my head and spat at me. They took me to prison and I was put in solitary confinement. The only person I saw for four months was the guard. I had only one set of clothes, no toothbrush and my family were only permitted to send me one meal a day, in the evening.'

'Then what happened?'

'Well, one morning Bob Denard came into the prison and freed me. He then asked me to go to the radio station and broadcast a message saying that the coup had been carried out by Colonel Mustapha M'hadjou.'

'What did you think of Bob Denard then?'

Abbas pondered for a few minutes and gazed at the roof. 'He was quite an intelligent man, who discussed things frankly. He was straight and upright. We clashed on some matters, but we stayed on good terms until he left – even while I was in the opposition.'

After making the radio announcement, Abbas, Denard and Abdillaï Mohammed formed an interim 'politico-military directorate' and started making plans for Abdallah's return. Denard had called him in Paris earlier that morning to tell him that the operation had been a success. He said that they would tie matters up before the president returned. Denard, exhausted, spent the night after the coup in Soilih's bed.

'We had one priority,' Abbas continued, 'that was to put things in order, to recover the arms that had been given to the Moissi and youth groups and to liberate Anjouan. We were the executors, awaiting the arrival of Abdallah, Mohammed Ahmed and Kalfane. Everything was in disorder, Moroni was a mess and there was no army to speak of. We had to start from square one, but we soon had Anjouan and the small island of Moheli under our control. Then it was only a matter of clearing up Moroni before Abdallah's return. We set gangs of prisoners – former Moissi and revolutionary youth – to work cleaning the streets of the capital and whitewashing the mosque and main buildings. A mercenary was assigned to get the post office running again, one to sort out the prison, another to each airport.'

'What happened to Ali Soilih?'

'Well, the official story was that he was shot while trying to escape. Denard said he had given him the choice to stand trial in front of a tribunal, or to take his chances in the middle of the night. He knew he had little chance of staying alive either way. They left his door open and he was killed by a guard on the way out of the compound. But, I don't really know . . .'

*

The next day, Mahamoud took me to the village of Choani, where Ali Soilih was born and spent his early life. Where the road trickled away, we parked under a tree and carried on walking up a stony track and headed into the centre of the small village to see Ali Soilih's grave.

It was planted in the front garden of an unfinished house. A short, white-washed, lava tomb with a simple inscription stencilled on the front in black paint:

ALI SWALIHI
Le 29/05/78
P.R.C.

(I presumed that stood for President de la République des Comores.) It was a pathetic testimony to a man who had led his country for the greater part of its first three years after Independence. A few metres away stood the identical – although slightly smaller – tomb of Soilih's mother, Mahamouda Mzé. The house looked as if it was being built especially to feature the two graves, which could have been statues or benches in a suburban garden.

Mahamoud led us through the building works to a small,

concrete house at the back. The door was open, but patterned cloths had been tacked over the windows to keep the temperature down. Inside sat Ali Soilih's sister, Fatime Soilih, and her pretty niece. Mahamoud introduced me and we sat down on metal folding chairs. The dank house was virtually undecorated.

Fatime Soilih was a large woman, with a great, flat moon of a face. She looked very similar to the photographs I had seen of her brother – and indeed to her half-brother, the present president, Said Djohar. Her head was shrouded in a dark shawl and she sat slumped in a tatty old armchair in the shadows, her swollen legs protruding from beneath her *chirumani*. She spoke only Comorian, but with the indispensable Mahamoud acting as interpreter, we soon struck up a conversation. She turned out to be rather jolly, frequently bursting into deep-bellied laughs, revealing a gold front tooth. She said that people came every day to visit her, mainly Comorians on a pilgrimage to Ali Soilih's grave. The Qadi and the Grand Mufti came on occasion to say prayers at the tomb.

Her brother was a good man, she said. He was especially kind to his family. When he became successful, he bought land and built the house we were sitting in. When he became president, he started building the big house outside. He died leaving it unfinished.

'But it will be ready soon,' Fatime said indicating her smiling niece, who sat quietly in the corner. 'Zahara is to marry my son and they will live in the house Ali started.'

'Did you think your brother was a good president?' I asked.

'Yes, I did. He always thought of everyone – the poor, the young, the workers – not only the rich. He was very thoughtful. Even when he was president, he used to come to bring my mother a little food. After he died, my mother went a bit mad and two years later she died of grief.'

Fatime said that she too was very sad and even now she thinks of her brother all the time and whenever she thinks of him, she cries. As if to demonstrate her point, tears started rolling down her large, friendly face. She sat silent and motionless, letting them fall unchecked. She turned to look at the big painted urn in the corner of the room and gradually her tears ceased.

'He was a good man,' she repeated. 'I miss him every day.'

When we got back into the car, I asked Mahamoud if he knew how Ali Soilih had died.

'Actually I have a friend who was in the army at that time and he told me that he had seen Soilih being killed.'

'What happened?'

'Well, after the coup, Ali was taken to the army head-quarters at Kandani, where he was kept under heavy guard. On the evening of the 29th May [sixteen days after the coup] the mercenaries told the Comorian guards to take the night off, that the "mzungus" would watch the president. My friend was curious. Instead of going into town, he stayed in his room with the lights off and peered out of the window. There was a lot of action that night, cars kept going up and down the hill from Kandani to where Abdallah was staying in Beit es-Salaam. Apparently Abdallah and his cronies took a vote on Ali's fate: Taki was the only one of them to vote against killing him.'

'Around midnight,' Mahamoud continued, 'the young soldier saw Ali Soilih being led out of his temporary prison by a mercenary. He stood in the open air, looking around, while one of the mercenaries put a gun to his head and shot him. He sunk to his knees. Another shot and another, until he collapsed on to the ground. He didn't shout or scream, but kept his pride and dignity while he died. I think he was probably very tired by that point.'

'What happened after he was killed? Was there an uproar?' I asked Mahamoud.

'Not really. The next day his body was taken to Choani, rolling around in the back of a military jeep. Everyone saw it. The mercenaries dumped him at his mother's house. Bob Denard told her that if she wanted, he would send some men over to dig a hole for the grave, but that he didn't want a full public burial. It was an undignified end to a dignified man.'

*

It was a plausible story. Who knows if it was true? I was fast coming to accept that Comorians love to tell stories and they don't really respect the distinction between truth and fiction. In such a small country, stories spread like Chinese whispers, often ending up distorted. They would be repeated so many times that people ended up believing them.

This ability to live half in the world of fantasy is, I was starting to understand, an important part of the Comorian personality. They are proud, insular, suspicious, intelligent people. They combine the wisdom of an ancient civilisation with the naïvity born of isolation. They have an Arab's love of bargaining and shrewd business sense, a Polynesian good-naturedness, and the appalling sense of timekeeping of an African. They are very class conscious, with the people of Arab extraction enjoying greater respect than the black Africans – and the family group is the central structure in their lives. They are always charming, but their charm frequently disguises another agenda. The men love women and the women are shy and accommodating.

1. Moroni Harbour

2. Colonel Bob Denard, head of the Comorian Presidential
   Guard (1978)

3. *Above left:* President Ali Soilih

4. *Above right:* President Ahmed Abdallah Abderemane

5. Ali Soilih, two days before his death (1978)

6. *Above left:* Kamil and Prince Naçr-Ed-Dine on Karthala

7. *Above right:* Mahamoud

8. Abdou, the *gardien*

9. Abdallah returns with co-president Mohammed Ahmed (on his left) and Bob Denard (behind)

10. Denard surrounded by his officers (Marquès is second from the left)

11. The officers' regimental dinner

12. Abdallah's tomb

13. Ali Soilih's grave

14. *Above left:* Demonstration against the mercenaries (1989)

15. *Above right:* Commandant Ahmed Mohammed showing the damage to his house

16. Moroni after the coup (December 1989)

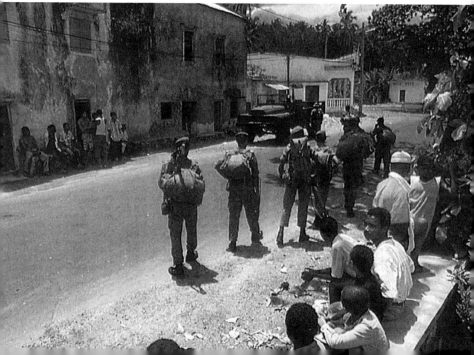

17. Denard outside the Friday mosque after the Grand Mufti
turned down his request for a Hitima: ten days later he
leaves the islands

7

Return of Abdallah

O NE MORNING, after waiting an hour and a half for a
contact – who never showed up – I wandered into town
to visit the Centre Nationale de Recherches Scientifiques
(CNDRS), the rather grandly-named museum in Moroni. I
walked over to a long white building, diagonally opposite the
post office and the bank. A plaque on the double steps leading
up from the road proudly proclaimed that it had been opened
by President Mitterrand in 1991.

Unlike most museums, it was baking hot inside. There were
four rooms depicting Comorian history, social and cultural
life, natural history and vulcanology. My favourite exhibit
was a huge stuffed coelacanth fish in a glass case in the natural
history room. It was about two-and-a-half feet long with
blunt, brown, slightly iridescent scales. Fins stuck out in all
directions, attached to the end of what appeared to be short
stocky arms and legs and a stubby tail. Its eyes were large and
bulbous and thick whiskers grew above its mouth.

The coelacanth, according to a sign beside it, was thought to
have been extinct for millions of years, before one was fished
up off the East African coast in December 1938. Experts at the
time compared the discovery to finding a dinosaur walking
down the street. An international search was immediately
launched, headed by a South African professor named Smith.

Smith spent fourteen years trawling around the western
Indian Ocean – to no avail. In 1952, he met a Captain Hunt in
Zanzibar and, almost as a last gasp, asked him to distribute
leaflets around the offshore islands, offering a reward for the

capture of a coelacanth. When Hunt pinned his posters up in the Comoros, they met with an immediate response: Comorian fishermen had been catching coelacanths for hundreds of years. A fisherman called Hussein hooked one the next day and rushed it to Hunt, whose boat was anchored off Mutsamudu, Anjouan. He pickled the fish in formalin and called Smith in South Africa. The professor jumped into a Dakota lent by his then prime minister, Daniel François Malan, and flew directly to the Comoros.

He wept when he saw the fish. The find made the front pages of newspapers across the world. Scientists flocked to examine the remains of the creature they called 'the living fossil', or 'old four legs'. Evolutionists declared the species to be at least 350 million years old and said it could be an important link between mammals and fish. The coelacanth, they learnt, lives at a depth of more than 200 metres, has a 13-month gestation period, gives birth to embryos instead of eggs and, when it swims, looks as if it is dancing.

Unfortunately, all this interest in the coelacanth resulted in large numbers being fished up from the sea. A ban was put on selling them for anything other than research purposes, but the black market price soared, until it could equal the equivalent of several years income to a poor fisherman. Now it is in great danger of becoming, once and for all, extinct. The CNDRS was involved in co-ordinating an effort to save the species.

'The Coelacanth is very important to the Comorian people,' the sign read. 'Its uniqueness to our islands has focused the world's attention on us. Please help to protect our coelacanth.'

*

I bought a copy of a video about Abdallah's life – in Comorian – and went to the bank to cool down.

Papa Claude said he would play the video for me on the hotel's in-house system. So I drove down to Mitsamiouli that afternoon. Comorian music started whining in the background and up on the screen came the picture of Ahmed

Abdallah Abderemane (1918–89). He was a charismatic presence. His face was round, with well-etched lines, his eyes and teeth protuberant, his nose pronounced. He looked regal, haughty. On his head he wore a green and gold turban, with a matching scarf draped around his neck. He stared, unblinking, at the camera.

The video worked through his life in chronological order. Abdallah came from a rich merchant family. He studied in Antananarivo before joining his father's business in 1940. Soon after, he became a deputy in the French government and later, a senator.

The video glossed over his unilateral declaration of Independence in 1975 and the coup soon afterwards was not mentioned. The next shot showed Abdallah and Mohammed Ahmed descending from a plane on their return to Moroni in 1978, being greeted by adoring crowds and smothered in flower necklaces. Neither Denard, nor any of his men, were at any time mentioned or pictured. The only white men Abdallah was shown with, were various heads of state. We saw him in China, Kuwait, Japan, South Korea, Egypt and Tanzania, meeting Saddam Hussein, Jacques Chirac and hugging Yasser Arafat, looking at all times grand and important. He appeared well-dressed, whether in the costume of a *notable – bou-bou*, turban, gold-braided robe and scarf – or in snappy tailor-made suits. He seemed always to be surrounded by pomp and finery: on Independence Day, when ranks of soldiers in white gloves, socks and belts marched past the government buildings and through Moroni, where the white paint didn't seem as weathered as today; in a 'pope-mobile' driving through Anjouan waving like the Queen; orating a speech in the People's Palace with visiting dignitaries. We saw him in his home town of Domoni, in green and gold, bags beneath his bulging eyes and ears sticking out from under his turban, delivering a rousing speech about Mayotte.

*

Abdallah returned to the Comoros on Sunday, 22nd May 1978. He embraced Denard after descending from the plane. In a symbolic gesture, one of his first acts after arriving at Iconi, was to bow towards Said Ibrahim's tomb and offer a prayer in the mosque for the victims of the Iconi massacre. A huge crowd had gathered to welcome him back and they were kept in line by members of the mercenary 'black commando'.

Abdallah then proceeded to Moroni to meet with the *notables*. He was impressed by the state of the capital.

'Was it like this before?' he asked Denard.

'President, had we not done this you would have been overwhelmed,' the mercenary replied.

Abdallah praised Denard for what he had done and adopted him as a son, bestowing upon him honorary Comorian citizenship in recognition of the 'exceptional services' he had performed for the country.

A significant amount had been achieved in the nine days between the coup and Abdallah's return. Denard had declared himself interim head of the army and chief of police. He had assigned ten of his men under the leadership of Lieutenant-Colonel Bracco to Anjouan, while Jean-Louis and three others were sent to Moheli. With another mercenary, Michel 'le Bosco', whom he had made commandant of the camp at Voidjou, Denard started recruiting men to form a regular army. From 5,000 volunteers, a core force comprising two companies was formed within ten days. They wore the uniforms and carried the arms left behind by the Tanzanian troops.

Denard's primary task was to create an élite, high-profile army-within-an-army, based around the members of his 'black commando' (so named after the black uniforms they wore on the night of the coup). He enrolled sixty Comorians to join the white mercenaries and embarked them on an intensive training course. After fifteen days, they were given heavy weaponry and put into position, patrolling the port and the airports. Their initial role was to reassure the population and they were given orders to respond to all calls, however minor the problem.

Denard and his 'directorate' marched Ali Soilih's younger revolutionaries off the streets and into the schools, which restarted within a week. Denard was working a twenty-hour day. He awoke at four in the morning and spent the hours before breakfast reading reports and writing notes. The directorate met at eight and at ten, he started his tours of the islands, visiting each village and all of his men to see if they had any problems. He ate either at the Itsandra Hotel with his men, or with his two fellow members of the directorate, Abbas and Abdillaï.

With the aid of the Grand Mufti, who was delighted no doubt to see the back of Ali Soilih, the scourge of Islam, Denard was rapidly becoming accepted by the Comorian people. And when the Grand Mufti embraced him in front of the *notables*, he put a seal on his goodwill.

Denard described his feelings in *Le Roi de Fortune*:

If one were to discuss my actions in Katanga, Zaire, the Yemen, Angola and elsewhere, I would say that my actions in the Comoros alone allowed no equivocation or ambiguity. I have never felt so sure of myself and what I have done. No, I could never forget it. The praises to God, to 'the angels of God' as they called us, the 'hadj' – those who brought back and saved the religion. How could I forget the grandfather who embraced my feet, or the teacher – one of the first Comorian teachers, a very old man – who cried and fell into my arms and then, suddenly, recited a poem in French that he had learnt when he was a child.

He described how he was taken by the chief *notable*, Ben Charraf, to his home village of M'beni, where he was solemnly presented with the habit of the *notables* – a similar green and gold embroidered cape and scarf to the one Abdallah frequently wore, and a sculpted stick. He was formally welcomed as a Muslim, 'Said Mustapha M'hadjou'. (Denard would later make a pilgrimage to Mecca, formalising his conversion to Islam and enabling him to add a Hadj to his name.)

'M'hadjou, you are a Muslim, a true son of Islam,' Charraf told him. 'You have saved the Comoros and in doing so, you have saved religion. God will protect you wherever you go.'

*

I had spent most of the day reading and had to stop only when the Prince arrived to take me out for dinner. He drove up in his government car and sat down for a whisky. He was looking dapper as usual and we set out to a restaurant. We picked up an extraordinarily beautiful, tall girl on the way, who Naçr-Ed-Dine introduced as 'Chumma's organiser in the village of Hahaya'. He explained once again that: 'We have all the beautiful girls in Chumma. Fatima is not even the most beautiful. But she and three or four others could easily get jobs as top models in Paris.' We both admired her high cheekbones, unblemished face and large, dark eyes. She had a hint of Arab in her face which, with the statuesque figure and bearing of a beautiful African, made a stunning combination.

We stopped at a new restaurant between Moroni and the airport. It was run by a Frenchman with a harsh southern accent. He called the Prince 'your Excellency' and punctuated every sentence with 'bieng, biengs'.

Naçr-Ed-Dine was in fine form. He was an expansive host and generous with his compliments. He ignored Fatima almost completely, only occasionally remembering to pat her absently on the arm. She sat silently, smoking cigarettes, eating little and looking bored.

'She is just shy,' explained the Prince. 'She is not used to meeting foreigners. That is why I brought her along, because if she is to be an effective campaigner for our party, she must gain confidence.'

I privately thought she was just sulking because I had come along. But when she turned down the lobster flambéed in whisky for salad with no dressing, I thought it served her right.

The Prince chatted away, ordering bottle after bottle of imported wine. Then he moved on to the brandy, and the prospect of the drive back began to appear increasingly frightening. It was approaching one o'clock when I finally convinced him that we had to go.

We tottered off to the car and drove full-speed to Hahaya to drop off Fatima. I moved reluctantly into the front seat, fastened my seat-belt and hoped for the best. It was a terrifying drive; Naçr-Ed-Dine sat well back, his diminutive frame swamped by the de luxe leather seat, his legs barely reaching the pedals. He belted down the middle of the road and I watched transfixed as our speed climbed to 140 kph. He talked continuously, often turning to catch my reactions, and laughed when I asked him to slow down a little. When we got back to Moroni, he tried to persuade me to stop at another restaurant for a drink, but I managed to plead with him to take me home. He was not very pleased.

*

Abdallah formed a new government with himself and Mohammed Ahmed as co-presidents, Abdillaï as prime minister and Abbas at defence. Denard stayed in the directorate. Their pressing task was to sort out the country's financial situation. The coffers were completely empty. Soilih's régime had received an estimated total of FF 460 million in external aid, but public debt stood at an additional FF 140 million. Revenue from exports was practically nonexistent. The two presidents and senior ministers were soon flying around the world, seeking aid from whichever countries would receive them.

France and the Arab nations were the first to respond to their begging missions. But Denard's continued presence on the islands was a hindrance to more aid. The Comoros were condemned by the member countries of the Organisation of

African Unity, who jeeringly referred to them as 'the Comoros of white mercenaries', and 'the islands of a white boss and a black state'. They called Denard 'the wolf of the Indian Ocean', while to the islanders, he was known by a more affectionate name; 'Bako', the wise one. The Comorian delegation was expelled from the OAU conference in Khartoum. And France, too, made clear her displeasure to the co-presidents.

Things were beginning to sour for Denard in his mercenary paradise. On 22nd July, the same day Abdallah awarded him the 'Great Officer Cross of the Star of Anjouan', he resigned from the directorate to concentrate on his positions of chief of the army and security. He hoped, doubtlessly, that if he stayed in the background for a time, everyone would forget about him. For he had, he admitted three weeks after the coup, been seduced by the Comoros. 'I hate the traffic jams of Paris but adore the scent of ylang-ylang,' he said.

However, the external condemnation continued, whipped up and egged on by the Marxist president of Madagascar, Didier Ratsiraka, who was known to fear Denard personally.

He tried to keep a low profile, focusing his efforts on organising a stable core of trustworthy, white mercenaries. A large proportion of the original team had already dropped out, exhausted from the continual pressure or sick with malaria, while others had been expelled for disorderly behaviour. Denard had kept an office running in Paris, which now busied itself with hiring new men to take their places. Denard specified that he wanted physically and morally appropriate men, and above all, sober ones. The new recruits arrived in dribs and drabs and by the time Commandant Charles (Roger Ghys, a sleek and charming middle-aged insurance salesman from Liège, who had worked with Denard before), arrived to take control, the team was beginning to take shape.

They were a mixed bag; some of the men were veterans of the Congo and Benin, loyal followers of Denard, while others had never even worn military uniforms before, but had been attracted by the scent of adventure in far-off lands. Ex-legionnaires joined ex-convicts, ex-clerks and ex-barmen. They weren't paid huge salaries – the base rate for juniors was $1,000 a month, increasing to only $1,500 for majors and colonels (although Denard, himself, has given so many different figures for his salary, that it is impossible to know which one to believe). Each of the original men had been paid a flat rate of $2,500 for the coup itself. Yet their standard of living was high. There were few expenses, the weather was good, the work fulfilling and there were beautiful girls everywhere, just looking for a 'mzungu' husband. Many of the men soon married local women and settled down to have children in houses they had built themselves. Denard himself was introduced to a young local beauty, Amina, by her uncle, the Qadi. They married the day after their first meeting and had two children, Hamza and Kaina, in quick succession.

She was Denard's sixth 'wife'. A man who enjoyed the company of women, he had collected 'wives' in the course of his travels. In addition to the first two; the Moroccan Giselle and Marie-Elisa, the Greco-Zairian nurse, Denard had 'married' three others; a Mauritian, an Italian and a Swiss girl. Each had borne him one child and he remained in constant touch and on good terms with all of them.

The pressures from outside did not cease. Denard believed that if he stayed out of the political spotlight, no one would be able to complain about his continued presence on the islands. But he had underestimated the reputation that mercenaries have around Africa. The leaders of the OAU member countries had not forgotten the era of *les affreux* and some of them had suffered personally at the hands of Denard and his men, or were afraid that he might move on to their countries next. They were not going to let one of the most feared men in Africa get away with controlling a country, albeit a small and remote one.

Internally, however, the Comoros were running more smoothly than they had since the French left. With Denard's help, a new constitution had been drawn up and accepted by the population. The assembly and governors had been formally elected and Abdallah was persuaded to take the position as sole president. Denard realised the time had come for him to leave.

The October meeting of the United Nations was looming. He knew that if he wasn't out of the country by then, the Comoros would once again be ostracised by the rest of the world. And they desperately needed a large injection of aid money that the UN meeting could have helped to generate.

Abdallah had mixed feelings about Denard's departure. He saw that it was inevitable and was in a way looking forward to being able to assert his power without the mercenary looking over his shoulder – but he was also scared of losing his protection.

They fixed a date and on 25th September 1978, only four and a half months after the coup, a leaving ceremony was held at the stadium in Moroni. It was packed with people and the entire new army was present. They marched past the stands and handed the Comorian flag to Denard, who took it, knelt on the ground and embraced it. Then he limped past all his men, looking each one in the eye. That afternoon the *notables* met in the presidential palace to say a personal farewell to the man they called M'hadjou.

Abdallah made a speech: '. . . Despite what certain people tell the world, you leave this country a hero, your head held high,' he concluded.

Three days later Denard, wearing jeans and a casual shirt, strolled in the sun through Moroni to pay the president a final visit. He found him sitting, as usual, under a large mango tree in the palace grounds.

'We talked of the future, then I said goodbye and we embraced,' Denard reminisced.

On 28th September, he left his villa carrying only a small suitcase and headed for the airport alone. Amina stayed behind in the house to hide her grief. One of Jock Malloch's planes had arrived especially to take him away. Denard saluted the ministers who awaited him at the airport, took one last deep breath of the sweet-scented air, before climbing into the plane and flying off.

8

Power Corrupts

I FOUND THE ABDALLAH FAMILY EMPIRE hidden up a short track off the main coastal road. A discreet yellow sign pointed the way to 'Etablissement Abdallah et Fils'. I passed the old presidential palace, its great white and lava speckled sides half-hidden behind high walls, and headed towards the office of Salim Abdallah. I parked in a large courtyard. The business looked sizable and busy: lorries were parked outside and blackboards were covered with chalked details of incoming and outgoing consignments. Inside, a young man was flicking through some files.

'Good morning, I would like to arrange an appointment with Salim Abdallah.'

The young man looked suspicious: 'Who are you?'

I told him and he disappeared down a narrow passage, muttering that he would see what he could do.

I waited. Some time later he reappeared with a well-built man with a confident air.

'Welcome, Samantha, I am Salim Abdallah and this is my younger brother, Cheik. Now, what is it exactly that you want?'

I explained that I was interested in the post-Independence history of the Comoros and I knew his father had been a pivotal figure in that period. Could we please talk about him?

'Where do you come from? Are you South African?'

'No, I'm from England.'

He looked reassured about this. But the inquisition continued: 'Do you know Bob Denard? Are you working for him?'

'No, I haven't met him yet, but I hope to.' I hurried on as he began to look uneasy. 'I want to hear all sides of the story. I want to learn the truth.'

Salim seemed decent enough. He invited me back to his office that afternoon, when there would be no one around (during Ramadan, the working day starts at 7 am and ends at 2 pm, without, obviously, breaking for lunch).

'We can talk about my father, but not about his death until I've spoken to my lawyer,' he warned.

I decided to leave my car there and walk around to the presidential palace. The high black metal gates were open, but when I approached them, my way was blocked by a sentry. 'C'est interdit, c'est interdit.'

I couldn't get him to say anything else and when I pulled out my camera, he started to look menacing, so I put it away again. I could see parts of the palace through the gates. It was a relatively modest, double-storied building, arranged in a three-sided square around a central courtyard. I couldn't see the mango tree which had been Abdallah's favourite resting spot, but it looked as if there was a garden around the back, so the tree was probably there. Two huge satellite dishes dominated the flat roof and all the windows were barred and shuttered. There was no one at home. I wondered if anyone had lived in the palace since Abdallah's death – I knew that President Djohar preferred the former residence of his late half-brother, up the hill in M'roudjou.

I still hadn't seen the new palace, as my meetings with Djohar were inevitably cancelled. The Prince, who as his second-in-command should have been able to arrange a rendezvous fairly easily, kept making excuses, saying he would discuss the matter when we next met and then proceeded to chide me for bringing up 'business matters when we're meant to be enjoying ourselves'. A local journalist I had met said the international press were rarely granted audiences with Djohar, 'because then they would see what an incompetent old fool he is'. I learnt that the ex-president of the supreme court had attempted to pull off a constitutional coup the year before, on the grounds that Djohar was mentally unfit to run the country. He had been relieved of his position and slapped into jail.

It was clear and sunny. Across the road three old men chiselled away at a new galawa, while several finished boats sat beside them like seals basking in the sun.

The offices of a businessman who apparently knew Denard quite well had been pointed out to me. They were just a few hundred metres along the road, so I decided to see if he was in. A secretary greeted me in the large storeroom downstairs and, when I asked to see her boss, she said he was out, but would return soon. I sat down to wait and was writing in my notebook, when a man with a boyish face came in and said hello. I couldn't believe this was the man I was waiting for; he looked as if he was in his twenties. But he introduced himself and said he would be happy to talk if I promised not to mention his name. I shall call him Ibrahim.

Ibrahim led me up some stairs. With his hands thrust deep into his pockets, scuffing his feet, he looked like a public schoolboy trying to appear casual. He was well dressed in western preppy clothes; baggy khaki trousers, a mauve Oxford cotton button-down shirt and black brogues. We went up to his large, light office and sat on the window seat. Books and pamphlets were scattered all over the desk, shelves and a large table, spilling on to the floor. Ibrahim got out a pad and started scribbling furiously. It was as though he had an immense store of pent-up energy that had somehow to be released, even while he was sitting down.

He said he was in his early forties (and was vain enough to look pleased when I expressed my surprise) and had returned to the Comoros over ten years ago after studying and working abroad. His first business venture on returning, he said, was to import a load of cement.

'At that time I didn't realise that the Big Three . . .'

'Who?' I interrupted.

'Oh, Abdallah, Mohammed Ahmed and Kalfane, an Indian

trader – the three who planned the coup against Ali Soilih. Well, they held a monopoly over cement imports – it was an informal one, but they were in a position to enforce it. When my ship arrived in Moroni harbour, they organised a week-long dockers' strike and my shipment was mysteriously destroyed. That is how the Big Three operated. I went to the customs people and said I refused to pay duties on the damaged goods – fortunately they agreed to let me off.'

He explained that the same three families had been the biggest businessmen during colonial times and when Ali Soilih came to power, they were determined not to lose their positions forever.

'When Abdallah returned to the Comoros in 1978, he broadcast a message on the radio, saying something like: "We have put our money into freeing you. Now you have to pay us back." That was how the monopolies originated, as a gift from the Comorian people to thank them for overthrowing Soilih. They also created monopolies in rice, vanilla and a partial monopoly in ylang-ylang. And Abdallah had the treasury as well. He used it as a purse, his to plunder whenever he felt like it.'

'And what about Bob Denard?'

'He didn't touch the state money, but was given a virtually free reign over income from abroad. Meat was one of his domains. A state-owned company, Socavia, held a monopoly over the importation of meat and Denard bought shares in it.'

Denard also received a percentage of whatever business was going on with the South Africans, Ibrahim claimed. 'And people say he was involved in arms dealings. It can't be proved, although on more than one occasion I did see the mercenaries loading cargo cases on and off planes at Hahaya.'

I had already heard rumours to that effect, that South Africa had been using the Comoros as a base from which to transit arms shipments destined for Iraq. While working for a South African newspaper the previous year, I had written a story producing evidence to suggest that a local company,

Armscorp, which manufactured the G12 'supergun' designed by Gerald Bull, had sold arms to both Iran and Iraq. I hadn't previously heard of any Comoros connection.

He said he had met Denard originally through a South African friend in Paris when he was involved in the movement trying to overthrow Soilih. 'It's ironic as now I would prefer Soilih to Abdallah,' he told me. 'Soilih was a genius, but he was surrounded by idiots who couldn't keep up with him. So he had to work twenty-four hours a day to make sure everything was done. If I had been in his position, I, too, would have smoked lots of marijuana and lost control.'

Ibrahim said that while he didn't see Denard often, people came to know that he was under his protection. This had helped with business, as his enemies were afraid to cross him, knowing Denard was behind the scenes.

'What was wrong with Abdallah?' I asked.

'He was very corrupt, but I must say that I'd prefer him to Djohar any day. At least Abdallah brought projects and financing into the country. Yes he took a large cut, but something was happening. His word was his word. He was a very clever politician, but above all, he was a clever business-man. Making money was his primary aim; he wanted to stay president because that was his way to ensure the billions kept flowing in – and there were billions and billions.' (Of Comorian Francs: approximately 500 CF are equal to one pound sterling.)

'But would you say he was a good man?'

Ibraham thought. 'Yes. Well, maybe no. He was very corrupt, but humanly speaking, he was a good politician. If people were in trouble or if they needed money for something, he would help them out. Not necessarily because he cared for them, or because he wanted the best for the country. He did it because he was a megalomaniac and was prepared to sacrifice anything to hold on to power. Now Djohar is altogether different.'

Abdallah never paid customs duties, he alleged. He

imported everything from soft drinks to corrugated iron and steel bars, all of which arrived in cases carefully labelled for the presidency. His sons, Ibrahim claimed, were even more devious; they paid their customs duties, but then went straight around to the treasury to tear up the cheques.

'What do you think of Salim Abdallah?'

'Well his father was a ruthless businessman, but his sons were his weakness, he always turned a blind eye to whatever they did. There is an old Comorian proverb which goes something like: "The woman who gives birth to a snake never throws it away." Abdallah was that woman.'

Ibrahim continued to spit figures out at me: how Abdallah took 10 per cent of this, and the minister of finance grabbed 5 per cent of that. Abdallah had sold the rice donated by the European Community as aid, he claimed. When the vanilla harvest time came, Abdallah would hike up the rice price, thereby forcing the villagers to come to work in his vanilla plantations at a minimal wage, just so they could earn enough to buy their staple food. This fitted in with Abdallah's reluctance to encourage the consumption of maize.

He was warming to his theme and I could see he was enjoying himself – rather too much maybe. There was a mischievous glint in his eye as he watched me scribble down his words. According to him, every politician on the island is completely crooked and if they are not, they are lazy and stupid; the princes are good-for-nothing Royalists ('Naçr-Ed-Dine is a good architect. Why didn't he work while he was in opposition for twelve years?'); Mouzawar is essentially devious – but probably the best politician in the country – although Ibrahim himself would probably vote for Taki, as he is a 'tough guy, no puppet to the French'. This was despite the fact that he is an office bearer in one of the other parties, a position he said he took so as to be in with the right people on the cocktail circuit, all of whom are involved with their own parties.

I suddenly got the feeling that this charismatic, sharp-talking Peter Pan figure was feeding me a load of dis-information.

It was the time I had arranged to see Salim, but when I returned to his offices, they were locked and no one was there. I wandered around. A large, dark green Mercedes 200E drew up, the first I had seen on the islands, a discreet display of wealth. Salim and three henchmen got out. After my conversation with Ibrahim, I imagined them to be the Comorian equivalent of the Mafia. Salim led me into his office, closely followed by Cheik, who was stubby and shorn and wore a gold chain around his neck. He told me he was in the army.

The office was large, air-conditioned and entirely brown, dominated by a huge, shiny, two-sided wooden desk. A photograph of Salim and his father, looking regal in a turban, hung over the doorway.

We settled into conversation. Salim was very charming and although his French was highly accented, I found it easier to understand as his vocabulary was only marginally less limited than mine. I suspect he is very clever. He evaded many of the questions I put to him and was always careful not to give his opinion on anything of which he didn't have direct personal knowledge. Instinctively I didn't trust him, but I don't know how much of that was due to the picture I had built up as a result of Ibrahim's description of his business practices. However, he was clearly devoted to his father's memory and didn't say a bad word about him.

Abdallah had, he said, become involved in politics because he wanted to defend the rights of the Comorians against the French colonial overlords. He lived like a good Muslim, collecting two wives, one of whom bore him six children. He was authoritarian, but at the same time, gentle and wise.

Trying to get Salim to digress from his father's saintliness, I asked what Abdallah had thought of Ali Soilih.

'I'm going to be honest with you,' he said, looking at the photograph on the wall. 'I handled my father's correspondence with Ali Soilih and I know that he never thought he was a bad man. He thought that by taking the political path he had chosen, he risked leading the country into a difficult situation. He thought Ali was maybe a bit druggy, but he never thought he was bad. Although,' Salim paused, 'in his opinion, Ali Soilih was being put under pressure, blackmailed, or ill.'

When I tried to get him to expand on this, he refused to answer.

'What did Ali Soilih think of your father?'

'He respected and held him in high esteem.'

'Then why did he overthrow him?' I persisted.

Salim dodged the question. 'You know, on two occasions when my father was in exile in Paris, Ali Soilih asked him to come back and help him here. But the family persuaded my father not to go – he wanted to though. It was soon after that he started to plan the coup.'

'So he contacted Bob Denard?'

'No, the first person contacted was not Denard, but an English mercenary.'

'Who?'

'I can't remember his name. Everything was set, but the Englishman needed too much time in which to research the Comoros, before he could carry out the coup. That's when we turned to Bob Denard. It worked out well initially. Denard knew the islands and he had some scores he wanted to settle with Ali Soilih. Because of that he was willing to work for less.'

'Who financed the coup?' I asked.

'I can't tell you. Lots of people have said it was France, but that isn't true. The only people who could tell you about the coup today are myself and Denard: my father's dead, Mohammed Ahmed's dead, the Indian's dead. I know all about it. I worked as the financial intermediary. It was me who carried the suitcase full of money.'

'So then the coup happened . . .'

'Yes, and all the Comorian people were very happy, they danced and they sang. But the problem was that Bob Denard's feelings got in the way of his mission and he decided to stay here.'

'Do you know how Ali Soilih died?' I asked.

'No one but Denard could tell you that. He wasn't there I don't think, but he knows. All I know is that when my father returned there was a meeting to decide Ali Soilih's fate. It took place on the first floor of the palace. I was on the ground floor and I heard everything. I know who was at the meeting and I know who proposed Soilih's death, who said yes and who said no. I know everything. I was there. But I can't tell you.'

'Who was there?'

'Well, it was the time of the co-presidency and the directorate. Denard was part of the directorate. That's all I can say.'

However much I tried to get Salim to open up, he wouldn't budge. He just kept telling me to ask Denard. I began to wish I hadn't told him I was planning to see the mercenary. He talked a lot about the good relationship between his father and Denard, managing at the same time to imply that Abdallah had wanted him to leave for years and that Denard was always looking for opportunities to two-time his boss.

I moved on to the subject of his father's business practices: 'They say my father stole, that he was corrupt, that he enriched himself,' Salim explained, 'but my father came from a rich family, he was educated and he worked. I inherited the business when he died in 1989, but I have been running it since he became president in 1978. Once he was president, he didn't have anything to do with running the business. It was me who did all that. I built all that outside, I put the money in the bank. If anyone says he stole, I can prove them wrong. They say he had bank accounts in France, houses in France and Switzerland. Well, if he did have them, he's not the only one.'

Salim was getting worked up, so I tried a change of tack: 'What were your father's main objectives as president?'

'He wanted the best for the country and he did an enormous amount for it. But all his politics were geared towards one thing: the reunification of Mayotte into the Comoros. It was his dream to see this happen. Now please excuse me, I have to go. I will speak to my lawyer this week and perhaps we can talk about my father's death another time. I would very much like to tell you our side of the story.'

With that he ushered me politely and firmly out of the door. I did not know quite what to make of him. He had the Comorian charm, but it was mixed with something else I couldn't define. It came across as shiftiness, but I think it could have just been that he was wary about revealing too much to an unknown foreigner and a journalist at that.

The next afternoon I dropped into the offices of Mohammed Ahmed's son and heir, Hassan Mohammed Ahmed. I wanted to give him a chance to refute Ibrahim's charges of wholesale corruption and cartelling by the 'Big Three'. We had organised a meeting for that morning, but he failed to turn up. This time, I was fortunate to catch him unawares.

It was not an easy meeting. Hassan was alternately aggressive and defensive. He said the idea that his father, Abdallah and Kalfane held monopolies was wrong. There were three of them, so they would have been oligopolies or cartels in any case. He blamed the old colonial legislation for creating a situation in which a few companies could dominate the markets, then said that other people could have entered if they had wanted to, but they lacked the guts. The sources of Abdallah and his father's wealth, he said, were the salaries they received as French deputies.

'Was there a cartel situation in cement?' I asked.

'No.'

'Did the Abdallahs pay their custom duties?'

'Yes, of course they did. They couldn't cheat because the chief customs officer and the manager of the central bank, at that time, were Frenchmen.'

Everything I asked, drawing on Ibrahim's information, met with a withering look and negative reply. Ibrahim, he said, was not one to complain. He had been a particular favourite of

Abdallah's and had benefited from bucking the system as much and as often as he could get away with it. Hassan was saying that he and his family were rich because they were clever. And why should he waste his time answering the foolish and impertinent questions of some foreign girl?

I was becoming increasingly frustrated by the Comorians, and by my own inability to work out what was going on, who was right and who was wrong, who was telling the truth and what was fabrication. Ibrahim and several other people had told me that Abdallah and his cronies were crooks – the sons, Salim and Hassan had, unsurprisingly, refuted that. Mouzawar had told me that Abdallah wanted power above all else and that money was his way of getting it. One of Abdallah's ministers, an elegant, soft-spoken man called Omar Tamou, agreed that power was the president's aphrodisiac, but disagreed that he had been at all interested in money. Ibrahim had thought the opposite. To some he was a patriarch, to others, a dictator.

*

After Denard left towards the end of 1978, Abdallah submitted the new constitution to the Comorian people, who accepted it with a rousing 99 per cent majority. The smooth and urbane Commandant Charles stayed to take charge of the small band of European mercenary soldiers and to advise the president on military matters. He quickly won the confidence of Abdallah and his family.

But Denard was not yet ready to hand over his hard-won island paradise. He planned to lie low for a time, before slipping back unobtrusively when the public spotlight had lifted off the Comoros. While Charles was busy transforming the original Black Commando into a Presidential Guard, converting to Islam and marrying a beautiful local girl, Denard bided his time in Paris. He kept in constant contact with Abdallah and his men on the islands.

In the spring of 1979, Denard was contacted by Clint

Eastwood, who suggested they collaborate on a film about the voyage of the *Antinéa*. He had read about the coup in American *Esquire* magazine. Warner Brothers agreed to a provisional budget of FF 200 million, of which $300,000 was paid in advance to Denard. They rented an apartment on Avenue Floquet in Paris for Denard and a small team of his men to use while they collated their reminiscences. Denard was flown to Hollywood three times and spent three weeks with Eastwood on his Californian ranch. 'It was the only time I earned a lot of money without having to risk my life,' he said later.

However, just as the script was coming together, everything started to go wrong. The producer fell ill, Clint Eastwood decided that he disagreed in principle with glamorising violence and Denard was left once again with only his dreams of the Comoros.

*

It was not an easy year for Abdallah. Rumours circulated about numerous coup attempts being plotted by the opposition, unhappy with the continued presence of the mercenaries – even minus their chief. The president could not decide whether he was better off with the mercenaries there to protect him, or whether opposition might die down if he got rid of them. He told Denard, waiting impatiently in Paris, that the time for his return had not yet come.

Instead, Denard concentrated on recruiting new men for the Presidential Guard and on trying to find alternative sources of finance. The death, in an aeroplane crash, of his 'protector' at the Elysée, De Gaulle's advisor on African affairs, René Journiac, had lessened the likelihood of France agreeing to pay for the Guard.

Denard decided to approach the South Africans, with whom he had maintained good relations since his Biafra days. He entered into negotiations with Brigadier Martin Cotze from the South African Defence Force (SADF), a key figure in military intelligence. Pretoria was keen to deal. They agreed to start funding the Guard from September 1979 and, in return, they were given permission to set up a secret listening station on the islands. A handful of South African agents slipped into the country and quickly blended in with the Presidential Guard, wearing the same uniforms and living in their barracks. Their job was to keep an ear on what was happening in the important African National Congress bases in Lusaka and Dar-es-Salaam and to monitor the continuing civil war in Mozambique, in which South Africa was playing an active, albeit underhand, role. Perhaps the idea of using the Comoros as a base for 'sanctions-busting', particularly in arms, had already been conceived.

Eyewitnesses told me of the regular arrival of mysterious planes after dark, when the airport had been sealed off and secured by the Presidential Guard; of heavy wooden crates being swapped from plane to plane; and of early morning departures. The crates were never opened in the Comoros, but it was a common assumption that they were full of arms manufactured by a South African company and destined for Iran and Mozambique. The shipments were flown in on Hercules C130 transport planes and reloaded into – normally unmarked – Boeing 707 or DC8 aeroplanes.

No one I talked to was able to confirm the content of the crates, but it is entirely feasible that they were arms shipments, probably 155 mm. shells and ground-to-air and air-to-air missiles. The operations were allegedly monitored by Israeli 'commercial agents', acting as intermediaries between the Iranians and the South Africans.

South Africa had been funding and arming the Mozambique National Resistance (then the MNR, later known as Renamo) since the beginning of the Civil War. A large portion of the guerrilla force's arms filtered through overland from Malawi, but those destined for the northern provinces probably came by air from the Comoros. The 'Comoros link' was, like the coelacanth, a well-kept secret until the end of 1984, when it came to light, to the embarrassment of Pretoria, who earlier that year had signed the 'Nkomati Accord', promising to cease support for the MNR.

While it has been proved that South African arms were sold to both Iran and Iraq, the route they took to the Middle East has never been confirmed. At that time, in the mid-Eighties, trade sanctions against South Africa were heavily enforced and the passage of anonymous planes between South Africa and Iran would surely have been noted. The Comoros, however, are on the flight path between the two countries. As an Islamic nation, it has always had close relations with Iran and at that time, there was a force loyal to the South Africans *in situ*, able to ensure the safety and secrecy of the operation. It would have been logical for the South Africans to use the Comoros as a transit station for arms – they were certainly being used for some heavy and illicit cargo – but then, as I was finding out, logic plays little part in Comorian life.

In 1979, South Africa gave 1.5 million Rand (around £750,000) to support the Presidential Guard. By 1985, the figure had risen to R4.5 million and in 1987, it had grown to R6 million (£3 million).

It was during the course of his negotiations with South Africa, in 1979, that Denard received France's discreet benediction to return to the Comoros. Under the alias of Remy Destrieux, an official government consultant, he was given a Comorian diplomatic passport and the status of an itinerant ambassador.

Over the next years, his life was busy. In addition to dealing with the South Africans, he travelled the world in an attempt to drum up financial support and investment for the Comoros. He visited Taiwan, Cyprus, Hong Kong and Tokyo. He was completely obsessed with the islands, which represented not only his dream, but his opportunity to make money. The country was in a mess. Corruption and disorganisation were the norm; the population was growing at an unacceptable rate; health and hygiene standards were very low;

deforestation was occurring on a large scale; and sand was being stolen off the beaches and used to build houses – leading to widespread wind and soil erosion. A large-scale injection of development finance was required if the situation was to improve.

At the beginning of 1981, South Africa came some way towards fulfilling that need. The link between the two countries was strengthened when Denard opened talks with a representative of the department of foreign affairs, a young politician called Glen Babb. In a separate deal from that already brokered through the SADF, South Africa expressed her enthusiasm to help with the country's development. Denard eagerly concurred, perhaps foreseeing the possibilities increased foreign investment would open up. With Babb, he hatched a scheme whereby South Africa would put money and technical expertise into the major areas requiring assistance: the infrastructure, health facilities, agriculture, housing and tourism.

At that time, South Africa was perceived as a villain across the world, and most especially in Africa. All the department of foreign affairs was looking for, in return for their investment in the Comoros, was recognition and the chance to demonstrate that they were not all bad. (The two departments – foreign affairs and military intelligence – enjoy a high degree of autonomy in South Africa. It is unlikely that the diplomats involved in 'development work' knew details of what the soldiers were up to.) An old crony of Denard's, Commandant 'Freddy' Lesage, was granted diplomatic status and installed in Pretoria as the 'Comorian trade representative'.

1981 also brought bad news for Denard. François Mitterrand was elected president of France. His new broom swept out many of Denard's contacts within the Elysée and the French services, and replaced them with dedicated young socialists. The witch-hunt had begun.

Within months, a warrant was issued for Denard's arrest in connection with the Benin affair. His wives were questioned and harassed. Abdallah was urged to break contact with him; Denard feared that the French parachutists might land any day to flush him off the islands. He placed the PG on full alert. But he need not have worried too much on that account. Abdallah and Mitterrand were old sparring partners. Although the French president, in his book of memoirs, *L'Abeille et l'Architecte*, described his Comorian counterpart as a 'corrupt trickster' and the situation in the Comoros as 'intolerable . . . morally and politically unacceptable', he owed Abdallah a debt of loyalty from the years when, as a senator, he had supported him.

For Denard, the socialists' ascension to power represented the end of an era: his relationship with the French intelligence service and consequent quasi-legitimacy, was severed forever – although he almost certainly did maintain links with his former controllers on a personal level. From that time onwards, however, he was unable – officially – to return to France or to see his scattered family. He was an outcast and his chances of being accepted by the French establishment appeared to have been scotched – at least for the time being.

So he turned instead to South Africa and threw his energies into cementing the relationship between the Comoros and its new protector. France still supplied around 60 per cent of the national budget, but it was an area over which Denard had little control. He was, however, in total command of the South African funds. The only problem was Abdallah, who was unwilling to be seen by the rest of Africa to be getting too friendly with 'the Racist Republic'. Abdallah wanted it both ways; he wanted to continue to receive their money, but not to give them the recognition they sought in return. He paid a secret visit to Pretoria and came away with a promise of a prompt increase in funds; but at the 40th anniversary meeting of the United Nations the following month, he spoke out vehemently against South Africa. Whenever Denard urged him to give something in return, he would reply that he 'didn't want to become the slave of anyone'.

In 1983, the president granted the South Africans permission to open a trade mission in Moroni, but refused to bestow on it diplomatic status. When the resident trade representative, Roger Harding, returned from a visit to his superiors in Pretoria with hundreds of specially-printed yellow T-shirts depicting a South African hand clasping a Comorian one in a gesture of friendship, Abdallah immediately sent Denard and his men to confiscate the T-shirts.

Denard himself was perhaps also not keen to promote easy relations between his president and South Africa – for fear of removing his role as the vital link between the two. The South Africans meanwhile appeared to be happy about dealing with Denard – although they were less pleased at never having been given a chance to advertise their good works to the rest of the world. Their department of foreign affairs continued to pour money into the country, all of which was channelled through the Presidential Guard: around R40 million between 1982 and 1989.

They spent millions building two hotels; the Itsandra and the Galawa Beach. They built a new village where the houses were made out of crushed volcanic rock. They set up a health evacuation scheme and founded a 1,300-acre pilot farm at Sangani. This was Denard's own special baby – he called it his crowning achievement. It was supposedly a presidential project, financed by South Africa and administered by the Guard, but in practice the Comorians had little to do with it. Two hundred thousand Rand were sunk into it in 1983, R400,000 in 1985 and R600,000 in 1987. Its aim was to demonstrate new methods of cultivation and develop strains of crops and animals more suited to the unique Comorian terrain. Denard put one of his mercenaries in charge.

*

It was time for the others to leave and thus, sadly, for me to quit our beautiful house. I can still recall the scent of the vanilla vines on the veranda. We bought Abdou, the *gardien*, a smart new *bou-bou* with gold tassles at the neck, and Mahmoud a new pen. Mac – as we called him – had arranged for me to rent a room from a young French couple who lived only yards away from the Choidjou restaurant. I left my bags and then drove my friends to the airport. I continued up the road to the Galawa Hotel where I had arranged to meet the elusive Tony Kaye for a drink. He had just returned from South Africa. He was tanned and fit-looking for his age, which I guessed to be fifty-something. His hair was cut *en brosse* and he wore a pink T-shirt. As soon as we had sat down at the bar, he struck up a conversation with the South African tourists on his other side. It was some minutes before he turned back to me.

'So, what exactly is it that you are trying to find out?'

I explained carefully, sensing his aggression and suspicion. 'What have you already learnt?'

Instinctively, I couched my findings in terms sympathetic to Denard as I guessed he would not talk to me if he thought I was at all hostile. He was careful not to compromise himself in any way or to give away sensitive information. A few times he said that if I printed some of the things he had told me, he would come after me with a machete. It was said jokingly, but there was a glint of seriousness in his eyes.

Denard is still, obviously, a sensitive subject. No one wants to arouse the ire of the present government by claiming close friendship with the mercenary. Yet those who knew him well when he was in the islands are afraid to speak badly of him – for fear of provoking his anger. They were caught between that proverbial rock and hard place.

Tony explained that he had arrived in the Comoros in 1985, having sailed from South Africa on his yacht, *Before the Wind*. He liked the islands and decided to stay. When the Galawa Hotel was built, he created his own diving and sailing operation, based in the boathouse at the end of the beach.

'I've heard you were a good friend of Denard's. How did you find him?'

'Who told you that? No, I wasn't a close friend, but we got

to know each other a bit. His men built the boathouse for me. But I don't speak French, you know, and he doesn't speak much English, so we could never get close. However, when Bob was staying in Trou de Prophete he used to come down to the boathouse every now and then with his son, Philippe, or one of his English-speaking men. He would ask after our health and was always charming and polite. He was always interested in anyone who had invested in the country.'

'How come his men built the boathouse? I didn't know they were involved in construction.'

'Yes, he created a company called SOGECOM, which was in both the security and the building business. The quote given to me by the company which built the hotel was far too high, so I asked Bob if he could do any better.'

'Was it a profitable company? Some people speculate that he made a lot of money in the Comoros – is that true?'

Tony shook his head. 'He always said to me: "Tony, I think I must be the only guy on the islands who isn't making money." He put most of the money he earned straight back into the Guard and Sogecom. He was upset that Abdallah was ripping off the country. I don't think Bob would have stooped to that himself. He was an absolute gentleman, a man of his word.'

'Do you think he was good for the Comoros?' I asked.

'Well, in my personal view, he had a stabilising effect on the country,' Tony said before taking off on the predictable South African rant about how African countries find democracy difficult and frequently work better under a dictator.

'But Bob wasn't a dictator, he was purely the head of the Presidential Guard,' he continued. 'And I would find it hard to believe that he is a blatant killer either. I saw him as a member of that class of British or French aristocracy who were sent off to fight as paid soldiers by their fathers. I could see him as the minister of defence or a general in any army. The only difference was that he worked for himself and was paid for it. The fact that he was a soldier of fortune was not, in my opinion, of any detriment to his character. I can think of numerous other generals who masterminded atrocities far worse than he is alleged to have done – in the name of war and defence.'

'So what was life like here for you before he left?'

'In the years between my arrival and 1989, life here seemed stable, the people appeared to be happy and the restaurants were full. There was a good ambiance to expatriate life; the tennis club was fairly busy as were the hotels. Tourism was quiet, mainly because there wasn't the infrastructure to support it – but Bob wanted to change all that. It didn't feel tense and as far as the expats were concerned, the PG was a stabilising influence. There was an overall feeling of optimism, until the "accident" [my inverted commas]. But I don't want to talk about that.'

'Do you still keep in touch with Denard?'

'Yes, I was rather fond of him. He never asked for anything from me and I suppose he had become a friend, although we didn't see each other too much. He admired my stance for hanging in here. Now I see him occasionally when I'm back in SA.'

'Are you going to move into his house?'

Tony shrugged. 'Well, he's said I can, but I don't know . . .'

*

I went into the casino, where South African tourists were smothering the roulette tables with chips. At the bar, I chatted with the young South African manageress of the hotel boutique. She said she'd been at the Galawa since it opened in 1988.

'So did you know Denard and the other mercenaries?'

'Yes, they were lovely men, always impeccably mannered. They used to come into the shop to chat. They were always very polite and if they weren't, the colonel would soon tell them off. It was fun when they were here.'

9

Cloud Coup-Coup Land

I WAS GETTING a very different picture of the mercenaries – depending on who I talked to. Almost without exception, the white expatriates praised Denard and protected his memory. They all described him as polite and well-mannered. One businessman told me that Denard had helped to stimulate and regulate the Comorian economy, while another – a Comorian – said that the only thing the mercenaries developed was the graveyards. The image of the mercenary band as described by the majority of Comorians I spoke to was altogether darker. I kept picking up rumours of torture and brutality – mainly during the late-Eighties, when there was a series of attempts to oust the mercenaries. And I heard that at one of their monthly regimental dinners, all of the 'European officers' – Denard had not been present – had worn red armbands sporting the Nazi swastika on a circle of white. It was not an image likely to make me warm to them.

I had told Ali Toihir that I was keen to meet and talk to a Comorian ex-member of the Presidential Guard. I wanted to find out what it was like to live and work on close terms with the mercenaries, or 'the European officers', as Denard preferred them to be known. Ali had urged me to meet Rambo, who now worked for the firm in charge of the hotel's security.

'He was in the Presidential Guard for a long time. I know he has some very interesting stories to tell.'

Rambo proved to be very elusive. While I was still staying at the hotel, I lurked around the grounds, trying to catch a glimpse of a Rambo-like security guard. I went to the staff canteen at lunchtime, where he apparently always ate. But he never turned up on the days I was there. I left messages with the gate-keeper, security guards, Papa Claude, Ali Toihir. To no avail.

One evening I was in my room, when the phone rang.

'Are you looking for me? Do you need me?' a deep, accented voice asked.

'Who is it?'

There was laughter. 'Do you need me? Do you need a man?'

'What? Who are you?'

'Have you ever tried a black man?' More laughter from the background. It was obviously a joke. I put the phone down.

It rang again. 'It is Rambo,' the voice said laughing, before in turn putting the phone down on me.

As I was getting into the car a few weeks later, after a visit to the bank, a short dark stocky man came over to me.

'Hello, Samantha,' he said.

He was wearing the uniform of the hotel security company. I glanced down at his badge. Rambo, at last.

'I've been looking for you everywhere, please can we talk?'

Rambo appeared confident. There was a sparkle in his eyes and his smile was full of mischief. 'Of course, please come and visit me at my room in the Maloudja on Friday at 16.00 hours.'

Rambo lived in a caravan at the back of the staff quarters. He was waiting for me outside the door when I arrived, punctual to the minute. His caravan was immaculate. His clothes were neatly stored away and peeking out from under his bed, I could see a perfectly polished pair of brown army boots. Rambo was also perfectly pressed, in a crisp shirt and trousers, striped socks and shiny black lace-ups. His hair was cut in a gentle flat-top and when he moved, even around the cramped living quarters, it was with grace and economy of movement. Any worries I might have had about coming to his caravan on my own – especially after the strange phone call – were immediately dispelled. He appeared so powerful and proud and sure of himself, that it was impossible to imagine him needing to take advantage of anyone.

We sat opposite each other on narrow benches. I gazed around his home. Photographs had been stuck in the rim of the roof and a torn-out magazine picture of Princess Bea with her tongue stuck out, was tacked on to the wardrobe door. He showed me a photograph of his Canadian ex-girlfriend, a pretty, bespectacled blonde, another of an American girlfriend and one of his wife and daughter.

'She married a gendarme while I was in prison. She thought I was dead,' he said.

I admired a team photograph of the Presidential Guard, mounted on grey card.

'That was taken when we went for a parachute course in South Africa in May 1984 with the 1st Para regiment in Bloemfontein,' he told me. 'Only the best guards were chosen for the course.'

Sitting in the middle of the front row, wearing an elegant pale grey suit and looking more like a diplomat than a soldier, was Denard. The corresponding name read Colonel Bako.

'Look, there I am,' Rambo pointed himself out.

He didn't appear to have changed much in the eight years since the picture was taken.

The name under his face was Sergeant-chef Anwar Aladin. 'That is my real name,' he explained.

'So where did Rambo come from?'

He smiled. 'Can't you tell?'

He was born in Madagascar, a member of the large Comorian community which had settled in Majunga on the west coast. After the 1976 massacre, he returned to the Comoros with the rest of the survivors in a Sabena aeroplane – this group of returned exiles were known from then on as 'the Sabenas'. The coup, he said, had been planned by the Malagasy who were jealous of the success and wealth of the Comorian people living there. He knew Denard's wife, Amina, he said. She was a Sabena.

His family went to live in Foumboni on the southern tip of Grande Comore, where he continued his schooling.

'Some months after the coup in 1978, I saw a crowd of young men gathered outside the prefecture. I went to see what was happening and was told that a mzungu, Captain Marquès, was recruiting for the army.'

He joined the throng of hopefuls, took the written dictation test, the physical – which included push-ups – and underwent the medical examination.

'I came out first,' he continued. 'Marquès took me in his car then and there and brought me to the military camp at Mdé.'

There he underwent more training, including combat training, running and assault courses. Again he came out top of the fifty cadets.

'Although I am small,' he told me, 'I am very strong.'

Rambo was obviously proud of his achievements, but he was not boasting. He told me he was the best because he believed he was and because the idea of false modesty did not cross his mind. It was a refreshingly simple statement of fact.

The rigorous training continued. He was transferred to Kandani, which was a hive of activity.

'This was when the Presidential Guard was really formed. It was divided into two companies, each with three sections. We were given black uniforms and green berets. We were proud to be in the PG.'

The regiment was given a motto: *Orbs Patria Nostra* – the World Is Our Country.

The PG's main duty was to guard the president, although they were also sent to deal with any problems that cropped up.

'We were the strongest. If there were strikes or demonstrations, we were called and when we came everyone was calm again. They were all scared of us.' Rambo looked proud.

After four months he was awarded his first red stripe and sent back to Itsoundzou to undergo the three-month training course to become a corporal. It was a difficult course but, not surprisingly, Rambo came out top and was promoted directly to corporal-chef. He moved into the training of new recruits.

'Those I trained were all admitted and in March 1980, I was made a sergeant. I enjoyed my job immensely, but I was beginning to get fed up with the mercenaries.

'Bob Denard was away a lot of the time and the other "petit mercenaires" did what they wanted. They would go into clubs, drink too much and insult people, threatening them with weapons. They raped women and got into fights. After a fight – regardless of who started it – they would take their adversary back to Kandani and lock him up. The Commandant Charles knew nothing of this behaviour, neither did Bob.

'At the start of 1982, I joined forces with Stofflet [the *nomme de guerre* of a French officer, Patrick Ollivier] to train more officers at Itsoundzou. He was a good bloke and very efficient in his job. I didn't like the Commandant Charles, though. He was a politician, not a soldier.'

Rambo got out a meticulously neat new notebook to check on a date, explaining that he had recently written an account of his experiences. His diary had been burnt when he was in jail.

'In 1983, my section was under the leadership of Henri Favreau, who although he spoke French, was not a Frenchman, I don't think. He was a racist and he insulted the black people. When my section was on manoeuvres one day, he insulted another sergeant-chef and called him a "fucking negro". I said: "It's not right for you to insult him in front of all the soldiers. Do you want to make war with me? You had better watch out!" After that we had "discussions" every day. He went and told Charles, who called me into his office and told me off. "It's not right," I told him. "You're black. There's the door, get out if you want to," he replied. I wrote out my resignation immediately. But all my friends and the people I had recruited and trained pleaded with me to change my mind. I said OK and went back, but I never forgot the incident and decided that one day the mercenaries would pay.'

Rambo was transferred to the Third Bureau, Operations, where he worked with Marquès [Dominique Malacrino], one of Denard's most faithful followers, who had served him in Benin and had been one of the original mercenaries who had come to the Comoros on the *Antinéa*.

'Marquès was much better. We worked well together. He was also small but very strong. We directed everything, including combat, from our office. However, I continued to fight with Favreau and I thought too much about him. When the élite went on the parachute course to South Africa, Favreau was also there and he talked about me in English to the South African instructors, saying that I was trouble. But Morkel, the teacher (he pointed him out on the photo, his name had been underlined), liked me and I always jumped first. Bob Denard came to watch the first jump and I landed right next to him. He shook my hand and congratulated me.'

On his return, Rambo went with Abdallah on a campaign trip to Anjouan. He showed me another photo of him in plain clothes, standing in front of a rostrum from where the President was delivering an impassioned speech.

'I thought that Bob Denard wanted to kill the President.'

'Why?' I asked.

Rambo glossed over it. 'But what would happen to us if he killed the President? I asked the other Comorians what we should do. They were scared but I wasn't. We talked secretly. I decided that we needed to get rid of the mercenaries as they were beginning to treat us very badly and I knew Abdallah was scared of them and would never get rid of them on his own. So I began preparations for a coup.

'I stole a Kalashnikov and hid it in a bag, which I gave to a friend – also a Guard – to hide. I started recruiting people. It wasn't difficult. There were lots of people who thought like I did.'

'Did you think you could overthrow the mercenaries with one Kalashnikov?'

'Easy. I could have attacked the whole camp alone if I had

wanted to. But I planned to have more weapons by the day of the coup and other soldiers with me as back-up. One day, however, the mercenaries searched the barracks and found the bag under my friend's bed. My friend talked under duress [something I suspected Rambo would never do] and the coup was over before it began. It was the end of 1984; the coup had been planned for 8th March 1985. I was arrested and taken to prison in Moroni.'

Only days later, Rambo jumped out of the window and went to Kandani to find a gun. The Comorian army, the PG and the gendarmes sent out search parties. There were announcements on Radio Comoros and the mercenaries broadcast orders that anyone who saw him should immediately inform the PG. They said he was as dangerous as Rambo. The name stuck.

Rambo became a Comorian Robin Hood. For three months he eluded capture on the main island.

'It was easy. I disguised myself as an old man, or a woman. No one would have recognised me, but I had a few people I could trust and they helped to hide me. One day, I was sitting in a tree, when a group of soldiers passed only feet away. If I had had a gun I would have killed all of them. No problem at all.'

He decided to leave the island. At night, he hid in some trees by the shore and saw a man refuelling his motor boat. At 2 am he waded into the sea and swimming, pulled the boat out past the reef, before climbing in, starting the engine and heading towards Anjouan. When he got there, he realised he was out of petrol. He found a man on the beach and asked him to get some more. The man said the nearest place for petrol was Domoni, but that he would fetch some. Rambo settled in the wood for a sleep, but the man rang the army and when Rambo awoke, he found he was surrounded by soldiers.

By this point in the telling of the story, Rambo was excited. He stood up in the low caravan and waved his hands around, re-enacting the scene.

'I thought, that's it, it's all over. I got up and took an empty petrol can in each hand. When I got near to the soldiers, I threw the cans at them on either side', he demonstrated vigorous throwing movements, 'and while they were trying to sort themselves out, I escaped again. I went and hid in the mountains. For five days I stayed up there, trying to avoid the people searching for me. At one point, they had almost caught up with me, so I dived into a deep hole and stayed there without moving while they passed.

'On the fifth day, I went to see a friend of mine, Malide, in Mutsamudu. I asked him where I could find another boat. He told me the army's speed boat, Karthala, was in the port, guarded only by two men. I planned to take it that night, after I had rested in Malide's house. But he gave me away. I should have known – he was an Anjouanais and they were always loyal to the president – in return they received many favours. I awoke in my underpants to see Jean-Pierre [one of the mercenaries, real name Dessales] and his men launching an attack on my bedroom. I escaped into another building. There was a crowd of women in a room, I told them to be quiet and moved into the shop next door. It had only one door; I was trapped. I climbed into the roof. Meanwhile I heard the soldiers hitting the women, demanding to know where I had gone. The Gendarme Commandant, Alani, appeared at the door and shot seven cartridges at me, but by ducking and rolling, I managed to avoid them. I shouted: "Stop, if not, I'll kill you!"

'I tried to take a little child as hostage, but they caught me, tied me up and then fifty men hit me with their rifle butts. They put me in a Peugeot 404 like a sack of rice, and took me back to Grande Comore. I was very pleased, it felt like a victory,' he told me, with relish.

'What happened next?'

'Well, I arrived back in Moroni to find I was a hero. People were in the streets shouting and crying "Anwar, Anwar . . ." I was taken to prison, where I found the other soldiers who had been implicated in the coup. I was kept in chains for two months, blindfolded and beaten every day.

'On the fourth day I was given some food; three spoons of rice. They would shut my fingers in the door and say "talk, talk".' He showed me his fingers, bent unnaturally back.

Rambo and twenty-five other soldiers were then taken to the military prison at Itsoundzou, where they stayed until Abdallah's death nearly five years later. One died.

He broke off his gripping narrative: 'I'm sorry, but I have to change as I am due on duty at 18.00 hours.'

I left, breathless from the story, and walked back to the hotel.

It was an amazing tale of adventure. The hero was as brave and as strong as his namesake. I asked a few people about him and they confirmed the basics of his story.

'Yes, he was a hero on Grande Comore for a while,' Ali Toihir told me. 'The whole army was frantic to find him, but the people were sympathetic. I think he was exaggerating about the coup, though. I don't think he planned it single-handedly and I don't think his motives were as pure as he said. The coup attempt went ahead without him, you know. It was a disaster. If I were you, I would go and talk to Moustapha Said Cheik about it. He went to jail too.'

*

There was a follow-up to this coup attempt, one that showed an even darker side to the mercenaries. Mahamoud took me to see Moustapha Said Cheik, leader of the Front Démocratique des Comores, one of the larger opposition bodies. For much of Abdallah's time, they were the only active – although still partly underground – opposition party. Many people I had talked to had dismissed them as a bunch of communists, but Mahamoud said that Moustapha was a great intellectual and that many of the young Lycée students supported him. Papa Claude surprised me when he also said that he voted for the FD.

Moustapha's house was in a compound near Itsandra petrol station. It was small but pleasant. Flowery curtains billowed out from open doorways and windows. His wife greeted us in the passage, saying that Moustapha was in the middle of a political meeting but that we should go in anyway. My first impression of the sitting-room was of piles and piles of books, tumbling down from tables and shelves, gathering dust on the floor. Several grave-faced and important-looking men in white *bou-bous*, were sitting around talking in low voices. Moustapha sat in a big armchair, looking more like a bemused observer than a participant. He motioned for us to sit by the window.

He had a wide and charming face, a bushy beard, fleshy lips, glasses and an easy smile. I instinctively trusted him, despite what I had been told about his politics and the apparent fickleness of his allegiances. Some of the men gathered in the cramped room, Mahamoud whispered, were current and past ministers. They were talking about a constitutional crisis that would ensue if something happened to Djohar who was, at that time, the only current elected member of the National Assembly.

'They said that if he dies, there is no one to take his place,' Mahamoud explained.

Moustapha, who had said nothing since I arrived, apparently decided it was time for the meeting to come to an end. He stood up and said a few quiet words, whereupon the grave-faced men filed out, still muttering.

He turned to me. 'So, what is it you want to learn?' he asked in beautifully modulated French. His accent, as far as I could determine, was elegant and his vocabulary extensive.

'I want to find out about the mercenaries and more particularly about the attempted coup in 1985,' I said. 'I was told that you would be a good person to talk to.'

'When Abdallah was in power, the mercenaries held the balance of power,' Moustapha explained. 'At first that was because they controlled the army, but little by little they started trying to penetrate into all areas of life. Through the cabinet director, Ahmed Abdou, they controlled the president and they had a hand in all the big deals. Their influence spread to agriculture and fuel and commerce. They were involved in massive corruption; together with Abdallah they were making large profits out of our poor country.

'It was a régime of terror. From Ali Soilih's mistakes, the mercenaries had learnt that it was not a good idea to attack the aged and the deeply religious. They kept them on their side and used them to cover up their corrupt deeds. In doing so, they crushed the little people.'

'Was it much more repressive than Ali Soilih's reign?' I asked.

'The same amount of people, proportionately speaking that is, disappeared under the two régimes. But towards the end of the mercenary régime, brutality and torture became daily currency. You see, as a result of the corruption, they were beginning to lose support and thus control. They had to resort to violence and because there was resistance, they had to use increasingly terrible means to suppress the people. Torture was commonplace and people disappeared. Some people who disappeared in 1985 have never been seen again.'

The story of the attempted coup of 8th March 1985, was gradually revealed to me.

On 30th September 1984, Abdallah was re-elected with 99.4 per cent of all votes cast. The Presidential Guard oversaw the voting and according to several accounts, was involved in the large-scale cheating and intimidation that took place during the run-up to elections. The Comorian people, and more specifically Comorian members of the PG, were becoming increasingly dissatisfied with the mercenaries. A plot was hatched to try to get rid of them.

The active members were a small band of Guards, all apparently from Rambo's section, and all Grande Comorians. Rambo was, by this time, hiding in the countryside – his fellow men had decided to proceed without him. Their plan was to attack the mercenary officers in their mess – into which they weren't allowed to take weapons – while they were having their traditional Friday night 'regimental dinner'. However, details of the plot were leaked to Marquès several days before, the dinner was cancelled and the mutineers were captured as they approached the camp.

At first the attempted coup was played down. Denard was out of the country and Abdallah was conveniently in France on a personal visit. The president issued a statement insisting the plotters were 'junkies', and saying that he had no plans to cut short his trip. On 14th March, the minister acting as president in his absence, put out another statement, which blamed the failed coup attempt on 'ordinary soldiers of the PG with the complicity of civilian elements'.

The panic began. There were a large number of arrests of Guard members – noticeably none from Abdallah's home island of Anjouan – and opposition politicians. Moustapha was one of the first to be picked up, accused of being the chief instigator of the coup. All other known members of the Front Démocratique were also detained and it was claimed that large sums of money were found in their houses. The FD faction in Paris issued a statement, on 18th March, denying any involvement and insisting that an 'unwavering consistency' of its political stance was the 'unreserved condemnation' of coups d'états.

The mercenaries demanded an immediate court martial, followed by exemplary executions, but they were persuaded not to go ahead by Denard.

An emergency committee which included the head of the regular army, Commandant Ahmed Mohammed, and the chief of police, Commandant Abdou Rezac, was appointed to decide what steps to take and to discuss new arrangements for the president's protection.

Abdallah returned from his trip to mounting mayhem. His previous tactic of underplaying the coup had changed. On a radio broadcast to the nation, he said it had been: 'A well planned operation, whose purpose was to transform the country totally by means of a revolution, make religion disappear and eliminate certain social classes.' The plotters were 'atheistic devils seeking to eliminate Islam,' he stated.

The hard core revolutionaries, the brains behind the guard members, comprised three groups: The Front Démocratique, the previously unheard of 'Mouvement Communiste Marxiste-Leniniste des Comores' and 'a clandestine group comprising our young cadres whose task was to provide the MCMLC with administrative documents, slow down the progress of our services, persuade villages and districts to rebel and spread false reports.'

Abdallah said that evidence seized showed the MCMLC to comprise seven members, with Moustapha Said Cheik at their head.

The seven were arrested between 18th and 20th March and taken to Kandani for interrogation, together with more FD leaders from all three islands and numerous senior officials suspected of being sympathetic to the coup. Some of Abdallah's ministers had their houses searched, while others were forced into hiding. The total number alleged to have been arrested varied from seventy to eight hundred depending on who issued the figures.

But the mass hysteria being whipped up by the coup attempt lacked a logical foundation. Thirty soldiers had been captured while trying to attack the mercenaries, who had full fore-knowledge of the event. Not a shot had been fired.

And there were several strange coincidences. A United States Navy ship, the USS *Jason*, had berthed in Moroni the night before the coup attempt in what was the first visit of its kind. Why was Abdallah not there to greet it? In the weeks that followed, the USS *Jason* gave all typewriters on the island a compulsory overhaul. This, presumably, enabled intelligence to be gathered about who had allowed their machines to be used for the production of anti-government pamphlets by the FD.

And why had Abdallah's stance concerning the coup altered so radically? His return was followed by a series of mass demonstrations, organised to show support for him. His popularity, which had been waning, soared (much as Mrs Thatcher's had after the success of the Falklands conflict). Most of the political opposition was safely behind bars, awaiting trial for treason.

The Front Démocratique organised rallies in Paris to protest against the 'coup' they claimed had been mounted against their internal leadership.

A French and a Belgian lawyer arrived in Moroni on 4th May. The Frenchman was there to defend a member of the FD and the Belgian as an observer for the International Human Rights Federation. They were picked up on their first day and denied permission to remain in the country, see any evidence, or meet any prisoners.

The trial was repeatedly postponed. There were widespread reports of torture. The FD claimed three people had been tortured to death. The official numbers of how many people were being held prisoner changed constantly. Abdallah's popularity may have experienced a quick boost, but the same could not be said for the mercenaries. On 13th July, three mercenaries pistol-whipped a singer in a Moroni hotel during a dance. The singer, 'Boulle', suffered fractures to the skull and other injuries.

The trial was eventually held from 4th to 7th November in the People's Palace. Thirty-six FD officials and thirty-one soldiers appeared in front of a judge from the Moroni criminal court. They all had to conduct their own defence. Moustapha Said Cheik and sixteen Guard members were sentenced to life imprisonment, despite the fact that no proof of Moustapha's guilt was provided to the court. The others received sentences varying between one and eight years. One man was acquitted.

The Guard members initially refused to answer any questions, saying that during the run-up to the trial, the Chief Qadi of Moroni had made them swear on the Koran not to say anything which might harm the authorities. They only agreed to answer questions after the Qadi relieved them of the oath. The aim of the mutiny, they said, was to get rid of the mercenaries in order to bring to the attention of the authorities the humiliations and bullying they had been subjected to.

'Who did they say was behind the plot?' I asked Moustapha.

'They didn't.'

'Were you?'

He smiled conspiratorially. 'I was informed of the intended mutiny by members of the Presidential Guard, but I did my best to try to dissuade them. They corroborated this in court.'

'So, to the best of your knowledge, the coup was all their idea?'

He shrugged. 'It was very nice to meet you, my dear. Please excuse me, but I am going to Anjouan tomorrow and I have many things to do.'

*

Mahamoud and I went to the small Coelacanth Hotel for a drink. Ramadan had ended several days earlier and there was a feel of spring in the air. The bush taxi radios were switched on again and sounds of laughter and Comorian music filled the town.

'What did you think of Moustapha?' Mahamoud asked me over a Coke.

'I liked him. He is obviously very intelligent. What does he do for a living?'

Mahamoud looked slightly shocked. 'Oh, Moustapha has never worked, he is an intellectual. He finished his scientific studies in Paris during Ali Soilih's time and when he returned to the Comoros, he founded the FD. He is funded by his supporters to be a full-time opposition politician.'

We talked about the coup attempt. Mahamoud said he couldn't remember it very well, but he knew it had provoked mixed feelings among the people.

'It was the first time anyone really tried to overthrow the

mercenaries, you know. In 1983, Prince Kemal hired some Australian and British mercenaries and planned a coup, but it never got off the ground.'

(I later asked Kemal about his abortive coup, but he refused to talk about it, saying only that he had been based in Paris at the time and had had to go to Clacton-on-Sea to meet the mercenaries. 'That is the mercenary centre of the United Kingdom, you know,' he told me.)

'1985 was the first time that the seed of rebellion was sewn in Comorian minds', Mahamoud continued, 'and it didn't stop there. The next coup attempt took place in 1987.'

*

On the night of 30th November 1987, thirty men left Moroni for the military camp at Itsoundzou. Their aim was to try to liberate Rambo and the other former members of the Guard still imprisoned for their role in the 1985 attempted coup. They crept along the road in the dark and ran straight into an ambush. The rescue attempt, it later transpired, had been betrayed to Marquès by a sergeant from Anjouan. This time the mercenaries did not hold their fire. Three men were killed and immediately buried by the side of the road. The rest were arrested by the mercenaries led by Marquès. They were thrown into jail, accused of plotting to obtain arms, to overthrow Abdallah and replace him with Moustapha Said Cheik.

The ministry of the interior admitted, ten days later, that 'a military plot had been foiled' and that 'three conspirators had been killed in the clashes'. They omitted to mention that the 'conspirators' had been unarmed and that they were shot without a word of warning. All the arrested men were former members of the PG, the Comorian armed forces or Ali Soilih's élite force, the Moissi. Reports seeped out of more torture at the camp. Sources claimed that up to ten people had died.

On the night of 6th December, the body of the first victim, Gaya, twenty, from Badjini in the south, was dumped at his family's door. On 8th December, two others: Addili, nineteen, and Boina Idi, twenty-five, were returned. According to those who carried out the ritualistic washing of the bodies, the dead men had been subjected to atrocious mutilation; their bodies were covered in cigarette burns and fierce weals, their teeth had been smashed and torn out, their eyes gouged and their wrists broken.

Itsoundzou had no morgue. If the bodies had died a week earlier, they would have been in a state of advanced decomposition. They weren't.

The Comorian members of the Guard were said to be shocked. They said that seven people had been killed in all – the bodies that had been too mutilated were buried at Itsoundzou. It appeared that the Comorian authorities had little to do with the treatment of the prisoners; the interior minister himself, Omar Tamou, was denied permission to visit them.

Opposition groups, including the FD and the URDC (Mouzawar Abdallah's party), issued a statement on 31st December, in Paris, in which they demanded 'the departure of foreign mercenaries' from the Comoros and the 'organisation of a national poll as soon as possible'. They said that 'by mounting their suicide operation of 30th November, our compatriots were expressing the despair of the Comorian people in the face of the confiscation of power by a group of mercenaries.'

A communiqué later issued by the Coordination Nationale pour un Parti Alternatif, stated that Ali Soilih's followers had not been involved in the coup attempt. Boina Idi had been Soilih's driver and bodyguard, but he had fled into exile in Marseille weeks after Abdallah's return, where he had become close to Mouzawar. It had been 'the Snake', together with Abbas Djoussouf, who had encouraged Boina Idi on his kamikaze mission, they claimed.

The reports of torture by the mercenaries were widespread. Rambo had certainly been tortured – although not to such a final degree – and the three bodies had undoubtedly been in a bad state when they were returned. Not having seen them, I am unwilling to judge the extent to which the stories of torture had been exaggerated by 'Radio-Cocotier' (the Comorian equivalent of the bush telegraph). Denard has always denied that heavy-handed torture took place and particularly dis-associated himself from any blame. In a long profile of the mercenary leader written by the French writer, Jean Lartéguy, and published in *Paris Match* in March 1989, Denard was quoted as saying 'I can kill a man with a bullet in his head, but I am incapable of torture, I find it repugnant.'

I believe this to be true, whatever horrors were perpetrated by the mercenaries nominally under his control.

He implied that the opposition was exploiting the coup attempt to show how the régime was becoming increasingly unpopular and sinking to brutality and repression. The reports had been grossly exaggerated, he claimed. Only three people had been killed and the torture had not extended beyond the bounds of reasonable interrogation. 'The PG was certainly not a group of choirboys, but it maintained order and guarded against excess,' he said.

*

There was another failed coup attempt in 1987, planned this time by a former 'European officer' of the Presidential Guard, Max Veillard. A French photographer friend in Paris, Eric, knew Max well and from both of them I pieced together the story of 'Servadac'.

Max Veillard was not a typical mercenary. He came from a well-off bourgeois family: his father was a director of the Banque Nationale de Paris. He went through officer training college at St Cyr (France's Sandhurst), but graduated bottom of his year. He went on to serve as a lieutenant in the first infantry regiment based in Sarrebourg. He resigned after a few years to pursue higher studies in commerce. According to my friend the photographer, 'Max was small, charming, not very

good looking, but polite and intelligent with a definite Machiavellian streak. He was extremely brave, but completely mad.'

In 1985, he gave up his degree course and went out to the
Comoros to join Denard, who was at that time trying to raise
the quality of the 'European officers'. Max chose as his *nomme
de guerre*, 'Servadac' after a character in the Jules Verne novel,
Les Enfants de Capitaine Grant. (It is also – perhaps co-
incidentally – an anagram for the French *cadavres* – corpses.)
He enjoyed his time there at first. He liked Denard and
described him as 'physically brave, cunning and street-wise'.
He thought, however, that the mercenary chief had the
mentality of a staff sergeant, not an officer, and that he
invariably surrounded himself with men of a lower calibre.
Marquès, Max described as 'a brute', as was another of the
captains, Jean-Pierre, while Captain Hoffman (real name:
Dominique Cuny) was 'incredibly stupid'.

He resigned his commission in 1987, disillusioned with the
mercenary outfit in the Comoros. But as soon as he returned to
Paris, he was contacted by various parties interested in getting
rid of Denard and Abdallah. A Monsieur Traufier, reputed to
be an international crook and smuggler, promised Max that if
he led a coup which succeeded in eliminating Abdallah, each
man who took part would be paid FF 200,000.

Fifteen days after leaving the Comoros, Max returned to
scout out the lie of the land. He told his surprised former
colleagues that he had come for a scuba-diving holiday. He
quickly recruited an adjutant of the PG, and with two other
mercenaries they started putting together a plan. It was simple:
a transport plane would land at Hahaya airport and disgorge
its load of jeeps and armed men. Simultaneously, a boat would
arrive at Itsandra beach with another contingent of soldiers.
The two forces would attack the PG base at Kandani and the
presidency at Beit es-Salaam.

However, Max's plot went the same way as the two other
attempted coups; one of the mercenaries he had recruited
confided in another mercenary who in turn told Marquès.

Max and his fellow conspirators were arrested and were lucky to leave the islands alive. Denard intervened, probably acting on orders from Paris and Pretoria. An officer of the International Police Cooperation Service was in the Comoros at the time and it was probably he who relayed Paris's wishes to Denard.

Max was bitter. He wanted revenge. He returned to Paris where he re-established contact with Taki, who had been behind the attempt to overthrow Ali Soilih in 1976, before returning to serve as the chairman of the Federal Assembly. He had recently fallen out with Abdallah as well and was living in exile in Paris.

It was during this period that Eric got to know Max. He was working as Taki's informal publicity agent, spreading anti-Abdallah, pro-Taki propaganda through the press. Eric said Max often spoke of his time on the Comoros and of his obsession to overthrow Denard. He told him that the PG had been particularly brutal following the 1985 and 1987 coup attempts.

Denard left the Comoros before Max had a chance to carry out his coup. He got his opportunity, however, in 1990. This time the aim of the mission was to depose Djohar and put Taki in his place. However, his plans were again foiled and after weeks on the run, the luckless Max was shot dead on a beach on Anjouan by Comorian soldiers. At the age of thirty-eight 'Servadac''s dream of taking over the Comoros had ended forever.

*

I knew I was coming closer and closer to finding out about Abdallah's death and Denard's subsequent departure. I wanted to know what had happened to force the mercenaries to leave the country and above all, I wanted to meet the charismatic Colonel Denard, whose presence on the islands had had such a devastating effect.

The mid-Eighties signalled the beginning of the end of

the mercenary era. After the way they had acted during the attempted coups of 1985 and 1987, their relationship with the majority of Comorians had been smashed and their eventual demise was inevitable.

The mercenaries faced further complications. In 1987, Marquès replaced Charles as Commander of the PG. Charles stayed on for some months as Abdallah's special adviser, before leaving the country with his Comorian wife and children to return to Liège. With his departure, a vital, close link with the president was severed. However, it was a relief for Denard, who had been increasingly forced into a position of uneasy rivalry with his second-in-command. 'When Charles left the Comoros,' he was quoted as saying, 'he left a big hole for the President, a hole I didn't want to fill. I couldn't afford to spend my whole time being charming.'

Denard had more important fish to fry. The special relationship he had enjoyed with South Africa for nearly a decade was threatening to crumble, as the winds of change swept over the Republic. President P. W. Botha appeared intent on starting a process of reform of the whole system of apartheid, in an effort to pave the way for South Africa's re-entry into the international community. When that happened, there would surely be no need for them to prop up a mercenary régime in the insignificant Comoro Islands.

Roger Harding, the South African trade representative on the Comoros, had become increasingly outspoken in his criticism of the mercenaries. After the episode when his friendship T-shirts had been confiscated, he had grabbed every possible opportunity to try to disassociate his country from Denard and his men.

'South Africa, given its negative image and its extreme desire to present itself in a decent light, is more or less at the mercy of the powers that be,' Harding complained in a press interview. 'South Africa is constantly reminded that if it doesn't do what is requested, it can leave.'

It was only a matter of time before South Africa decided to

pull out on its own account. The mercenaries' bad reputation was rubbing off on their already heavily tarnished image. All the development money South Africa poured into the Comoros was channelled through the PG's bank account. The farm was known as the 'mercenary farm', the luxury new hotels under construction were 'the mercenary hotels', Guard troops had moved into the houses South Africa had built to test lava-to-bricks technology, and Eduard Jonas, the Afrikans doctor running the medical evacuation scheme, drove around in a car bearing the distinctive Presidential Guard licence plates. After the attempted coup of November 1987, when at least three Comorians had been tortured to death by the mercenaries, village children yelled 'assassin' at Harding's car.

In March 1989, Roger Harding was called in to see Ahmed Abdou, Abdallah's cabinet director, and asked to leave the country. His main offence, it appeared, was to have openly criticised the mercenaries' presence on the islands.

France too, was becoming fed up with the mercenaries, who were always referred to as 'French', yet who had become increasingly tied to Pretoria. At the end of December 1988, the then South African defence minister, the hawkish General Magnus Malan, visited the Comoros. France tried to persuade Charles to influence Abdallah not to meet him, to no avail. The next year, Abdallah paid several visits to South Africa. The French made one thing clear: they would not be prepared to continue to pour money into their former puppet nation if the strings were truly out of their grasp. The scene was set for a showdown.

10

Death of a President

THE COMOROS AWOKE on 27th November 1989, to the soothing sounds of classical music on the radio. They knew what it meant even before the official announcement on Radio Comoros. There had been a coup d'état. Their President was dead.

President Ahmed Abdallah Abderemane, the first and fourth president of the independent Comoro Islands, died at around midnight on Sunday 26th November 1989. The man who had been at the forefront of Comorian politics for forty years, who was known to his people as 'the father of Independence', was finally out of the picture.

The country was thrown into turmoil. People stayed in their houses to await the latest news. For several hours, Moroni was empty; the streets were deserted, the market was abandoned, no prayers were said at the mosques. Whispers travelled from house to hut, town to village.

The first rumour to be disseminated by Radio Cocotier blamed the murder on the former head of the ragged Comorian Armed Forces (CAF), Commandant Ahmed Mohammed. He was known to have been dissatisfied with the way he had been dismissed from his position months earlier and this, it was thought, was his way of exacting revenge on the President. He had been the brains behind the RPG7 missile, which had been shot through Abdallah's window, the rumour went. But this story was greeted with scepticism; the Commandant was from Anjouan, he was known to be completely loyal to the President, he could not possibly have killed him. When, hours later, the news hit the streets that Ahmed had been asleep in his home on Anjouan at the time of the President's death, suspicions inevitably turned to Bob Denard.

An official statement released on Radio Comores at 8.30 am stated that: 'The presidency was attacked by unknown elements. The Presidential Guard, who assure the President's protection, riposted. There was an exchange of shots and the President was mortally wounded.'

All lines of communication with the outside world had been cut. There were only three satellite phones on the island: Denard had one, the head of the United Nations Development Project had another, and the new South African trade representative, Marco Boni, had the third. The story was slow to hit the international press and first reports were confused.

The early newspapers placed the blame on Commandant Ahmed, adding that after killing the President, he in turn had been shot by the Presidential Guard. Who told them? On the BBC World Service midday news, South African foreign minister, 'Pik' Botha, in an unfortunate *faux pas*, stated: 'my representative on the ground assures me that the security forces have everything under control'.

The exiled Comorian opposition party, 'L'Union Nationale pour la Démocratie aux Comores' (UNDC) was the first to come up with an alternative explanation. They announced from Paris that: 'It is clear that from now on, the Comoros are hostages of the mercenaries, led by Bob Denard and his companion, "Marquès", who according to all the information we can find, assassinated the President Ahmed Abdallah Abderemane.' They demanded the immediate intervention of France under the terms of the bilateral defence pact signed in 1978. 'The President may have been a dictator, but he was a man of the Comoros, who wasn't a hostage to anyone,' said the general-secretary of the UNDC, Mouni Madi.

A radio announcement stated that, under the terms of the Comorian constitution, the President of the Supreme Court,

Said Djohar, would hold the position of interim-president until new elections were held. Djohar followed the announcement by declaring a 40-day period of national mourning. Denard refused to talk about the events of 26th November until the period of mourning was over. But that did not stop the accusing whispers.

The same day, the remains of the President and his bodyguard, Djaffar, who had died at the same time, were taken to their native island of Anjouan, where an autopsy was performed at the hospital in Domoni. Sergeant-Chef Djaffar was buried that evening, while the President's family decided to wait for the return of his twin sons from France.

The words 'assassination' and 'murder' were banned from the pages of the Comorian weekly newspaper, *Al Watwany*. The Presidential Guard kept a twenty-four hour watch over Radio Comores, monitoring the content of their broadcasts. Members of the CAF were rounded up, photographed and then released. Most returned to their villages.

The foreign press started to trickle into the country incognito. People discovered to be journalists were summarily thrown out by the Presidential Guard. But some remained undiscovered and facts began to leak out, many of them contradictory; numerous witnesses said they had heard heavy gunfire around Moroni from 23.56 to 00.44. There were reports of five dead Comorian members of the PG, one dead and three injured gendarmes. But the president's palace showed no signs of a shoot-out – no bullet holes were visible.

The PG patrolled the island ostentatiously. 'We are on full alert,' explained a Comorian Guard. They occupied all the strategic points, including the airport and the CAF headquarters, and patrolled the streets in landrovers and jeeps, displaying their insignia: a black bat on a yellow shield. The interim-president, Djohar, in a private meeting with a French diplomat, held his wrists together apparently to indicate that he was being held hostage.

Abdallah's sons arrived on Anjouan at 5.30 on Tuesday

28th November. Their father was buried in the heart of his home in the presence of the entire government. The funeral was marked by the absence of any foreign dignitary or diplomat.

Work officially re-started on Thursday 30th, but the schools were still empty and many of the workers who turned up showed a marked lack of concentration and motivation. The opposition held their first meeting at the home of Mouzawar Abdallah. He and Abbas Djoussouf called for a mass demonstration the following Saturday to protest against the occupying mercenaries. The island was relatively calm. The rest of the week passed without incident.

On 4th December, Marco Boni announced the cessation of all South African support to the Presidential Guard and demanded the immediate departure of the mercenaries.

On the afternoon of 5th December, Denard held a first terse press conference for the benefit of the journalists who had managed to avoid being thrown out and whose presence he had obviously decided to tolerate. Flanked by Marquès and Siam, he denied any involvement in the President's death:

'I am not the murderer of President Abdallah. Nor are any of the men under my command.'

He did not once open the file that lay on the desk in front of him. 'It will be put in the hands of the authorities,' he said.

He refused to answer any questions.

'Islam and the customs of the Comoros prevent me from talking during the mourning period,' he explained, as he tried to convince the journalists of his good faith and lack of motive.

'We pass for professionals, so don't you think we would have arranged this a bit more neatly?' he asked.

That was his only concession to reason. For the most part, he spoke from his heart which, he insisted, 'is Comorian'.

He had 'for more than fifteen years, enjoyed daily personal relations', with Abdallah, he said, who he considered to be 'like a brother . . . He sometimes called me at 4 o'clock in the morning, just to say; "Bako, I can't get to sleep." I never had a single stormy conversation with him.'

Denard was particularly upset that: 'We failed in our mission,' of protecting the President.

That morning he had tried to clear his name in the time-honoured Muslim fashion; he asked his wife's uncle, the Grand Mufti of Moroni, to organise a 'Hitima' – a cleansing ceremony.

'I am a Muslim, my family is Muslim,' he explained.

During the ceremony, all guilt and suspicion is meant to be washed away as the Charifs, pious descendants of the Prophet Mohammed, lecture from the Koran. Witnessing the act of faith, the gathered *notables* testify to the benediction of the one who has undergone the Hitima.

'It is often practised around here,' said a believer waiting outside the mosque. But a serious Hitima had not been said in the great Friday mosque since 1986, when the Grand Mufti had exonerated the members of the opposition accused of setting the Lycée on fire. If Denard had received his Hitima, he would have been able to walk away from the mosque cleared of suspicion, with his head held high. But it wasn't to be.

From nine in the morning, small groups of young people and believers started assembling in the square in front of the mosque.

'It's a sham,' said one of them to a watching reporter from *Liberation*.

'Denard may be a Muslim, but he's not devout.'

The elders, solemn in their traditional gowns, started to gather.

'The Mufti will never accept this masquerade,' said the observer.

'You may well say that, but remember, it was he who married him, who gave him his name, who instructed him in the ways of Islam,' another retorted.

The Charifs, however, were of the same mind as the majority of the population. They stayed outside the mosque, refusing to take part in Denard's Hitima.

Shortly after ten o'clock, a cream Peugeot 505 drew up and parked in the square. A European captain in plain clothes climbed out, his mini machine-gun barely hidden beneath his pressed white shirt. He stared menacingly at the crowd. Minutes later, Denard's car arrived. He parked at the foot of the mosque and in silence, surrounded by his Comorian bodyguard, he limped towards the central stairs. He wore a pale grey suit and an open-necked sky blue shirt. On his head he sported a *koffia* embroidered with the words; 'In the name of Allah the merciful'. At the foot of the stairs he paused, and with some difficulty, took off his sturdy black ankle boots. Slowly, he climbed up the steps and entered the mosque. Alone.

Inside, he lowered himself carefully to sit cross-legged on a heavy, red carpet representing the Kaaba of Mecca, the sacred tomb of the Prophet. He leaned back against a pillar and looked around. The mosque was empty. Only one ancient *notable*, Nze Abdallah, a yellow scarf around his shoulders, came to sit next to him. Denard took his hand and kissed it. Outside, the crowd murmured their discontent.

The Grand Mufti arrived. Without a word, he walked into the mosque. He stayed just long enough to let Denard know that the Hitima would not take place. He said a short 'fatiha', a prayer asking forgiveness, before leaving the mosque, closely followed by Denard. The mercenary was obviously shaken and humiliated. He knew his attempt to prove his innocence to the Comorian people had backfired. He quickly put his boots back on. His bodyguards cleared a route back to the car. The crowds started to hiss quietly, almost hesitantly: 'Denard, assassin!' It grew to a hoarse whisper as more people joined in: 'Assassin, assassin!', quickly building up to a cry: 'Denard, assassin! PG nalawe! [get out]'. 'Where is France?' the crowd demanded as a mercenary captain took photographs of the demonstrators.

Overnight, slogans appeared on walls and daubed on to the

side of the mosque: 'End the pillage, out with the thieves and assassins!' On Thursday 7th December, a demonstration was organised by the students. A large group from the Said Mohammed Cheik Lycée crossed the town, waving banners and shouting for the mercenaries to leave. They were intercepted at a PG barricade on the coast road, near the Coelacanth Hotel. Guards in jeeps charged towards the students, while the men behind the barricade let off tear-gas. The students turned to run. The PG pursued them towards the market, hitting them with rifle butts and clubs. They rounded up the photographers who had been present and confiscated their films. The troubles continued until evening. One Guard was dragged out of his car by the demonstrators and beaten up, his vehicle was set on fire.

President Djohar and the Grand Mufti appealed for calm. Mouzawar and Abbas cancelled the demonstration planned for Saturday.

Marco Boni released a statement to the press:

The minister of foreign affairs, Mr Pik Botha, declared today in Pretoria that in the light of the tragic events surrounding the assassination of President Ahmed Abdallah Abderemane in the Comoros, the South African government has decided:
– to suspend assistance to the Presidential Guard and all other forms of co-operation with the Comoros which had been agreed in the past with Abdallah and to wait for the situation to normalise.
– to demand the immediate departure of all expatriate elements preventing the Comorian people from exercising their democratic right to self-determination.
– to support all efforts permitting the Comorian people to decide the correct path leading to peace and democracy without outside interference.

Botha also affirmed that the shape of the future relationship between South Africa and the Comoros would be decided after consultation with the democratically elected leaders of the archipelago, with the aim of promoting the population's well being and reinforcing existing ties between the two countries. He said that South Africa was at present exchanging information with all parties interested in bringing the current situation to some conclusion by way of a co-ordinated approach.

Behind the scenes, through their diplomatic representatives, both Pretoria and Paris were frantically trying to cut a deal with Denard, which would lead to his departure from the islands before any more blood was shed. While in Mayotte, the French were hastily assembling a task force, ready to attack Grande Comore if negotiations failed. The purpose of the force, they claimed, was to remove all French citizens on the islands away to safety. But they fooled nobody. Denard and his men would have to leave the islands if the French were to retain any credibility, both with the Comorian people and in the eyes of the world.

At 9.30 pm on Tuesday 12th December, Denard held a second press conference at the PG headquarters in Kandani. He looked pale as he sat behind a large table, surrounded by his men.

'I, Colonel Said Mustapha M'hadjou, solemnly swear on my life and my conscience, before God and men, that the declarations to follow are true and sincere. Having talked to the interim-president as well as to the Abdallah family about my respect for the memory of President Abdallah; having consulted my Comorian friends and my men; in the light of the terrible accusations that weigh heavy on our minds; in the light of the South African and French pressure being exerted to chase us off the islands in a state of dishonour; in the light of the deployment of an armada which threatens to intervene at any moment, creating a situation in which it would be impossible to avoid a blood bath, I have decided to break my silence during the mourning period.'

He gave his version of the events leading up to the death of the President. He talked about the disintegration of the Comorian Armed Forces and the forced resignation of their chief, the Commandant Ahmed Mohammed.

'After the Commandant's departure, they had no leader, no mission, no money. Abdallah had decided to disband them so as to reduce expenditure. But certain elements of the CAF weren't too pleased.'

In the night of 26th November, the president's palace was attacked by automatic gunfire. The source was assumed to be dissident members of the CAF, Denard explained. The PG section on duty replied. They alerted Marquès, who called Denard and Captain Siam, a recently-arrived officer. Together they went directly to the palace and into the President's study. Denard urged Abdallah to sign an order to disarm all members of the CAF on Grande Comore and Anjouan, to prevent a further attack. Denard showed the document to the assembled journalists. It was hand-written in spidery black ink on a piece of the President's headed paper. 'The order is given to the Presidential Guard to disarm the Comorian Armed Forces. The civil and military authorities, in this case the gendarmerie, must give their help whenever requested.' There was a scrawled signature at the bottom.

'Later, Staff-sergeant Djaffar arrived. He was half-dressed and carried a Kalashnikov in his arms. He was obviously in a state of panic. He was told to stay on guard in the hall. A bit later, two soldiers from the PG came in to report to Marquès that they had been injured by bullets and shrapnel. The President was sitting in an armchair in the next-door room, talking to the Colonel [throughout the press conference, Denard referred to himself in the third person], who sat in front of him. Some time later, while they were still conversing, there was a sustained burst of gunfire directed at the study. Djaffar burst into the room and aimed his gun at the Colonel and the President. The Colonel, surprised, threw himself to the floor as Djaffar opened fire, hitting the President full-on in his chest. The Captain [Siam] returned fire and Djaffar fell to the ground.'

Denard read the statement in the formal tones of a police officer in court. He once again refused to answer questions, but as he rose to leave, he muttered almost to himself: 'Yes, Djaffar's attitude was inexplicable . . . panic. The President's death was an accident arising out of a state of general madness. I am fed up with being called an assassin. It's really too damned stupid.'

The negotiations moved inexorably towards a conclusion. On Thursday 14th December – two and a half weeks after Abdallah's death – the first batch of about half a dozen mercenaries, accompanied by their families and Denard's wife and two young children, Hamza and Kaina, left on the night flight to Paris, via Nairobi and Marseille.

Earlier that day, at another hastily-convened press conference following a rainy awards ceremony at Kandani barracks, Denard had said he was prepared to leave, but 'not like dogs kicked out into the street. If we depart, we must do so with our heads held high.' The aim of the parade ostensibly, was to promote Comorian members of the Guard to replace the departing mercenary officers. The three hundred ordinary soldiers, smart in their camouflage uniforms, presented arms (in their case, Kalashnikov semi-automatic rifles). Denard, wearing a soon-sodden safari suit, stood at the end of the lines, his head held high.

At the press conference, he stated his demands for an orderly withdrawal. They included: a parade with regimental flags flying, bands playing and a farewell address to his men, compensation for their 'moral and material investments on the island', an amnesty for him and his men in connection with the death of Abdallah, six months severance pay for his officers, the re-integration of all Comorian members of the PG into the new security forces of the country and an official salute from the French military.

Negotiations continued into the night. Late on Thursday, Denard announced that they had come to an agreement and that the remaining 'European officers' of the Presidential Guard would depart the next day.

At dawn, the battleships of the small French armada inched their gunmetal grey noses over the horizon and anchored off the west coast of the island. By 2 pm the South African Hercules transport plane had taken off, carrying its load of mercenaries to Johannesburg, where they would remain in transit overnight, before returning the next day to their countries of origin. At the request of his country, which was unwilling to accept him, Colonel Bob Denard was granted temporary residence rights in the Republic of South Africa.

11

Inconsistencies

THE EPISODE WAS RIDDLED with inconsistencies. No one had been charged with killing the President. Most of the contemporary press reports were sceptical of Denard's story, but none came up with a thorough, logical version of their own. Two-and-a-half years after Abdallah's death, I decided to reheat the trail.

Anjouan seemed to be a good place to start. A year earlier, President Djohar had appointed Commandant Ahmed Mohammed, the man on whom the initial suspicion had fallen, to be governor of Abdallah's old island. He was willing to see me and I thought I could take the opportunity to pay my respects at Abdallah's grave. There were spare seats on the plane, which was expected to leave on schedule the next morning.

It was a clear day and the little Fokker was only half full for the thirty-minute hop across the water. Anjouan soon came into view and I had the impression we were flying into the apex of a boomerang, with its long green arms stretching into the choppy sea on either side. We landed at the tiny airport and walked straight through the small stone hut and out to the front, where a large acacia tree shaded a few hawkers from the platinum-bright midday sun. A taxi driver took me into the island capital, Mutsamudu.

I left the taxi in the centre of town and wandered along the wide, sandy streets, fringed with smaller concrete houses and palm huts, outside which girls sat, their faces painted with yellow sandalwood paste, the traditional Comorian equivalent of a facial, which is meant to restore nutrients to the skin, while protecting it from the sun. All their *chirumanis* were red or aubergine and white, instead of the variety of colours favoured by the main islanders. Few of the men wore *bou-bous*. Amazingly, at midday, there were signs of activity; shops were open selling patterned cloth and brightly-coloured or fluorescent surfer shorts. On the balcony of one charmingly tumbled-down house, sat half a dozen young men, chipping busily away at large pieces of wood. Mutsumudu appeared to be cleaner and busier than Moroni. It represented the tail-end of Abdallah's chauvinism towards his own island.

I stopped for lunch at the only tourist hotel in town, the government-owned Al Amal. It was empty and dreary, giving off the distinct ambience of the 1970s, the colour brown and communist North Korea. I decided against staying there and wandered out into the streets. A young man accosted me: 'Hello, my name is Hassan and I am a student of English. Please can I be helping you?' I got the feeling his teacher may well have come from the Indian subcontinent.

'Thank you, I am looking for somewhere to stay. Not', I looked back at the Al Amal, 'there.'

'Well, I can be helping you then. You must go to Charly's, on the airport road. I would be taking you there myself, but I have a class. But please be calling me for help if you need it.'

I took his address and went by cab to Charly's.

Hassan's recommendation turned out to be excellent. Charly's was a small, irregularly-shaped white building, with balconies it seemed in every crevice. It overlooked a graphite-grey beach next to a long jetty, unfortunately close to what must have been the oil and petrol terminal. Charly was rather spooky to look at. He reminded me of Baron Samedi, the bald voodoo zombie in the film *Live and Let Die*. His lips were thin and lined with black and his eyes bulged. He showed me to a white, cell-like room, immaculately clean with a diamond-shaped window, without glass, made of stone lattice work. It was by far the most stylish hotel room I had seen in the

Comoros and it was considerably cheaper than any of the government-owned hotels.

'What are you doing here?' Charly asked me.

'I'm just on holiday. I've spent a couple of weeks on Grande Comore and I wanted to see one of the other islands before I leave. Unfortunately, I've had so much trouble getting a flight, that I have very little time left and I have to go back to Moroni tomorrow afternoon. Do you know where I could hire a car?'

Charly laughed. 'There is nowhere. We don't get very many tourists here. But I'll run you into town and maybe we'll be able to find someone with a car to drive you around.'

We stopped beside a couple of cars on the way into Mutsamudu, to ask whether they could be hired. It didn't take long to find one; a Renault 4 in reasonably good condition with day-glo pink nylon seat covers. Its driver's name was Youssouf and he had thick, curly eyelashes, but not, I was to find out, much in the way of personable character traits.

I told him I wanted to visit Abdallah's tomb and we set off for Domoni on the other side of the island. He growled that we would have to be quick as he had to be back for prayers at sundown. The one fact I knew about Anjouan, was that it was home to Livingstone's giant fruit bat, one of the largest in the world, with a wingspan of over a metre. It had first been discovered by Dr David Livingstone when he visited the island in 1863, my guidebook said. There used to be an abundance of them, living in the thick forests that coated Anjouan's hills, but progressive deforestation and the underplanting of the primary forest had led to the disappearance of most of them until, in 1989, it was estimated that only about sixty remained.

I asked Youssouf where I could see a Livingstone's fruit bat and he shook his head and scowled.

'Why? Do you want to buy one?' he asked aggressively.

I asked what he thought of Abdallah.

'I liked him because he was Anjouanais. He helped us. All the other presidents were from Grande Comore. I didn't like them.'

We drove along a country lane that wove its way past beaten metal huts. There were people, and goats and yellow-faced girls everywhere. Children played with rough wooden go-karts, skipping up the inclines with their vehicles bumping behind attached to a piece of string – then bounding down the rough road at great speed. The island looked densely populated, but there also appeared to be more cultivation than on Grande Comore or Mayotte. All the way along the side of the road there were fields and thickets of cloves and ylang-ylang, whose presence was heralded by a hefty belt of sweet scent.

Youssouf appeared to be in a bad mood, but I didn't know why or what I had done wrong. He refused to answer any more questions and drove in stony silence. But the heavy atmosphere inside the car could not detract from the breathtaking scenery that was unfolding on the outside. Sheer wooded slopes soared into the blue sky and plummeted to fast-running streams and waterfalls, nestled in deep green folds. We drove up and down quilted hills as I gazed out of the window. Although I had become fond of the unrelenting harshness of the black volcanic rock on Grande Comore, the rich red soil of Anjouan was a welcome change. The grass verges along the side of the road, neatly clipped by goats, could have been in Dorset or Wiltshire. It was as lush as England in spring, but the landscape was more varied.

As we approached the town of Bambao, the centre of the ylang-ylang industry, crouched at the bottom of a fold, I noticed large piles of coconut husks laid out on the side of the road. I asked Youssouf what they were doing there, but he merely grunted. I couldn't recall copra figuring on a list of Comorian exports. When we reached the ylang-ylang refinery, their purpose became apparent. Dozens of grimy men in tattered working clothes were stuffing them inside hungry furnaces. The foreman gave me a quick guided tour and showed me how the furnaces heated up the ylang-ylang flowers to produce the essence. The room was very hot and the machines, which looked almost prehistoric, were falling to bits. Youssouf started shuffling his feet, so, armed with a gift of a tiny bottle of pure perfume essence, I said goodbye to the foreman and jumped back into the car.

The outskirts of Abdallah's home town of Domoni were clearly marked by their neatness. The sides of the road were primly fenced with palm weave. Green and white signposts – the first I had seen on the Comoros – pointed the way to the harbour, the town centre and the main outlying villages. Even the roads appeared to have identifying numbers. We passed Djohar's Domoni residence, a monstrous pastel-coloured ice-cream dream and headed into the heart of toy town. Domoni was still overcrowded and dirty, but it would have won the award for the best-kept village in the Comoros, hands down.

It was hard to miss Abdallah's former residence and final resting place. It was situated right in the middle of the old town, which was delineated by thick crumbling walls, relics of the era of the battling sultans and raiding pirates. I got out of the car and stared in disbelief. Even Youssouf had a hint of a grin on his face. Abdallah's mausoleum was like a shimmering white and gold Walt Disney pagoda in the middle of what was, relatively-speaking, still a shanty-town; it was a shrine to money and power. A thin man said he was the 'Gardien' and offered to show me around. Unfortunately he spoke only Comorian, but I was happy just to follow and let his long-winded explanations waft over my head.

From the outside, I could see that four, tall, gold-leafed smaller minarets stood guard over the large, gold, central dome. Marble steps led up to a sumptuous tiled and carpeted mosque under another side dome. A giant chandelier hung from its ceiling. I gathered from my guide's somewhat explicit gestures, that this was the men's mosque. He led us – Youssouf had been sufficiently enthused to follow – to a small spiral staircase in a tiled oval tower and we emerged into a minstrels' gallery overlooking the heart of the mausoleum. The walls of the huge central building were coated with shiny blue, white and orange tiles. Below us, in the centre of the room, lay the ex-president's white marble tomb, inscribed with gold Arabic writing and half-covered by a gold-embroidered, green velvet shroud. Four carved gold minarets supported the heavy, green rope which surrounded the tomb. Six Korans on carved wooden holders stood at intervals around it, in front of matching Persian prayer carpets, each one with a string of worry beads laid carefully on top.

Green marble pillars, studded with green spotlights, led up to the gallery where we stood staring. This was not the Comoros. A vast chandelier hung from the big windowed dome. Everything was sparkling clean. The *gardien* conveyed in sign language and a Pidgin French that the building had been started a month after Abdallah's death, constructed around the central tomb and had taken a year to build. He said that the money had been donated by the Chinese, but Salim Abdallah had told me that they had only given FF 400,000. Morocco had contributed a whole lot more (Abdallah was distantly related to King Hassan), Air France had transported all the goods and equipment for free and the family had made up the balance, which totalled around FF 10 million.

We left through the women's mosque on the other side of the central salon. It was a mirror-image of the men's, but I think a little smaller. A plaque on the outside wall of the building read:

D AL MAKHOUM PRES HADJI CHEIK
AHMED ABDALLAH ABDEREMANE
PAIX A SON AME

Was it to further his aim of peace that Ali Soilih had been killed in 1978? I couldn't help comparing the tombs of the two former presidents; the one so humble, the other so opulent.

I asked the *gardien* if I could meet Abdallah's wives, who still live in the adjoining house – which wouldn't have looked out of place on a prosperous plantation in the American south. He said they didn't receive unexpected visitors and would be asleep anyway. On our way out, he asked me for CF 500 to buy some cigarettes and sauntered out of the gates into town. I realised that he probably wasn't the *gardien* at all, just a freelancer trying to earn cigarette money.

I took advantage of the fleeting look of happiness on Youssouf's face to ask him if he knew where I could find members of the bodyguard, Djaffar's, family. I knew they were from Domoni. He asked a man in the road, who said he knew another man who knew the Djaffars. I set off towards the port, with an ever-growing retinue. We passed fishermen displaying their catch of fat tuna and the Friday mosque with its tall tower, half-white, half the pistachio green of Islam.

Papa Djaffar was sitting outside on his stoop. He wore a pale blue short-sleeved shirt and matching slacks. A sparkling white vest showed through the shirt's opening. On his head perched a prayer hat and he sported fashionable gold and tortoise-shell half-rimmed shades. He didn't speak good French, but there were by this time many people eager to act as a translator.

'I'm a journalist from England. Please tell me how your son was killed,' I opened.

'The mercenaries killed him.' He addressed all his remarks to the young translator. 'Please tell this girl I can't talk to her anymore.'

'Please sir, I know it is hard for you to talk about it, but Denard accused your son of killing the President. I don't believe that and I want to find out the truth.'

At which point his voice rose and he started jabbing a finger at the air: 'The truth is that my son was killed while he tried to save Abdallah. He was a good boy. I was in the French gendarmerie, but I know that he was killed by mzungus and that is why I won't talk to mzungus!'

He hadn't looked at me once during the whole exchange, keeping his eyes fixed firmly ahead. Quite a crowd had gathered and were leaning forward to catch his every word. I felt shaken and went back quickly to the car.

Youssouf was waiting with a smirk on his face. He had heard every word of the exchange and agreed with Papa Djaffar's sentiments. We drove back to Charly's at high speed, only stopping once for him to buy his wife a heap of wild raspberries, crammed into a green banana palm basket.

When I got back to the hotel, I still felt uneasy. I sat on a wall and described my emotions in my journal:

'Rarely have I been less proud of my journalistic ability, more ashamed of my profession,' I wrote. 'I blundered in without tact and respect, behaving like an arrogant colonial and managed to upset – but not to shake the dignity – of a proud and sad old man. I feel guilty, so ashamed. The only recompense is to prove his son's innocence.'

I watched the water slapping on the graphite beach. The sea was lit by the golden setting sun and the vast bulky mountains were silhouetted in the background, draped in a shawl of soft clouds. Large bats – although not large enough to be Livingstone's fruit bats – were swooping and gliding through the palm trees. I gradually grew more peaceful.

*

Youssouf came to fetch me promptly the next morning. I had been afraid he would forego the money I had promised and ditch me. We arrived at Commandant Ahmed Mohammed's offices in the hills above Mutsamudu promptly at nine. He was expecting me, said a charming hello and led me into his large office. Out of the windows, I could see the ruins of the canon-ringed citadel, set against the backdrop of the bustling town and port. The Commandant explained that the citadel had been built, using British money, by Sultan Abdallah I at the end of the eighteenth century to help defend the town against Malagasy pirates. It was partly destroyed by a vicious cyclone in 1950, he said.

I liked the Commandant immediately. He was a large imposing man with a rich and resonant voice that sounded as it emanated from the depths of his impressive girth. When he stood up, I was surprised to see he was shorter than I, but he appeared large and strong. His head was a massive shiny dome, hard and smooth as a bullet, fringed around the edges with unhealthy ginger fuzz. His eyes were large and bloodshot. He wore casual clothes and docksiders and his relaxed frame filled a wooden armchair. His French was not much better than mine – despite the fact he had served several years in the French army, rising to the rank of warrant-officer, first class. It was when he returned to the Comoros, however, that his ascent in the ranks of power became meteoric and before long he had been promoted to colonel and later to commander of the Comorian Armed Forces (CAF). Whenever I had talked to anyone about the Commandant, they had immediately mentioned his wife, rolled their eyes and smiled. When I asked why, they would shrug and laugh. All I could make out was that she was a pretty tough business woman. Her sister had married Commandant Charles.

I tried to start off subtly, saying that I wanted to find out about tourism on Anjouan and also about what had happened to him on the night of Abdallah's death. Ahmed brushed off the tourism diversion and launched straight into the background to his role in Abdallah's death. He had known in advance, he claimed, about the 1978 coup:

'Voila, I was the only person who knew it was going to happen. I had been in close contact with Abdallah in exile [but since Abdallah himself didn't know the date, this is unlikely]. I told a friend who I was living with at the time, also a former soldier, and together we made arrangements to help. And so it was that when the coup took place, all the international phone lines were cut.'

Soon afterwards, Abdallah made his fellow-Anjouanais head of the CAF.

'Bob Denard had his militia, the PG, and I had the national army. We had several disputes, but at the beginning they weren't very serious.'

But the Commandant became increasingly disillusioned

with the mercenaries and was vocal in his criticism. The contretemps came to a head in September 1989 when, he alleges, the mercenaries framed him for smuggling cigarettes – when it was actually they who had done the smuggling – into Anjouan.

'Why did they want to get rid of me? Because the mercenaries knew very well that they'd gone too far and that I wouldn't tolerate it. For example, they held a monopoly over everything and put the shopkeepers and traders out of work and they never paid their customs duties – nothing at all. Abdallah let them get away with it. One could easily have believed that there wasn't a state, that the mercenaries controlled the country and did what they wished.'

He appeared to me to be more concerned about the loss of business opportunities, than about mercenary brutality. The Commandant then sidetracked, for the first of many times, into talking about his famous wife, with whom he is obviously obsessed.

'She's a businesswoman now,' he said, 'but she used to be a builder and built the hospital in Moroni. Now she owns a number of boutiques and imports general foodstuffs and construction materials from Reunion, South Africa and France.'

After the Commandant was accused of the smuggling, he went to Abdallah and handed in his resignation. The council of ministers accepted it, but a successor was not chosen, so he hung around his office, waiting for someone to whom he could hand over power.

'That brings us to 24th November. I remember 24th November very well. The President came to Anjouan and I telephoned his head of protocol to request a meeting. One was arranged for 16.00 hours. I arrived at his house in Domoni and he said to me: "Ahmed come and sit down and let's have a chat." Before that my wife had written a letter saying that the attacks on my reputation were unjustified and were the work of jealous people who wanted us dead. The President said to me: "Ah, Ahmed's wife sent me a letter." I asked if it was impolite, but he said: "No, never. She wrote me a pretty letter, very explicit."

'Then I asked him please to appoint my successor. I told him he could always count on me, that even if I wasn't head of the army I would never turn against him. I was never in favour of the mercenaries because their behaviour was not noble. They behaved as if they had conquered the country, the population could not rely on them, but I was always loyal to the President. He said: "No Ahmed, I know very well what happened. Therefore, I am not going to accept your resignation. You will stay on as head of the army." I said to him: "If I accept, Mr President, it will be under certain conditions. You must clear the names of my wife and I and it must be understood that I take orders only from you."

'He agreed and said he was going back to Moroni on Sunday and we could go together, if I wanted, and sort out all the problems concerning defence and security. "I want to put my security in your hands," he said. I replied that I had things to sort out on Anjouan, but that I would follow him the next day. "Good, until Monday then," he said. I left and went home. He went back to Moroni on Sunday and it wasn't until 10 am on Monday that I heard he was dead.'

'Who do you think killed him?' I asked.

'Well, I wasn't there, but I think it was Marquès or Siam. They were trying to pressurise the President into signing an extension to their contract, but he refused. He was fed up with them. He sounded the alarm and Djaffar came running into the room with his gun. He was taken out straight away – what Denard said is wrong, everything is wrong from start to finish! He was speared with a dagger. That is what I was told by men who saw his body. They said he was torn apart, then he was shot.'

'You don't think that Djaffar could have shot the President in a moment of panic?'

'No, you see Djaffar was a member of the family, Abdallah's family. He was totally loyal. And he was not the type to get panicked. He was technically very intelligent, quite big and very solid. No, Djaffar could not have done it.'

'So then what happened?'

'The one pressed the alarm, the other came with a gun and they killed him and then they said, therefore we must kill the other. They killed one, then a second and a third . . . I was the third.'

The excitement of telling the story had made the Commandant difficult to follow. I tried to slow him down by asking only about the parts that directly related to him.

A Parisian friend of his was staying at the Ylang-Ylang Hotel in Moroni that night. As he drove home from the Galawa, he heard some gunshots from the direction of the president's palace.

'He phoned my home as soon as he got back to the hotel and got hold of my wife. He told her: "Madame, something's wrong . . ." She reacted quickly and telephoned my office. The soldier who answered said, "Madame, it's true, but don't come here because the mercenaries have attacked our camp." My wife took our small child and rushed to her parents' house. Five minutes later three trucks arrived, carrying fifty soldiers with guns, grenades and rockets. They stormed into the house and took everything, everything that belonged to me, everything, everything, everything! They knocked over all the cupboards and broke everything they could. They found my gardien and asked him where I was. He said he didn't know, so they beat him up and left him on the ground.

'Siam was in charge of the search. He discovered that I was in fact on Anjouan – which they hadn't known at all. That was why the plan failed. They wanted to find me straight away, bring me to Abdallah and riddle my body with bullets. They would have killed me and then everyone would have been invited to see my body, the body of the man who had murdered the president. They had already sent telexes to Paris saying that Abdallah had been assassinated by Ahmed. But Ahmed had not yet been captured.

'The next morning in Moroni, my wife heard the rumours and she became mad. That Ahmed would have done this without first consulting her . . . but she thought it was true.'

In the meantime, when Denard heard that Ahmed was on Anjouan, he ordered his men to fetch the Air Comores pilot and fly to fetch him. Led by Jean-Pierre with two other mercenaries and forty-seven members of the PG, the plane flew to Anjouan. It was delayed, however, for a few hours at Hahaya, owing to mechanical problems and only touched down at 4.30 am.

'They thought I was staying at my house here,' the Commandant pointed out of the window, 'but when they arrived, they only found the guard, who said I was at my other house near the military camp in Patsy. They came to find me and on the way they met my driver, who was coming to pick me up. They stripped him, searched him and took the money from his pockets. They stopped at the military camp and demanded to be let in. "Voila! We're on manoeuvres, we want to come into the camp, have breakfast and see the Commandant when he arrives," Jean-Pierre told the sentry. But once they had been let through the gate, they disarmed him and took control of all the dormitories.

'Then they came for me. It was between 6 o'clock and 6.04. I was asleep. I heard noises on the track and thought it was soldiers out on exercise, or peasants on their way to the fields. But the noises continued and I said to myself that something strange was going on. I got up and as I put my hand on the door knob, the mercenaries broke the window and threw a grenade into the room. It exploded. I was surprised, I didn't know what was going on. My first thought was that there had been a coup d'état, that Abdallah was dead and that they were trying to neutralise me. I got dressed hurriedly and was in the process of loading my revolver, when they shot two rockets through the window into my bedroom. One exploded a metre and a half to my left, the other shattered the door through to the sitting-room. Others were shot at the roof, which collapsed on top of me.

'I was stunned, badly wounded. I had eighteen open wounds, all on my left side, seven fragments of shrapnel inside my body and a broken eardrum. I was stuck inside that house, while they fired their Kalashnikovs through all the openings. There are signs of more than four hundred impacts on the walls of my bedroom.'

'You were lucky,' I said, somewhat inadequately.

'I was extraordinarily, uniquely lucky. I was bleeding all over. I've still got three pieces of shrapnel in my body.'

He made me feel a hard nobble under his skin, around the waistband.

'It was a miracle?' I suggested.

'Yes, a miracle. I've still got the clothes in Moroni. I keep them as a souvenir. One can count the eighteen holes in them. But the good God gave me strength enough to crawl out of the house. I managed to walk the 200 metres to the military camp, where I found a mercenary with a Kalashnikov. I demanded to speak to Jean-Pierre. "Jean-Pierre, what is it you wanted to say to me?" I asked. "We called you but you didn't reply," he told me. "But this is my home, is that how you behave at your home?" He didn't reply except to say that the Colonel had asked for me. "Which colonel?" I said. "Bob Denard," he replied. "OK," I said, "let's go and see him."

'But Denard wasn't there. Jean-Pierre looked scared stiff. We went to the camp and saw all the soldiers lying on the floor. Jean-Pierre called Denard on the radio. But he wasn't very clever because he spoke loudly and everyone overheard his conversation. Bob Denard spoke to him. "So is the operation over?" he asked. "Yes, Colonel." "And the Commandant Ahmed, is he dead?" "No Colonel, only badly injured." '

The Commandant proceeded to explain – in minute detail – his brave journey back to Moroni.

'When we got there, I went into Marquès's office and Marquès held out his hand. I said: "Never. I will never leave the traces of my blood on your hand. My only regret is that my blood will stay on your floor and that I can't bend down to wipe it off." He said, "But Commandant, I didn't tell them to do all this." I said to him: "Ah yes, Marquès, for once you tell the truth. You told them to kill me and bring me here in a jute sack. I want you to tell me what's happening." "President Abdallah has been killed." "Stop, that's not possible! With the security you put in place at night? They say it's as tight as the beads in a rosary."

'Marquès dismissed me and said I could go home. "Stop, you did this to me and now you're saying I can go home, grievously wounded? Why on earth did you do all this?" "The President had given us orders to disarm all members of the CAF. We were afraid what your reaction might be." I said: "Very good, so these were preventative measures?" You have to understand, these men were inhuman.'

He complained about his subsequent treatment – he was prevented from being evacuated to France as a medical emergency until two days after the mercenaries had left. When they attacked his house, he claimed, they not only destroyed it and all the contents, but they killed a thousand of his chickens that lived in the breeding-house beside the house. He was aggrieved at not having received any compensation.

'I had to pay for the flights to Paris and for my operations. I had some medical insurance in Paris that reimbursed me for some things, but otherwise it was me who had to pay all these expenses. I had to pay for the evacuation and for my wife who accompanied me – she's a professional nurse.'

He insisted on taking me to see the ruins of his house at Patsy, where he took me through the mercenaries' attack, move by move. The house was certainly a mess; the roof didn't exist, the bedroom wall was indeed pock-marked with holes that could have been caused by bullets and shrapnel, but just as easily by weathering and erosion, and where there should have been doors, there were just gaping spaces. The chickenry next door, which looked suspiciously small to house a thousand birds, was also a complete wreck. They looked like ancient ruins, not just two-year-old ones.

We said goodbye, and I promised to go and meet his wife in Moroni the next week. I believed most of his story, although there were parts he had undoubtedly embellished to make himself appear brave.

Youssouf was in the car with a sour look on his face. Obviously waiting for me was as disagreeable a task as driving me around. We went for a quick trip to the northern end of the island, before he deposited me, thankfully, at the airport in good time for the return flight. I don't think either of us were upset to see the back of each other.

The flight back to Moroni left twenty minutes early. I sat next to a small Italian doctor called Sevario. He told me he had lived on the Comoros for fifteen years and had spent most of that time running the leprosy hospital. He lamented the fact I would not be able to visit him there. I was not so sorry.

'How many cases of leprosy do you have there?' I asked.

'About fifteen hundred, but we have it under control and there shouldn't be any more.'

'Did you know Bob Denard?'

'Yes, he was a splendid fellow. It was he who found the leprosy camp in a terrible state in 1978. Everyone had forgotten about the lepers. He arranged for funding and for medical assistance. He was definitely a force for good in the Comoros.'

*

Mahamoud was waiting for me at Hahaya. I felt as if I had arrived home. His eyes were shining and he obviously had news of some import to tell me. He couldn't even wait until we were in the car.

'I'm going to get married,' he announced.

'What? But who to? I didn't even know you had a girlfriend.'

He looked pleased at the impact of his news.

'Yes, she is from my village. I have known her a long time

164

although we haven't exactly been going out. But you'll never guess what,' he barely paused, 'she lives in France. I will be able to get my papers and go to live with her!'

To live in France was the grand ambition of most Comorians.

'That's wonderful, congratulations. How did it happen?'

It had only been about five days since I had last seen him.

'Well, she came back from France – she lives in Lille – and proposed to me straight out. Of course I accepted. She's doing the same accountancy course as I am. We will be able to study together – although at first I may have to work. I will go and live with Jacques and Kiki in Avignon for a while and earn some money, then we will rent a flat and live together.' He beamed.

'What's she like?'

'Well, she's quite good looking. Not too fat or too thin.' He held his hands out to approximate the width of her waist. 'I think we will be very happy. And as soon as we are married we will come and visit you in England!'

I told him about my meeting with the Commandant. 'If what he said is true, then Bob Denard is definitely lying. Why would he try to kill the Commandant, if Djaffar had indeed shot the President?'

Mahamoud agreed. 'But we must go to see the gardien. He has a story that I know would interest you.'

*

We drove straight up the hill to our old house in Daché. Mahamoud told me on the way that it had been bought the previous week by a young Comorian waiter who had won FF 50 million in the French national lottery. He hadn't yet moved in. It was lovely to go back and whistle for Abdou through the gate. The garden smelt as intoxicating as ever and some more hibiscuses had come into bloom. Abdou was delighted to see us and went straight back into his small room to change into his new gold-tassled *bou-bou*. He came out grinning. We went to sit on the veranda, where the vanilla vines framed his nut-brown face.

Mahamoud acted as translator: 'Gardien, Samantha is interested in finding out about what happened the night the President died,' he explained.

Abdou started chuckling and grasped his hands together in pleasure, before launching into his story. I felt sure he had tried to tell me a number of times before, as some of his accompanying actions looked familiar. Once he got going, we couldn't stop him. His lyrical voice soared and swooped as he varied his rhythm and timbre with the true sense of drama of a professional storyteller, illustrating his tale with extravagant gestures. As he warmed to his theme, he relaxed on the wicker-work chair, his elbows resting on the arms.

This is Mbae Abdou's story:

At the time of the President's death, a French pilot (or pilottee, as Abdou called him) working for Air Comores was living in the house. At about one in the morning of 27th November (barely an hour after Abdallah's death), Abdou was resting in his room, sitting on his bed, chin in hand (he demonstrated), when he heard a voice calling at the gate. 'Gardien, gardien gardien.' He peeked out of the window and saw two strange mzungus at the gate. They were accompanied by a Comorian.

He came out of his room and walked towards them. One of the mzungus shouted at him: 'Open the gate!'

'No!' he replied.

'Are you going to open it or aren't you?' He explained he wasn't as the pilot was asleep and it was not usual for people to come visiting in the middle of the night. 'Open!' 'Never, never!' 'I'm going to shoot you,' threatened the mzungu brandishing a large gun. 'Go away and come back in the morning,' said Abdou.

A shot was fired into the air. Abdou unsheathed his pocket knife and waved it in the air, shouting, 'No, no, nooo!'

He told me that he thought, at that moment, if there was any further trouble, he would kill them! One of the mzungus fired a shot at the ground near his right foot; he jumped to the left and then decided it was an opportune moment to find the pilottee.

He woke him and was told to go to open the front door. The pilot got dressed in a hurry and went to the gate and started to shout at the mercenaries: 'You're mad to come here and shoot at my house, you're mad!' They laid their arms to the floor. 'The gardien's not stupid, he's not going to let you in without permission,' went on the pilot (although I suspect this could be a little embroidery by Abdou). The mercenaries apologised to the pilot, who gestured for Abdou to open the gate. The two mercenaries went into the house, while the Comorian stayed outside.

Abdou made coffee and the mercenaries sat on the floor. The pilot then gestured for Abdou to leave the room. The pilot came out of the house shortly after with the two men, got into his car and left. He came back the next morning and said he was returning to Anjouan with the President's body.

I'm pretty sure it was a true account of what happened on the night of the President's death. If so, Abdou can claim some credit for delaying the mercenaries' departure to Anjouan, and thus perhaps for helping to save the Commandant's life.

*

I went to see the former head of the gendarmes, Commandant Abdou Rezac on the way back. His house was a stone's throw from the gendarmerie headquarters. He greeted me pleasantly and offered me a cup of ginger tea.

His version of the events of the night of 26th November 1989 went like this:

'I arrived home from a nuptial ceremony at 22.00 to find a message telling me to call the President. I tried calling his direct line, but there was no reply. I tried all the other numbers, including the Guards' post, but I still couldn't raise anyone.

'At 23.00 I received a telephone call from one of the technical advisers who lived close to the presidency. He told me he had heard the sound of shooting coming from the palace. I switched off the TV and I could hear the shots and also rocket fire over the telephone. I put the phone down and immediately received a call from the gendarmerie, saying they too had heard the noises and what were they? I called the PG, who told me that no manoeuvres were planned for that night.

'The gendarmerie called again and I put them on full alert. My phone didn't stop ringing, everyone was in a panic. At around 23.45, I received another call from the duty officer at the gendarmerie, who signalled that vehicles were approaching and firing shots. I told them not to attack unless they were attacked. I dressed hurriedly, but the phone rang again. It was the duty officer once more, who informed me that they were under attack and advised me to stay away. I heard cries and shots. The noise continued for half an hour. When I called again, a mzungu answered and when I identified myself, he just said "merde!" and put the phone down. There was no further communication from the gendarmerie.

'I stayed at home until 02.00 when the cabinet secretary phoned and told me to come to the presidency at Beit es-Salaam. I said I couldn't as I was surrounded by mercenaries. I heard him talking to someone who was probably Bob Denard, who said: "He can leave, I will give instructions." I drove down to the post office, where I was stopped by a couple of white mercenaries, accompanied by Comorian members of the Presidential Guard. The mercenary in charge put a gun to my head and asked where I thought I was going. However, he received the go-ahead over the radio and escorted me to the presidency.

'When I got there, I found a number of ministers sitting down. They were all very subdued, no one said anything. Ten minutes later, Bob Denard came in and told us that the President was dead, that uncontrollable elements had attacked the presidential palace and that the President's bodyguard had killed him in a fit of panic. I found this completely idiotic.'

*

I decided to try to track down one of the ministers who had been present at the early morning meeting at Beit es-Salaam.

Abdallah's former minister of the interior, Omar Tamou, was the first to respond to my notes. He was an elegant man, and, like all the Comorian politicians I had met, very charming. He folded his long legs neatly and settled gracefully into a large chair on the terrace. He was helpful, but at the same time careful about what he said and especially careful not to say anything compromising about the mercenaries. We spoke first about Abdallah, who Tamou had begun to support in 1973, having changed his allegiances from the Prince Djaffar.

I moved the conversation on to the events of 26th November.

'At 10 pm I heard shots, but I dismissed them. A few months earlier, the PG had performed some manoeuvres in Moroni and I thought they were at it again. I called the PG head-quarters and a mercenary answered. He said that the president's palace was under attack, but that they had the situation in hand. The noise continued. An hour later I called the finance minister, Said Ahmed Said Ali, who knew nothing more. He said the situation was now calm and he would call me if anything changed. I went to sleep.

'At around one in the morning, I was woken by a phone call. It was Said Ahmed Said Ali saying that they were all at the presidency and that I should come along. I got dressed in a hurry and started out for Beit es-Salaam. Barely one kilometre from my house, I was stopped by members of the PG who had set up a roadblock. I started to be afraid and regretted not asking for an escort. They eventually let me past and I drove on to the presidency, taking the long way around, so as not to pass the president's palace. When I arrived I found a number of ministers present including Said Ahmed Said Ali, Ahmed Abdou and Said Kafé. Colonel Abdou Rezac was then summoned. Denard was also there with one of his lieutenants – Marquès, I think. Everyone sat in silence, not knowing what we were waiting for or what was going on. I didn't even know who had called the meeting.

'At around half past two, when we had been there for nearly an hour, Ahmed Abdou started getting fed up with the waiting. He asked Denard: "How's the President?"

'Denard shrugged his shoulders.

"How's his morale?"

"Very low."

"What exactly happened?"

"There was an attack on the president's palace. The Presidential Guard was informed and went to the palace. They stayed with the President to protect him. While they were in the President's office, the adjutant-chef Djaffar burst in, his gun in his hand, and aimed it at them. He had a furious air and Bob Denard [again speaking of himself in the third person] sensed he was about to shoot, so he threw himself on the ground and the President was hit with a bullet. The Lieutenant shot Djaffar and Djaffar is dead . . . "

"And the President?"

"Dead also."

'At which point everyone lost their heads and there was pandemonium.'

'Then what happened?' I asked Tamou.

'Denard showed us a paper signed by the President empowering the PG' to disarm the army here and on Anjouan. Ahmed Abdou was the first to recover his speech and question Denard again:

"Those elements that attacked the palace – do you know who they are?"

"No."

"Did you catch any of them?"

"No."

"Was anyone on either side killed or wounded?"

"No."

'There was total silence. Everyone started to feel scared. I couldn't think clearly. I was full of emotion and that overtook my imagination.

'By about three, we had recovered enough to think coherently. Denard said we would have to start to plan how we were going to run the country. We turned to the constitution and found it said that in the event of the death of the President, the head of the Supreme Court takes over for a 40-day period, leading up to a general election. Commandant Abdou Rezac went to fetch Djohar and while he was away, we tried to devise a communiqué to issue to the people. We argued about the wording; Denard said to put that the palace was attacked by members of the CAF. But there was no proof to suggest they had done it. He got quite angry and went into Abdallah's office to use the satellite phone. We finished the statement. It was very laconic; it didn't say who had killed Abdallah. It just said that the president's palace was attacked by unknown elements. The PG, who ensure the protection of the President, riposted. There was an exchange of shots and the President was mortally wounded . . .

'Djohar arrived and without a word of warning, was given the communiqué to read. Someone from Radio Comores was summoned and recorded Djohar reading it out. He looked very shocked. We all were. It was a nightmare night.'

'What do you think happened?'

'I don't know.'

'Don't you think it was odd that none of the attackers were captured or wounded?'

'Very bizarre – for that reason one asks oneself whether there really was an attack.'

And why, I wondered, had Denard waited nearly two and a half hours to announce the President's death?

Omar Tamou excused himself very politely, saying he had to return to his village of Foumboni that night.

*

The next morning I went to meet his fellow minister, Said Ahmed Said Ali. He lived in a large, but rundown house. The garden was littered with rubbish and seven defunct Citroën DSs. I asked him what they were for. He said they were his father-in-law's obsession and he kept buying additional ones to use for spare parts. The last one had given up several years ago. Only one remained in action in the whole country, and that was President Djohar's.

Said Ahmed Said Ali – known to his friends as Charif – had served as minister of finance and public enterprises since September 1985. Like Tamou, he was still fairly loyal to his former President, calling him 'the best of a bad bunch', although unlike him, he was quite open about the existence of corruption:

'Yes, there was corruption everywhere – from the President, to Denard, to the ministers, to the customs officers and from there down.'

The Comorian economy, he said, had been on a downhill slide since the mid-Eighties. They were faced with falling world prices for their exports and on top of that, they had a heavy burden of foreign loans to pay off, legacies from the period of heavy investment at the start of the decade. The number of public sector employees was spiralling and the state could no longer afford to pay them. Abdallah knew he would need an increase in French aid and he knew he wouldn't get it while the mercenaries remained.

'For the year before he died, Abdallah knew things weren't going well. He tried to get rid of the mercenaries. All the money donated by South Africa was channelled through the PG, the ministry of finance never saw a cent. South Africa wanted to come out into the open, but Bob Denard didn't.'

'I thought it was Abdallah who didn't want to acknowledge the South Africans?'

'Well, he was persuaded by his "private adviser", Bob Denard. A few months before his death, Abdallah made contact with a man called Paul Barril, the former number two in the Elysée's anti-terrorist squad, who had set up a private security company. They had several meetings in Paris. Abdallah wanted Barril to organise the mercenaries' departure and to replace Denard. France must have been "au courant". Abdallah knew all about French politics. In October 1989, he told me that I would need to include the Guard's salaries in the next year's budget. That could only have meant one thing; an end to his relationship with the mercenaries. He started putting pressure on Denard to leave. He exaggerated what he thought about him, claiming to all and sundry that he was a "hostage to the mercenaries", because he knew Denard would hear about it. He knew Denard knew about the meetings with Barril.'

'Do you think the French put pressure on Abdallah to get rid of the mercenaries?'

'I certainly don't think they put obstacles in his way. But I don't know who was the first to come up with the idea. I think Abdallah asked France for help and they put him on to Barril. But they exerted subtle pressure through the budget and also, Mitterrand was due to pay a visit to the Comoros in 1990 and he had intimated that he wouldn't while the mercenaries were still there.

'Abdallah was scared of Bob Denard. The climate between the two of them had deteriorated. Things weren't going well and contact wasn't as frequent as it had been. Abdallah knew the presence of the mercenaries wasn't good for the Comoros. He made a final decision to get rid of them and he was prepared to sacrifice his life to that end.'

12

Suspects

THE COMMANDANT was clearly out of the reckoning and I didn't think Djaffar had done it. According to the autopsy performed by Dr Roger Izarn, a surgeon from Domoni Hospital, on the afternoon of Monday 27th December, Abdallah had died as a result of five bullet wounds clustered around his heart. All were potentially fatal. Two had entered his cardiac muscle, while the remaining three all pierced his aorta. The autopsy report is brief, but it does state that at least three of the bullets had entered the President's body at a significant downward angle, and that the exit wounds had been larger than the entries – both of which would imply that he was shot at a fairly close range. They didn't appear to be the shots of a man in a state of panic – who hadn't meant to aim at his victim.

That left three suspects: the three Frenchmen who had been in the room with the President and his bodyguard, Djaffar – Colonel Bob Denard, Major Marquès (Dominique Malacrino) and Captain Siam (Jean-Paul Guerrier). They were the only witnesses and they had their story; and I knew they would stick to it whatever. There was no proof either way. All I could do was to look for inconsistencies in their stories.

*

I went back to see Salim Abdallah, who had called to say that he was willing to talk about his father's death.

'By 1989, my father knew Denard had to go. He contacted

France and with the tacit consent of South Africa, they drew up plans to integrate the PG, the CAF and the police into a single Comorian force. The President's close security was to have been assured by a new special team set up and trained by Paul Bàrril. France was prepared to help with the financing but some other countries – South Africa, Morocco, Senegal and Gabon – would have provided financial support. My father told Bob Denard about his plans; he was too much of a sentimentalist. He called Denard into his office and said: "Voila, this can't continue. I am the head of state and I have responsibilities to my people and they want you to go. But I am prepared to let you stay in the Comoros with your wife and all your goods. But no more military camp, no more diplomatic passport, all that is finished." Denard agreed to my father's terms, but one doesn't know whether he was sincere or not.'

'So what do you think happened on the night of 26th November?'

'Well, I can't tell you too much, but I will say one thing: there were blunders in this affair. I am persuaded that the coup was premeditated, prepared for a long time. I will give you the clues at my disposal. First of all, my father called a referendum on the Comorian constitution.'

'I've heard about that, wasn't he trying to become president for life?'

'No,' Salim replied. 'That is what the opposition say. I think they say it because they were accomplices in the affair. No, he wanted three main changes to the constitution; he wanted to reinstate the post of prime minister, he wanted to change the rules of succession so that if anything happened to the president, the head of the federal assembly would take over, not the president of the Supreme Court. And lastly, he wanted to remove the clause limiting the president's mandate to two six-year terms. That was what was misinterpreted. During the six months before the referendum, my father had been under considerable pressure to seek a third mandate, but he was not too keen. He had always said that he didn't want to die in power. But one thing had persuaded him that he should stay: he had been in contact with Mitterrand over the Mayotte question – the reunification of Mayotte into the Comoros was his greatest dream – and I think the French president must have given him a positive indication. His envoys, Said Kafé and Dr M'tara Maecha, had returned from Paris only three days before my father's death. Maybe there was a deal linking the departure of the mercenaries with the return of Mayotte.'

I had heard the conspiracy theorists – of which there were many on the Comoros – mention this French deal on several occasions, and it was certainly not outside the capabilities and compunctions of Paris's notorious foreign policy. But it was also well within the realms of the Comorian imagination – it would have taken just one person to mention the idea and Radio Cocotier would have seen to its dissemination and circulation until everyone believed it to be fact.

The result of Abdallah's referendum, however, was never in question, it was just up to him to decide on the exact figure he wanted to release. This time he was remarkably moderate; a hefty 7.5 per cent of the population was allowed to have voted against him. It was a rousing victory for the wily old campaigner. He hailed it as proof of his continuing popularity. 'Even the goats and the cows have voted for me,' he claimed. They must have, as there were widespread protests and burnings of ballot boxes by the opposition, who were remarkably vocal for such a tiny proportion of the population. The Presidential Guard were in charge of ensuring the elections were 'free and fair'.

'I believe my father's death was a result of a conspiracy between the mercenaries and some Comorian opposition members who were unhappy at my father standing for a third term,' Salim continued.

'How do you feel about Denard now?'

'Personally, I had feelings for him, but they finished when my father was killed. I spoke to him soon after my father's death. We were in the palace and my father's body was in the next-door room. I said to him: "Bob Denard, you have given me three different versions of his death, tell me the truth, I want to know the truth."

'What were the three versions?'

'Well, first of all he said that people came from the outside to kill my father. Afterwards he talked about a political faction here who planned an uprising using the Commandant . . . and then there was the story about Djaffar.'

'Do you think Djaffar could have done it?'

'No, I do not think so.'

'So what do you think happened?'

'That Sunday I came back from Anjouan on the plane with my father. We ate together at 19.00 and all that happened at midnight. I'm going to tell you the truth: my father knew about it. When I said goodbye to him that night, he told me two things. He told me not to come back that evening and he said: "If he kills me, don't let him stay here."'

'Denard has his version, but why won't he go to Paris to tell it to a judge? I would like to believe it wasn't him – perhaps he didn't pull the trigger, but he knew about it. When I saw him at 4 am he was armed, he had a pistol and some small grenades on him, but taking into account the relations they had with one another, I don't think he can have done it. Someone else did the shooting, and it wasn't Djaffar.'

*

I dropped round to see the Commandant and his wife, Soila, at their house near Volo-volo market. He was a changed man in her presence. He appeared nervous and lacking in confidence and trotted around the house at her beck and call. He had also suddenly developed an annoying nervous tic – he kept making loud sucking noises. She was an attractive woman, considerably younger than her husband. She wore a tight white skirt and a crimson T-shirt decorated with beads and glitter. She was animated, eloquent and her charm was obviously a powerful and well-oiled weapon.

She spoke good English, which effectively cut her husband out of the conversation. I soon gave up trying to reply in French so that he would be able to understand.

I asked her who she thought had killed Abdallah. She said that without doubt it had been Denard or one of his men.

'I'm trying to find some eyewitnesses who were at the palace that night,' I explained.

'Well, it will be difficult, now that Abdallah, Djaffar and Monique Terrasse are dead.'

'Who?'

'Monique Terrasse. She was Abdallah's mistress, a French co-operant. She was found dead the next morning. It appeared to be suicide as she had left a note. But I don't think so, it is too much of a coincidence. She was at the palace that night and she was supposed to have left shortly after ten, but I don't think she can have. She knew something had happened because she rang Salim Abdallah in a panic at four in the morning. He wasn't there, but she told his wife that she had to speak to him urgently. The next morning she was found dead in her apartment.'

It certainly looked fishy. I was surprised Monique Terrasse hadn't been mentioned in the press reports. I later went back to Denard's account in *Le Roi de Fortune*. It confirmed that Terrasse had been to see Abdallah that night, but had left at 22.15. The President's private phone had rung after midnight. Siam had answered it and told Abdallah that a French woman, probably Terrasse, wanted to speak to him. He had said to tell her that he would ring back. It mentions only in passing that Monique Terrasse had killed herself hours after the catastrophe.

Soila's phone started to ring. She said goodbye and then turned to me and continued in English, her husband looking on smilingly: 'Ahmed has changed considerably since the episode with the mercenaries. He used to be a strong man with intellectual capabilities, now look at him,' she paused to regard her husband, 'he doesn't trust anybody and is unwilling to make decisions on his own.'

*

That evening, I asked my landlord, Michel, a Frenchman who had lived in the Comoros most of his life, about Monique Terrasse, the mistress whose death had been so timely. He said he had known her quite well, although not as well as his mother, Christianne Mille, who had been Abdallah's secretary. Monique was a French co-operant, who taught maths at the Lycée. She was thirty-eight when she died. She had no family of her own and had grown close to the President during the months of their affair. Her body was found the day after his death; she had supposedly killed herself with a cocktail of sleeping pills and alcohol. In her will, she left her jewellery to her Comorian servants and asked to be buried in the Comoros. Rumours spread by Radio Cocotier said that she had been present at the palace while Abdallah had been killed and that traces of blows were found on her face.

'She was a very proper, very correct person,' Michel continued. 'You know, she worked out in the gym. But she was also very neurotic. She was so miserable after her dog died that she hardly ate anything for two months.'

'So do you think she was the kind of person to commit suicide?' I asked.

'Yes, it would not surprise me at all.'

That took the pressure off another piece of damning circumstantial evidence. To be sure, the coincidence of Terrasse killing herself was great, but if she was unbalanced as Michel urged me she was, then it was possible that the news of Abdallah's death could have pushed her over the edge.

*

My time was running out and there were still a couple of people I wanted to see. First on my list was the former chief prosecutor of the Supreme Court, Ali Salim. He was in disgrace following his unsuccessful attempt in 1990 to dislodge Djohar in a constitutional coup, on the grounds of mental incapability. His phone had been cut off and the first few times I went round to his house, he was out. I caught him on the day before I left. He lived in a small apartment upstairs from his mother – unusual for Comorians, who tend to live in their wives' houses. But Ali Salim, I discovered, was married to a French lady, a former co-operant like Monique Terrasse.

He was young and well-spoken. We sat on the balcony and his wife brought us tea.

'I am terribly sorry, but I cannot help you much,' he said. 'I was in charge of the investigation into the President's death and I completed it last year and turned over my findings to the French authorities. But now, unfortunately, I no longer hold the same position and I am not able to talk about the case.'

'Did you come to a conclusion as to who had killed the President?'

'Well I certainly cut down the list of suspects.'

'Who was on your final list?'

He smiled: 'I am not at liberty to say.'

'Did you come up with sufficient proof to convict someone or some persons of his murder?'

Ali Salim nodded. 'If I were you, I would talk to the Abdallah family's lawyer in Paris, Jacques Vergès. He has my file and he is able to talk.'

It was tantalising. We spoke for a while in general terms. He told me that his investigations had been severely hampered. He was unable to gain access to the president's palace until several days after the mercenaries' departure and when he got there, he found it had been completely cleaned. There were no remaining clues; the carpet showed no traces of blood, the cupboards were empty and all the bullets and cartridge cases had been removed. All except for one bullet which he discovered wedged in the air-conditioning vent.

'Who removed all the evidence?'

Ali Salim shrugged: 'I don't know. Maybe it was the mercenaries or maybe it was the special French "demineurs" – bomb disposal experts – who came to the Comoros supposedly to disarm the bombs that Denard and his men had left in the Palace.'

I had heard about the *demineurs*; some reports said they arrived in the country after the mercenaries' departure – while others said they came only days after the President's death and locked themselves in the palace for hours, before disappearing quietly back to France without making contact with the Comorian authorities. Ali Salim couldn't help me there.

Another strange coincidence was that the President's regular close security section had not been present at the palace on the night of 26th November. Instead they had been on night exercise 20 kilometres away, patrolling the beaches for smugglers under the direction of the French director of customs, a Monsieur Calvet.

Then there was the strange fact that none of the 'uncontrollable elements' who were said to have attacked the president's palace, had been caught or injured. Against the well-armed, well-trained and well-equipped Presidential Guard? Who were the so-called 'elements'? In an interview, a Comorian officer of the Presidential Guard said the shots appeared to have come from two or three gunmen at most, armed with assault rifles, grenade-throwing guns and a portable 60 mm mortar. Would dissident regular soldiers, unpaid and undisciplined, really be able to pull off a coup like that? And where would they have come by the mortar?

Add this to the rumour (which I was unable to confirm) I had picked up from several sources, that the Commandant was a well-known smuggler and was thought to have smuggled drugs into the country, and he too enters the category of an unreliable witness. Was there a 'coup' mounted against him by the mercenaries? Did he and the President make up on the Saturday? Or was he after all the brains behind the plot, providing himself with an unbreakable alibi? I had to admit this scenario was very unlikely.

But these were all coincidences, all with possible alternative explanations. If Denard had concocted his story – which he would have had to do at speed in the middle of the night and under pressure – he had covered his tracks well. I doubted I would get to the root of the problem in the Comoros. I hoped I would be able to go to Paris to see the file prepared by Ali Salim, maybe it would give me the answers I sought. But if so, why had no one been convicted of Abdallah's murder?

There was only one person with all the answers: Bob Denard. I was by this stage almost certain that he was still living in South Africa. Tony Kaye had seen him there only months earlier; I knew he had not returned to France as the mandate for his arrest was still out and I suspected that rumours in the British press that he had been hired by Mobuto Sese Seko of Zaire to train his personal bodyguard, were false. Mobuto would have to be crazy, after the role Denard had played in trying to overturn him during the ill-fated mercenaries' revolt in 1967. Yet how would I find him? I was half-surprised that he hadn't caught up with me, he must have known what I was up to.

*

My final two days in the Comoros were hectic. The day before I left I drove to the Galawa Hotel. It was the last time I was to go up the coastal road I had come to know so well. Ali Toihir was in reception when I arrived.

'Samantha, I'm so pleased you're here. There's a French journalist staying, who's been looking for you everywhere. I gave him your number, but he said he couldn't get through.'

'Do you know what he wants?'

'No, but I'll tell him you're here.'

I went down to the pool and settled in front of a large club sandwich. Before long, a tall, thin, dark-haired man came to sit opposite me.

'Hello, you must be Samantha. I'm Philippe Chapeleau.'

'Hello.'

He ordered a beer.

'I have heard you are writing a book about Bob Denard. I

have just come from Pretoria, where I was staying with him. I
told him about you and he wants to meet you.'

It had happened – contact had been made.

'I'd very much like to meet him too. I was going to try to find
him when I got back to South Africa. Do you have his
number?'

'He has just moved house and does not have a phone yet. But
I will give you my pager number and I will make sure that a
meeting is arranged.'

'Are you going back to stay with him again?'

'Uh, non, but I will be in contact with him.'

*

It was sad to say goodbye to Papa Claude and Ali Toihir. Papa
looked almost tearful. Ali Toihir's farewell was more
restrained, but I was just as sad to take my leave of him. I drove
back as the sun was beginning its descent into the sea. The sky
was lit up in shades of pink and orange, casting a strange,
warm glow on to the jagged, black lava.

But my last hours weren't as peaceful as I had expected them
to be. A Comorian journalist I had met with Mouzawar turned
up for a couple of whiskies before dinner. M'changama had
worked in London and Paris before returning home to start an
independent newspaper, *L'Archipel*, which he and another
journalist were still struggling to produce, on an ever-
decreasing shoestring.

'This country is in a very bad state. There are twenty-four
parties competing for seats in the up-coming elections. The
majority of them are in there for the money. Whoever wins is
bound to continue the rape of the Comoros. What we have
here is anarchy loosely masquerading as democracy. But what
is going to happen to us? We are totally reliant on international aid – for the most part French. But the French have
threatened to withhold their donations if the present corruption and theft doesn't halt. The International Monetary Fund
and the World Bank have set targets, but there is no way we are

going to be able to keep to them. There is huge unemployment, the civil servants are only being paid one month out of every four and a small number of people are pocketing large sums of money. How are we ever going to get out of this quagmire? It would require a truly visionary and powerful leader to do that – but we don't have one. And who can blame the politicians? The country is going to the dogs; they might as well try and grab what they can before it self-destructs.'

'But why do you think the Comoros is in such a state?'

'Oh, there are so many reasons. But at the heart, I think, is the Comorian nature. We don't have a real identity. We are Africans, but we want to be Arabs. In our consciousness Africans are slaves, so we try to ignore our Africanness. But we aren't Arabs either, despite Islam. Our Arab days are long gone. We are sort of schizophrenics; you say many people have lied to you. We don't see it as lying. We do it to try to show the sunny side. We believe that if you tell the truth to someone, maybe you'll hurt them. Everyone goes around telling people what they think they want to hear. You have noticed that many Comorians have two names? It is a way to hide themselves. This is why the true story of what happened on the night of Abdallah's death has not yet been revealed and may never come to light. There is no such thing as a reliable witness in the Comoros.'

*

It was with those words still ringing in my head that I went to dinner with the Prince for the last time. On this occasion his entire family were there; his beautiful wife had returned from Paris with their new daughter, Fatima Nawar Naçr-Ed-Dine, and her elder sister. In addition, the Prince's three children from his first marriage to his present wife's elder sister, had come back for the university holidays from France. He told me in a jocular manner that several government informants had come to him and denounced me as a spy. It was further proof of the power and inaccuracy of the Comorian rumour machine.

It was a happy evening; my host was at his most genial and as flamboyant as ever, his wife was quiet and gentle and his children, intelligent and friendly. We ate and drank a lot and on about my third protestation of fatigue the Prince, a fat cigar between his teeth, said he would drive me home. He kissed his wife goodbye.

'I may be late,' he told her, 'I am thinking of going dancing. You are coming with me, aren't you Samantha?'

I blushed. 'No I am not.'

He continued to try to persuade me on the way down the stairs and it degenerated into a full-blown argument when he turned the car in the opposite direction to my house and started heading at top speed for the nightclub.

'No, look, I have to leave tomorrow. I want an early night. Take me home. Please.'

He just grinned and took another turn leading even further away from where I wanted to go.

'I'm getting out,' I said, opening the car door.

He slammed on the brakes.

'Are you crazy? What do you think I am doing? Kidnapping you? No, you have just eaten a large meal and it is not good for you to go to bed with a full stomach. I am taking you for a drive to give you time to digest your food.'

I wanted to laugh, but the Prince was in deadly earnest. We completed the journey in silence. He didn't even look at me as I said goodbye. It was sad, he was one of the more amusing people I had met on the Comoros.

*

I left the next day. The drive was beautiful, the rain had stopped, coaxing the most powerful scent from the omnipresent ylang-ylang flowers. I was leaving the perfume islands.

But I was on my way to South Africa to see Colonel Bob Denard.

13

The King of Fortune

I WAITED by the phone for ten days before Denard called. Then one morning I was woken by its persistent ringing.

'Allo, can I speak to Samantha Weinberg please?' The accent was strong.

'Speaking.'

'Do you speak French?'

'Yes.' I was not yet fully awake.

'Philippe told me to phone you. It is the Colonel Denard.'

It was. It was really him.

'Yes, yes, please can we meet?'

He said he would come to Johannesburg to see me at the end of the week. We arranged to have lunch at the Japanese restaurant at the end of my road.

*

The next day I met Marco Boni, the former South African diplomatic representative in the Comoros.

'I had an interesting time during my two years there,' he told me. 'I really miss it now.'

He was maybe in his late-thirties, with a large, round face, and a warm smile under a thick, manicured moustache.

'What did you think of Denard?' I asked.

'He struck me as a very charming man. I had a considerable amount of contact with him, mainly during the negotiations for his departure. I think he was proud of his role as an international statesman, a broker of the relationship between South Africa and the Comoros. His motives were, I think, mixed. He wanted money and power, but he also wanted to settle down and to do some genuine good for the country.

'I saw him as a tragic figure. He had fallen in love with the islands and had probably reached the stage where he wanted to stop being a mercenary. But, unfortunately for him, I don't believe he had a firm enough grasp of local and international politics. De Klerk coming to power was the final nail in his coffin. South Africa just couldn't afford to be seen to be associating with the likes of Denard.'

'What was your brief on the Comoros?'

'From the beginning, my mission was to try to terminate relations between South Africa and the mercenaries. But Denard had some pretty powerful contacts here. I was his contact in the field, but he had other strings to his bow: obviously within the South African Defence Force and the others too, probably.'

'Like who?'

'I shouldn't think it would take too much imagination to guess.'

'What sort of relationship do you think he had with these "other strings?" '

'Well, there were all sorts of rumours.'

He clearly wanted to change the subject. If the 'other strings' were who I thought they were, they weren't the kind of people you talked about in the 'new South Africa'.

'What you have to understand is that the Comoros has always been completely Franco-centric. The relationship between the two nations is a bit like ours with "the home-lands" and I think that is a mistake. The French had double standards – and we had so much to offer. We really wanted to make our first real foray into Africa a success. We provided all sorts of aid – the hotel alone involved a complicated loan agreement for 58 million Rand and in the beginning we ploughed R1 million a year into the farm.'

But the relationship, Marco bemoaned, was never really allowed to prosper as it could have. He accepted that South

Africa was too closely associated with the mercenaries in the eyes of the Comorian people and claimed that Denard had never really encouraged the two countries to become close to each other, as he was afraid of jeopardising his special position as the middle man.

'What do *you* think was the real story behind Abdallah's death?' I asked.

'I don't really know. I first heard that the Commandant Ahmed was behind it. However within hours we knew that he wasn't involved and I thought then that if it wasn't him, there was only one other person it could have been. I tried to contact Denard all that day and finally collared him in the evening. We met at the officers' mess. He told me in great detail the story about rockets coming through the window, Djaffar appearing in a state of panic and firing, and him throwing himself to the floor. He was wearing his habitual beige safari suit and he had a revolver tucked discreetly into his pocket. It was at that moment, I think, that I realised it was the real thing, not the movies.

'I never felt at all threatened by him; he always conducted himself in a thoroughly gentlemanly fashion, he never wore a uniform, or brandished a pistol, or anything. But I could see things had changed by the anxious look on his face. He kept repeating; "Je suis le porte-chapeau [I have to carry the can]. Everyone is blaming me because I am an easy target." '

'Did you believe his story?'

'No. But I didn't know what had really happened, though I doubted he was directly involved. During the next days, it was as if winter had arrived and all the squirrels had gone into hibernation. The streets were deserted. I was paranoid that my phone had been tapped. I started making contact with prominent Comorians – my main aim was to convince them that we weren't in any way involved. It was an opportunity for us to distance ourselves from the mercenaries and to offer support, assistance and friendship to the Comorian people. That was all we could do because it was obvious at that time that the French were pulling all the strings on the negotiations front . . .

'Denard's conditions for his departure were, I think, an attempt to keep face and salvage his pride. I don't think he really believed they would be met, but he wanted to leave his kingdom with his head held high.'

Marco had been unhappy, he intimated, that the mercenaries were allowed to depart on a South African plane in full uniform, carrying their guns – a flagrant violation of international air law – and with sealed trunks suspected to contain the President's archives. He wouldn't be drawn on why this was allowed to happen but the inference was clear – it was part of the deal brokered with the French. Denard's blackmail had begun.

'Are you seeing him?' Marco asked.

'Yes, tomorrow.'

'Please send him my regards.'

*

I arrived at the restaurant early. I asked for a table for Denard, but they told me they had no bookings under that name. I studied the list and saw he had used 'Bako', his Comorian pseudonym. I sat down and watched the car park.

An old red Nissan Cherry estate drew up. It was him. He took a while to park, fussing over the sign reserving the space for patrons of the restaurant. He got out and carefully locked his door, opened the back door and took out his blazer, which he put on over a pale blue shirt (through which I could see the outlines of a vest). He was wearing subtle grey linen checked trousers and a discreet tie. He could have been a prosperous businessman or a retired diplomat. He limped towards the restaurant, shorter than I had imagined and quite stocky. He wore large tortoise-shell glasses, which I hadn't seen in any photographs. His black ankle boots appeared from a distance to be reinforced. He looked like an old man.

But when he came over to the table, I changed my mind

about that. He was a powerful physical presence, his eyes behind the spectacles were a piercing turquoise, the same mesmerising colour as the Comorian sea. They were the eyes of a younger man and a hard man.

Immediately we said hello, I knew instinctively that conversation would not be difficult; we had a lot of common ground. The time we spent in the Comoros represented a bond that not too many people could share. And we were both Africaphiles: it is often said that once you spend time in Africa, you can never get it out of your system. I think that is true – up to a point – but it is also a certain type of person that is drawn to the barren chaos and desperation of the 'dark continent'. Denard and I might not agree on many things; we might not like each other; but we were still bound by Africa.

He sat down and produced two copies of a magazine called *Fire! Le Magazine de l'Homme d'Action*.

'It's my new venture,' he explained. 'I am now a man of the press.'

There was a large picture of him staring sternly from the front of the first edition of the 'new series'. I noticed he was wearing the same elephant-hair bracelet and gold chain around his right wrist as he wore now, tucked discreetly under his sleeve. *Fire!* was, he explained, the flagship in a publishing empire he was planning to create.

'I feel young, about to embark on a new career. My life has passed so fast, I haven't had time to grow old.'

We talked about a range of subjects. I didn't want to discuss anything too deeply as I wasn't taking notes and I also didn't want to talk about Abdallah's death yet. The main aim of this meeting, I thought, is to make sure he likes me enough to meet again. We talked about the future; he assured me he didn't want to return to the Comoros, as he was 'fed up with the hypocrisy and constant lies of the Comorian people'. He said his time on the Comoros was now just a memory, an *histoire d'amour*.

We ordered. Denard wanted lots of sushi and sashimi.

I asked him if he had kept Ramadan this year.

He smiled: 'Not here, although I did when I was M'hadjou in the Comoros.'

'But are you still a Muslim?'

'I am a Muslim, as I could be Jewish, Catholic, Methodist, whatever. In the Comoros it was best for me to be a Muslim, because that was what they wanted me to be. But when I went to the mosque to do "Hitima" and they wouldn't let me – that was when I really stopped being a Muslim.'

We talked about his seven wives (he had recently added another one) and eight children, all of whom live in France: 'I love women,' he proclaimed. He said he wanted to return to his motherland. The Benin sentence, however, still hung over his head. 'But it is an honourable sentence. Four of the "criminals" I was alleged to have "associated with" were heads of state. There is no dishonour in that.'

In the meantime, he was being kept busy by the magazine and ideas for books. He had plans, he told me, to write five, about separate episodes in his life; Katanga, Zaire, Biafra, the Yemen and the Comoros. 'Le Roi de Fortune was like a summary. There is still much to say.'

His conversation was full of bravado – I felt he wanted to convince me of his continuing importance. But what was he, I wondered, but an exile living out his enforced retirement far away from the battlegrounds of his prime, in a country that was not his own, among people who didn't speak his language?

He rose to leave, having paid the bill out of a thick wedge of large notes. We had both eaten an extraordinary amount of raw fish.

'I trust you,' he had said. 'You have clear eyes and an open countenance. I am willing to be interviewed by you. Call me in a few days to set up a meeting.'

He limped towards his car and suddenly he was an old man again.

*

I had to wait a week before our next meeting. I faxed off a list of questions which I had tried to make searching enough for him to take me seriously – but not too critical in case he changed his mind about seeing me. We set a date and he gave me directions to his house.

It was drizzling as I drove up the main N1 motorway linking Johannesburg to the administrative capital, Pretoria. Following his instructions, I took the Atterbury Road turn-off and passed the Hypermarket and a Kentucky Fried Chicken drive-in restaurant.

I turned into a short hilly street in a comfortable suburb – all barbeques and water-sprinklers – just after four and parked in Denard's leafy drive. The garden was well-tended and there was a frangipani tree just under an ivy-smothered arch. The smells brought back sharp memories of the Comoros, perhaps that was why he rented the house. It had stopped raining and there was a faint hint of steam rising from the crazy paving. The house was low and honey-coloured like both his houses in the Comoros.

I knocked on the heavy, wooden, arched, double doors. Thick, metal rings turned as Denard opened the door. He ushered me through a tiled hall into a small sitting-room.

'Would you like something to drink?' he asked.

'Coffee, please.'

I followed him through to the cavernous kitchen, spartan neat. He began to search through the cupboards for the coffee. I noticed he was wearing the same black, reinforced ankle boots.

'It doesn't matter if you haven't got any,' I said. 'I'll have tea.'

'I have, I had some this morning, but I don't know where the maid put it.'

We moved back into the sitting-room with cups of tea. I got out my tape-recorder and he went off to fetch a large dictaphone machine. I gazed around the room. It was very bare, even for a house that had just been moved into. There were no pictures on the walls, no ornaments, only a buff-coloured, *faux*-velvet sofa and chairs, and a glass coffee table covered with a glittery, embroidered, brown mat. The floors were bare, an ancient television and video stood by the window. And sitting on top, I could see two videos Philippe had made for him; 'Comores '92' and 'École de Chasse'. A small, neat pile of copies of *Liberation* magazine sat on a low table in the corner and I saw an edition of *Soldier of Fortune* magazine – the accepted bible of the mercenary world – on his desk.

We switched on our respective recording devices and immediately the tone changed. He was alternately aggressive and defensive, rarely relaxed. I was tense. Sometimes I caught him repeating whole passages from the book about him – other times he contradicted things I knew to be true. I got the feeling he expected me to accept whatever he said, that he believed he would be able to convince me by the force of his personality alone.

'What were your greatest achievements in the Comoros?' I started.

'The most important thing was to have come, to have changed surely the course of history, to have re-established democracy. Of course it's not democracy they have now, it's anarchy.'

'So do you think the Comoros were a better place when you left to when you arrived?'

'Oh yes – that's indisputable. When we arrived in 1978, there wasn't a state. Ali Soilih had destroyed the administration and everything. It was necessary to start again from scratch. The process of decentralisation that Soilih had started wasn't, in my opinion, a bad thing, but he tried to do it all too quickly. He relied on children and they quickly got out of control. His other error was to underestimate the importance of religion and the traditional leaders. He wanted to change customs and traditions and he went about it in a brutal manner. But he had some good ideas.'

'If you could go through the period again, what would you have done differently?'

'Nothing. I believe that one should accept the passing of time. We arrived, took responsibilities – the country was in a state of abandon, there was no money, nothing worked. The town was empty and dirty. We cleaned it and fixed everything.'

'No regrets?'

'Non, je ne regrette rien. Not at all. I can't think of anyone today who could have done what I did better. We were thrown out of the country in 1989, the year of International Human Rights, because some people wanted to get rid of "the mercenaries". But we weren't mercenaries, no, we were pioneers. Look at the evidence; go and see the farm, the hotel, the houses, the roads. We were responsible for all that. No, we were labelled mercenaries because the Comoros has a tradition of mercenaries. It dates back thousands of years, there were mercenaries in the Comoros before there were parish priests.'

'And you didn't want to be king . . .'

'No,' he laughed. 'That's a myth, a legend. It comes from the Sean Connery film. I regret being called that.'

'Not the King of Fortune?'

More rueful laughter: 'More often misfortune. The "fortune" in soldier of fortune doesn't refer to money, but to luck.'

'Surely you made some money in the Comoros?'

'I had a salary like everyone else, but how can one make money in a country where there isn't any? I made some money before in military operations and war and I have saved it. I am not a man who wastes money or throws it around. Look around you. I risked my life to make money, I am not going to throw it away.'

'How much did Clint Eastwood pay you?'

'Not much, but it was the only time I made money without risking my life.'

All his Comorian assets, he reminded me, had been left behind. He came away with nothing and he is, at present, waiting for his lawyer to clarify his position with regard to those goods and investments. He denied, however, that he had ever had a meat-importing business or that he had made money from commercial enterprise in the Comoros.

'Can we talk about the events of 1989?'

'No. My two colleagues [Marquès and Siam] are on bail in France. The whole matter is sub judice. I have nothing further to add that you can't read in the book and in the magazine also. I can't say anything else, because if I talk, perhaps it will affect their bail. I don't want my words to prejudice their case. The subject is closed. There is nothing to be said that hasn't already been said. Except that France broke their word. One of the terms for our departure was that my men could return to France without being exposed to prosecution. But they broke their word. [Siam and Marquès were arrested in Paris on 14th and 26th September 1990 respectively.] Their sole fault was to have believed France's word. I received an assurance from France that none of my officers would be sought by French justice. It is unfair. Marquès is a good man. He became Commandant of the PG in 1986. He always respected laws and he was perfectly loyal to me and to Abdallah who gave him an audience every week. As for Siam, he had only been there three months. I recruited him to be an intelligence officer and in this task he acquitted himself with dedication.'

The two men were released on bail a year later — against the wishes of the instructing judge, Chantal Perdrix. Throughout the interview, Denard kept returning to the subject of France's perfidy. It was obviously a subject that weighed heavy on his mind.

'I accept that,' I said, 'but perhaps I could still ask some questions that wouldn't jeopardise their case?' He nodded. 'What was the plan to reorganise the armed forces?'

'It needs to be said that at the time,' Denard replied, 'the CAF was completely rotten, it didn't really exist. The Commandant Ahmed had resigned and the soldiers hadn't been paid for four or five months and many had deserted taking their arms with them. The President had decided, in conjunction with the French, to reorganise the army.'

'What happened?'

'Everyone submitted their plans; the French, the South Africans and us. But none were carried through because the President died. Under our plan, Marquès would have remained as Commandant of the Guard – there would still have been a Guard but it would have been much smaller, there would perhaps have been five or six Europeans and a hundred men charged with the close security of the President. The rest of the soldiers – that is to say the Comorians – would have been integrated into the defence force.'

'You don't think the French were keen for you to leave?'

'No, I don't think so. It suited everyone that I was there, the French too. There was, perhaps, a political problem with having expatriate foreign officers, but that was why I formed Sogecom – to involve some of my men in the development side. The Comoros needed us and we were dependent on them. But they never made decisions; they said, as all Arabs do, "Inshallah" – if God wills it. The President's favourite saying was "what must be done must be done". He never did anything until it was totally necessary. Like with Sogecom; it needed to be inscribed in the statutes, but it never happened. It was always the same story: "tomorrow, tomorrow". We had to live every day with tomorrow. That was the Comorian mentality and we had to adapt ourselves to their philosophy.'

'But if there hadn't been the troubles of 1989, if '89 hadn't happened . . .'

'With "if" one could put Paris in a bottle.'

'Don't you think the changes in South Africa would have made a difference to your position?'

'Not really. They might have stopped financing us

eventually and maybe we would have had to leave – but with compensation, they would have paid us our dues and reimbursed our investments. We weren't given a centime of compensation.'

'Do you think the French wanted you to leave?'

'No, they used the President's death as a pretext, they grabbed the opportunity. Of course one can say, "but who provoked the President's death?" Not us. The only evidence for us having provoked it was purely circumstantial. Look at it logically – who was the victim? OK, the dead President was the victim but we were also victims because we lost everything, twelve years' work gone up in a puff of smoke. So you see, we were the victims too. Where is the logic? One speaks a lot of logic: the logic of war, the logic of peace . . . there are always logics. The logic for us wasn't for the President to die.

'Look at what happened; we were given no option but to leave. If we had stayed and fought, some French would have been killed and in the end I couldn't accept that. We were given the opportunity to negotiate. There were negotiations, all sorts of negotiations, including for compensation. However, as soon as we relinquished our arms, there weren't any more negotiations. But there are still recourses to justice. They accused us and there is justice for the accused. They need proof . . . two and a half years later, what do they have in the way of proof? There isn't any proof. There isn't any proof. There is no proof that it was anything but a tragedy.'

Who was he trying to convince – himself or me? I had noticed that sometimes, once he was on a thought track it was hard to get him off it. Sometimes, I thought, he just caught himself short as he started to criticise Abdallah – as he had done on numerous occasions, and frequently in public, before Abdallah's death. He was very keen for me to think that if the terrible accident hadn't occurred, he and his men would still be living happily together with Abdallah in the Comoros.

'My men were killed – for to put a man into prison is to kill him, to ruin his life. And what about me? Will I be here forever? I don't have the money to stay here forever. And when I don't have any more money what are they going to do? They will throw me out. What do I do here? I live quietly, I pay my rent, buy my food, I have an old car, I am not extravagant. While I have money it is all right for me to stay, but when I run out? We shall see.'

'Sorry, I don't really understand. Do you think the French plotted to throw you out?'

'No, I don't think there was a plot, I think there was an opportunity. There were people who wanted to see us go – that's for sure. They wanted to see us go because we represented order and while we were there they could not scheme or steal.'

'Comorian people you mean?'

Denard shrugged.

'How were the French involved in the Comoros?'

'I don't know. France didn't tell me anything. The French weren't involved in 1975 or in 1978. Maybe they knew about what was going to happen and turned a blind eye to it, but they didn't give any money.'

'I thought you said in the book [*Le Roi de Fortune*] that you had worked for the French services?'

'Yes, but indirectly. All the sleeping partners for whom I worked were states or future states, never private people. But not France. France was behind Gambia, behind Gabon, behind Morocco, but they never directly gave the orders. It was always the people who represented the state, or who were going to represent the state, who gave the orders. I never had direct contact with the French services. But it's their job to watch, to control, to manipulate . . . of course we were manipulated.

'All that was in the period of decolonisation, but after 1989 they wanted the decolonisation to be over. But it will never be over. France failed at decolonisation, she botched it up. It started in 1960, now thirty years later they want to change the process, to introduce democracy. Democracy? In countries where there are tribes, ethnicity, where the centre of life is the village, where there isn't a national spirit? We can't make a United States of America or a Europe out of Africa. It can't exist, too much is still rooted in ancestral customs.'

'But France was involved in your departure from the islands . . .'

'Yes, and this gave them responsibilities. It's all very well for them to say; "those men there, chuck them out", but they can't leave it like that. I worked for twelve years there, paid by South Africa and by France – for they gave the PG subsidies for materials, equipment and arms, and our soldiers and officers went on training courses in France. These are responsibilities they can't deny.'

'Do you think many Comorians were against you and your men?'

'Not many. They liked us, because in creating and paying the Guard, we were feeding in total about 10,000 civilians. And now we've gone, there's no one there in our place and no one capable of taking it. You have seen what is happening there now – it is too painful to speak about. The Comoros needed us. The Guard was organised, the Guard was structured, the Guard had an administration . . . when there was a problem in the Comoros, the Guard was called. If there was a fire, the Guard was called; if there were bees in the roof, the Guard was called; if there were problems in the village, the Guard was called; if your house was falling down, you called the Guard. Voila!'

'If we can't talk about his death, can we talk about the President himself?'

'The President . . . the President was a formidable man. One can say what one wants about him, but the Comoros won't have another president like that for a long time, a very long time . . . maybe never. One can accuse him of some things – he had his faults, but what man doesn't? He wasn't a realist and, of course, he made errors like all humans. Who has never made a mistake in their lives? One can always criticise, but don't look to me to criticise the President. The President was my friend and I respect his memory . . . One can, of course, always find things . . . one can always find people who, out of jealousy and meanness, out of self-interest, spit on his memory. But don't count on me for that. I knew the President well, I knew his qualities and his faults. He led the country in the Comorian manner and it wasn't worse then than it is now.'

'They say he liked money . . .'

'I don't believe so. They talked of Abdallah, the richest man in the Indian Ocean. But where would one make a fortune in the Comoros? How? Are there gold mines? Or diamond mines, or oil? No, no! It's always journalists who make up this kind of thing. He was no more corrupt than others. Do you know a president who hasn't been accused of corruption? Even Mitterrand has been accused of all sorts of things, Giscard too. Everyone has been accused of corruption. Me too, I'm corrupt, the whole world is corrupt. But those who tell you Abdallah was corrupt are perhaps corrupt themselves. What does it really mean, to be "corrupt"?'

'Do you think Abdallah wanted you to leave?'

'Not at all . . . at one time he was solicited, I think . . . it's very blurred, it's not clear because we didn't involve ourselves with these things. Abdallah knew he needed us, that we were his security. He had already resisted lots of people who wanted us to go. They say he wrote a letter to Mitterrand – I'm still waiting to see that letter. But we would have tried to make him promise, tried to influence him to keep us, that's for sure. He had no reason to make us go; we didn't cost him a cent, we didn't cost the Comorian state anything, or the Comorian people. On the contrary, we gave them security.'

'What was the story with the Commandant?'

'The Commandant is a friend, as were all the commandants of the CAF and the gendarmerie. But Ahmed is a Comorian; he was given responsibilities, but not enough means. The means he did have, he used perhaps for other things, but I don't want to throw stones at the Commandant. What happened on the night of the President's death was that it was decided to disarm the CAF, because they had lots of arms – they could fire at anyone. Once the decision was taken, it was carried out within five minutes. We went to Anjouan to disarm the CAF there – and of course the Commandant – but we made a mistake, we didn't phone him before. He was frightened in my opinion. It was a reflex of fear, he climbed into a roof and a soldier fired a bazooka . . .'

'Why?'

'They were under orders to disarm him. But they fired the bazooka and the roof fell in – he was lucky. I have spoken to him since, we have stayed good friends.'

I was getting tired and my French was beginning to falter. I apologised to Denard and said that when I returned, I would be fluent.

'You need to find a French boyfriend,' he informed me.

'I had one once.'

'Wasn't he any good?'

'No.'

'You've got plenty of time. You're still young, enjoy life, acquire experiences. You need a mature man. You need to come here to work with me. Why not? You will learn good French and we can write a book for the Anglophone market. Give it some thought, I'll give you my address.'

He gave me a sticker with a box number printed on it.

'What name should I write to?'

'Robert Denard. It's no longer Bob. Bob was my "nomme de guerre", Robert is my "nomme de presse".'

'Don't you have another nickname, like "Mad Mike" Hoare, or "Black Jacques Schramme"? Something like "Bad Bob Denard".'

'No, I am a soldier, I am not a "mad" . . . what does that mean, "mad"?'

'Fou.'

'No, I am not mad. I may have a hole in my head, but I'm not mad. I've a hole in my head – didn't you know? Here, give me a hand . . . can you feel it? It was in Zaire, I was wounded, I should have been dead. That was in 1967.'

'Did you always want to be a soldier?'

'Yes always. I wanted to be like Surcouf . . . the English know Surcouf, he was an enemy of England, a sailor like Nelson. He fought against Nelson. He was a pirate.'

'Would you have preferred to be a soldier in the regular French army?'

'No. I served in the French army for seven years and I soon learned that there weren't any possibilities. I left the army and went abroad, first to Morocco and then to Katanga, where I rapidly climbed the echelons. I was made a colonel in 1965 by Mobuto.'

'Have you always been anti-communist?'

'Yes, but when it comes to ideology, I don't wear blinkers. I don't immediately see red when I see a communist. But I am against a certain doctrine. My main aim is to liberate people, to avoid massacres. I have saved many people – I don't only do war. You can't do war 365 days a year.'

'What is a mercenary?'

'A mercenary is a man of arms. It is a man who fights for a country that is not his own, who fights for a wage. He is paid by the country he fights for. He doesn't kill for wages or work for individuals – the people who do that are not mercenaries, they are killers.'

'Do you think it is an honourable profession?'

'That all depends on who practises it. But I can tell you one thing; a mercenary who doesn't respect a certain code of honour cannot last thirty years.'

'What characteristics make a good mercenary?'

'One has to be courageous. You have to be more than a good soldier. A soldier works within an army structure with logistical support, a pension and social security. A mercenary doesn't have all that. A mercenary is paid and that's it. He needs to be not only a good soldier and brave, but also organised and willing to take risks. One cannot be a good mercenary only for the money, it's not possible. One can't kill oneself for money. The salaries of mercenaries in any case are often less than the salaries of regular soldiers in the French or American armies.'

'What do you think is the future of the mercenary?'

'For two thousand years people have been saying that the mercenary era has ended, but here we are still today. I don't think the mercenary's time has passed. I don't know what will happen in the future, but things will turn up. The period of decolonisation may be over, but who can know what will happen in the future? I think that, as long as there are people who enjoy adventure, there will be mercenaries. But adventure is like love, it needs to be done well and one needs to have partners.'

Again his face was inscrutable. I couldn't work out whether he was being suggestive, or whether I was misreading the situation. I didn't want to become his partner in adventure but I was, I realised, envious in a way of what he had done, of the history that he had witnessed – and in some cases contributed to.

I wasn't really getting anywhere. He was a man who never quite let himself lose control. I needed time to assimilate what he had said, to try to read between the lines. I still felt that he thought he could make me believe whatever he said, despite my having, in some cases, collected corroborated evidence to the contrary. I thought, suddenly, that maybe he had convinced himself that his version of events and situations was the truth.

I was surprised to feel sad when I left. I felt sorry to leave him alone with his dreams, so out of context in his empty suburban house.

14

Testimonies

WEDNESDAY 25TH NOVEMBER, 1981. MAHÉ INTER-NATIONAL AIRPORT, SEYCHELLES. Shortly before sunset, the orange and white, Royal Swazi Fokker Friendship landed on the short runway and taxied over to the terminal buildings. Among the disembarking passengers were forty-seven burly men carrying cricket bags inscribed with the initials A.O.F.B. They were members of a philanthropic rugby club, the Ancient Order of Frothblowers, apparently eager for their two-week holiday on the beautiful Indian Ocean islands. Outside the airport, their four friends waited anxiously to greet them and bear them off to a welcome cocktail party at a nearby hotel.

The first man through was older than the rest, a trim grey-haired figure with a goatee beard and an upright bearing. One by one, the other members of the party emerged into the humid evening, smiling as they grouped around the three minibuses, waiting for the last stragglers. One of these was Kevin Beck, who passed safely through passport control, but inexplicably turned into the red, 'Goods to Declare', customs hall. The man before him, a Frenchman who had boarded the plane at Moroni, had been caught with fresh fruit in his luggage. The customs officer, Vincent Pillay, was suspicious when Beck said he had nothing to declare. He began to search his bag. Beneath the toys ('Christmas presents for poor Seychellois children'), under the beach clothes, Pillay felt a hard outline. He asked Beck to accompany him to the guardroom.

He emptied the bag to discover parts of a weapon neatly

packed in polystyrene. The woman police constable took it for a spear gun and was in the process of writing Beck a receipt, when her superior officer, Sergeant Esparon, had a closer look. He asked what it was. Beck replied that he didn't know, but added, fatally: '. . . there are forty-four more with bags like mine outside.'

The game was up. Sergeant Esparon, holding the muzzle of the AK 47 from Beck's bag, came running through the aiport, shouting that 'they' had guns and must not be allowed to leave. There was chaos. The men started reaching for their bags, tossing toys and clothes out of the top and rapidly assembling their AK47 semi-automatic rifles. One man fired a shot into Esparon's shoulder at close range. He fell to the ground. Shots were whizzing in every direction. Night was falling. One of the mercenaries was killed by accident by a bullet from his own side.

In a matter of minutes, the mercenaries had asserted their control. They herded the airport staff and passers-by into a passenger lounge and disconnected the telephones. The man with the goatee, whose passport had been issued in the name of 'Thomas Boareau', but who was far better known as the Irish mercenary, 'Mad' Mike Hoare, tried to reassess the situation. The original plan, to stage a bloodless coup to overthrow President France-Albert René, was clearly a write-off. The primary concern now was damage-control. Hoare ordered four members of his party to go to the army headquarters to 'seize the barracks'. They were followed by fifteen men in commandeered minibuses. But the attack on the barracks failed and a mercenary was badly injured. Hoare ordered the men to fall back on the airport.

The succeeding events are ones that 'Mad' Mike would probably prefer to forget. The army counter-attacked, a soldier was shot by one of his own side. Hoare decided that the coup attempt should be scuppered and tried to contact the British pilots of the Air Swazi plane who, unsurprisingly, were not keen to fly them out. A scheduled Air India flight was guided in to land, at which point the Seychelles army reopened fire. After some hurried negotiations, the mercenaries boarded the plane and the pilot agreed to fly them to Durban – if his passengers and plane remained unharmed. They took off and soon after the army once again launched an attack on the airport, now empty of all but the hostages in the passenger lounge.

On arrival in Durban, the mercenaries were arrested by the South African authorities, charged with hijacking under the Civil Aviation Act, and sentenced to terms of imprisonment ranging from one to twenty years (Hoare was released after serving a quarter of his time).

The attempt by Colonel 'Mad' Mike Hoare to return to mercenary action, two decades after his triumphant period in the Congo, was a dismal failure. One of the aspects that must have rankled most bitterly, was that his despised rival, Colonel Bob Denard, was still sitting happy and wealthy on the nearby, larger, more populous Comoros. The Royal Swazi plane that had conveyed the Frothblowers from Swaziland to the Seychelles had even stopped in Moroni on the way to refuel and take aboard passengers.

Patrick Ollivier, then a captain in the Comorian Presidential Guard, described the events of 25th November in Moroni in his book, *Soldat de Fortune*. He had been expecting Denard to dinner at the camp at Itsoundzou. The chef had prepared a special langoustine feast. However, a motorcyclist arrived at dusk with a message for Ollivier. He informed him that the Colonel was unable to come for dinner, but was expecting him at Kandani, the PG headquarters.

When Ollivier arrived: 'le Vieux was pacing up and down his office like a caged lion, in a state of great excitement. ". . . Have you heard the news? There is fighting at Mahe airport. There is a coup in the Seychelles," he said and asked us to place our companies on full alert.'

Denard toyed with the idea of rushing straight off to the Seychelles, but because of a total lack of information as to what was happening and who was behind it, he decided to stay behind. The next day he hovered around the airport until he heard that the coup had failed, and then took the companies off full alert.

I asked Denard what he thought of Hoare's Seychelles coup: 'I thought he was stupid not to have spoken to me . . . he would surely have succeeded if he had. If he had spoken to me, I could perhaps have helped him and he would have been in the Seychelles today.'

It was another example of Denard's arrogance and, perhaps, self-delusion. That Hoare had excelled himself in the Congo in a way that Denard could never emulate, is accepted. After his year as chief of the Fifth Commando, Hoare had briefly turned mercenary soldiering into a respectable profession. He was a British hero. But since then, he had lain low – until, that is, the Seychelles débâcle. In theory, it should have been an easier task for him than the Comoros was for Denard – the Seychelles are much smaller than the 'perfume isles'. So why had Denard succeeded and won the bounty of twelve years in virtual charge of a sovereign country – when Hoare had failed and spent the following five years in a South African jail?

Patrick Ollivier credits Denard's tactical advantage: 'The superiority of Bob Denard in this kind of operation is evident,' Ollivier wrote. 'It is a typically French superiority. With less than nothing, he put together a troop of soldiers capable of taking the initiative during the heat of the action. The Seychelles coup failed terribly. The mercenaries fought and then retreated. They lacked the aggression to carry out decisions.'

I don't know. I found it an extraordinary coincidence – of the kind that perhaps is not so strange in the bizarre and twisted world of the modern mercenary – that the two most famous names in the profession should both attempt to overthrow governments on Indian Ocean islands only a few years apart from each other. It is perhaps even stranger that one should have succeeded and the other come so close. The Seychelles episode only served to reinforce the impression that the mercenaries lived in a completely different world from most of us – one with different morals and codes of conduct and different horizons.

*

Eleven years after the coup attempt, I caught an Air Seychelles flight to Mahé International Airport. Even in the plane, an air of barely-suppressed excitement was evident. The next week, on Sunday 26th July 1992, the Seychellois were to be given the opportunity to vote in the first democratic elections to be held on the islands for eighteen years. The main protagonists were well known to their people; there was President France-Albert René and there was ex-president Sir 'Jimmy' Mancham, from whom René had wrenched the country in a bloodless coup only a year after independence in 1977. It was in Mancham's name that 'Mad' Mike Hoare had led the mercenaries into the Seychelles in 1981 (although not at his express command).

When in power, Sir Jimmy had done his best to live up to his nickname, 'The Playboy President', playing host to the international jet set, holding all-night parties and driving around his islands in a blue Rolls-Royce Corniche, inevitably accompanied by a beautiful starlet. He used as his anthem his favourite song, 'La Paloma Blanca' and his aim as the Seychelles' first president was to turn them into 'the love islands'. Thus when a well-known film director was caught making love with a young girl on the airport runway while waiting for his plane, instead of telling him off, Mancham invited them to the presidential residence for a drink.

It was dark when the plane landed, but as we disembarked I breathed in that familiar glorious heat and the sweet salty smell of an Indian Ocean island. The crickets' chorus was out in full voice to greet us; the Seychellois at the airport were friendly and beautiful. I felt as though I was coming to somewhere at once familiar yet not quite real.

I was covering the elections, but the other aim of my trip was to see Christianne Mille, and try to determine what, if any, difference the separate mercenary-led coups had made to the respective archipelagos.

I called Madame Mille as soon as I arrived and we arranged to meet at her office after work one evening. She was employed as a secretary at the French embassy in Victoria, capital of the Seychelles. She was well turned-out and well preserved, I guessed she was in her fifties. I sat beside her desk as she finished up.

Our conversation turned slowly, inevitably, to the Comoros. She told me she had lived there since Said Ibrahim's time. He had been, she said, a wonderful person; very strong, very wise, very dignified, with a regal yet humble manner. His sons, Kemal and Naçr-Ed-Dine, have nothing of his presence. Said Mohammed Cheik was also a good man and a good president. 'There was no corruption in those times. They genuinely wanted the best for their country. Abdallah too . . .'

'But wasn't he very corrupt?' I asked.

'Abdallah was a rich man when he became President and he didn't abuse his powers . . . I don't know about his sons.' She shrugged.

When Abdallah died, 'it was like a black hole'. She kept stressing that she didn't want to talk about his death as she had left the islands to get over it. I did not want to push her.

'People told me it was Allah's will that Abdallah died and that I should accept it,' she said. 'But my God didn't will it. However I have decided not to think about it and not to try to find out who was responsible. For then I will hate someone. Now I do not hate anyone. I want to keep all my good memories, not to taint them with bad ones.'

'What do you think of Denard?' I asked.

'I liked him, he was a good man and close to the President. If he did not do it, then he was unlucky in his treatment. If he did, then he was even more unlucky for he will never forget it, it will always be in his heart. I feel sorry for him, he is a virtual prisoner now.

'I'm sorry,' she said, 'it's not that I don't want to help, but it still hurts so much that I don't want to talk about it. Abdallah was like a father to me. It was a catastrophe. Every time I think about it, it wrenches my heart. I came to the Seychelles to get away from what happened and to forget about it. After two years I am beginning to do so.'

I liked Madame Mille and that was why I could not push her. The events in the Comoros had obviously had a terrible and long-lasting effect on her. I wondered if maybe she had seen or heard more than she admitted to. According to numerous sources, she was closer to Abdallah than anyone else. She could have been the only person to know what he was thinking and feeling in the months, weeks, days, leading to his death. She saw him only hours before he died. I did not know whether she was just unwilling to talk about it, whether she had somehow blocked off her memories, or whether someone had persuaded her to forget about it. It seemed strange that she should not want to know what exactly happened the night of Abdallah's death. The family of Monique Terrasse – Abdallah's late mistress – had also made no fuss, demanded no inquiry. Why not, I wondered?

*

I left the Seychelles far too soon. Despite his immense charm and bonhomie, Jimmy Mancham failed to win the elections. The so-called Marxist dictator, René, had called his bluff, held democratic elections – and won. The Seychelles appeared to be happy, harmonious and prosperous. The mercenary coup wasn't a taboo subject and many Seychellois I spoke to – of all political persuasions – appeared proud that their country had managed successfully to beat off the invading mercenary force.

It took me several days to discover what seemed strange about the islands: and then I realised. Unlike any other country in Africa I had visited, there were no visible signs of absolute poverty, no beggars, no slums. The differences between the

Seychelles and the Comoros could not have been more manifest. Sure, both were beautiful Indian Ocean islands, full of natural bounty; but where the Seychellois were open and unafraid, the Comorians were wary and secretive. The Comorians habitually dressed in long robes, the Seychellois wore as little as possible. The mercenary coup in the Comoros had succeeded, whereas the one in the Seychelles had failed. However, I did not think that had it been the other way around, the countries would have fared too differently.

I did not know why the two archipelagos were so different, I suppose one could put it down to culture; the Comoros had an ancient, Muslim history; the Seychelles had none. And that, in the end, is why I liked the Comoros more, despite the Seychelles' clear physical upper hand: the Comorians had a sense of being their own people, whereas the Seychellois were only really what the thousands of tourists who visited their beautiful islands had made them.

*

Mouzawar Abdallah, 'the Snake', had given me the number of a friend of his who lived in exile in Marseille and urged me to visit him if I was near-by.

'He will show you what life is like for those people who were forced out of the country by Abdallah and Denard,' he told me.

I drove from Toulon, where I had rented a small cottage in which to work, along the coast to Marseille. Huge, chalky, cragged hills, sometimes topped by medieval stone-walled villages, towered over the autoroute on my right, while the sea slopped calmly on my left.

I phoned Mouzawar's friend, Aboubacar, from town and he came to meet me outside the gates of the Hospital 'la Timone'. A middle-sized man in a fake, black leather jacket came striding towards me. He had an open, friendly face and gave me to understand that any friend of Mouzawar's was a friend of his. He jumped in my car and asked if we could stop in town to fetch a large sack of rice, after which he would give me a tour of Marseille. We chatted away about the Comoros, life as an exile and whether his country would have fared better had it been an English colony (he said yes, I thought not necessarily).

He was very keen to hear my impressions of the Comoros. 'Is it very bad there now?' he asked.

'No, it's beautiful, I loved it.'

'But it's very bad,' he stated.

I realised he wanted me to agree. He was missing his homeland and wanted to be reassured that he had made the right decision in leaving.

'Yes, the economy is in a terrible state.'

At this, he looked a little happier. He showed me his French ID with its 'Refugie, origin Comorian' status.

'I am the only Comorian political refugee in Marseille,' he told me proudly.

'Why did you have to go into exile?'

'It was very bad. I was against Abdallah and they kept putting me in prison.'

'Why?'

'Because I was against Abdallah.'

It transpired that he was a longtime friend and supporter of Mouzawar's and that every time he greeted Mouzawar in public, he would be arrested and sent to jail for around ten days.

'How many times were you in jail?'

'Many. Many.'

Eventually the persecution got so bad that, fearing worse, he fled to Marseille.

'Abdallah was very corrupt and the mercenaries killed lots of people. If they saw you walking up the street with your wife and they fancied her, they would just come and take her away. If you tried to stop them, they would threaten you with a knife.'

So in 1982 he left a good job as superintendent of roads and came to Marseille, leaving his wife and children behind. Life for an exile was not easy. In the early days, he said, he was scared that the mercenaries would come and find him and kill him. And finding a job was hard. At first he lived in a tiny room in the city centre which he shared with other Comorian exiles.

He showed me around his former neighbourhood, locally known as 'le panier' (the basket). From a tourist's point of view, it was picturesque. Steep, cobbled streets were bordered by a mélange of pretty, old shuttered houses and tatty tenements. I thought it was vaguely reminiscent of the shabbier parts of Paris, but Aboubacar insisted that living conditions were terrible: there was overcrowding, shared bathrooms and no heating or water. He told me of the problems that he and his countrymen faced in getting papers allowing them to stay and work in France. He explained that only about half of the two and a half thousand Comorians living in Marseille manage to find jobs, while the rest are forced to live with, and be supported by, their fellow, employed countrymen who, in turn, are trying to save money to send back to their relatives at home. It had taken Aboubacar six years to save enough to send for his family and to be able to rent a large enough flat in which to house them. He works as a concièrge from 6 am to 1 pm, six days a week (earning FF 5,000 a month) and then as an odd-job man for three hours every afternoon. His rent is FF 2,600 a month. And he considers himself to be one of the fortunate ones.

We drove up and down the narrow streets. The occasional window was brightened by a window-box overflowing with red geraniums, but as we drove, the streets seemed to get narrower and more oppressive. I kept catching glimpses of the chicken hutches behind the attractive stone façades. It was a *quartier* of immigrants, teeming with Arab and African faces. We drove past the Place d'Aix where, according to my guide, the Comorians go each day to meet and talk, a sort of substitute for the squares outside the mosques back home.

I wondered whether life on the breadline in France was

better or worse than life in an economically-defunct country like the Comoros. I did not come to any conclusion: in France there was always the possibility of striking it rich, but if you didn't, poverty must have been worse than in the Comoros where there was always home, the family, mangoes on the trees and fish in the sea.

*

In Paris, I arranged to see the writer, Jean Larteguy, who had written the seminal French book on mercenaries, *Les Mercenaires*. He had spent twenty-five years fighting for the French in Indo-China and when he returned, brought out another book entitled *Le Carrière d'Écrivan Baroudeur* (The Career of a Fighting Writer). It was in his long profile of Denard, written after a visit to the Comoros in March 1989 and published in *Paris Match*, that he described mercenaries as men 'who fight for twenty or thirty years to reshape the world ... they fight for their dreams and the image of themselves they have invented. Then, if they haven't been killed, they resign themselves to living like the rest of the world ... and then die in their beds of a stroke or cirrhosis of the liver.'

The man who opened the door of a plush apartment in a fashionable district looked like an ex-mercenary himself. I judged him to be in his late fifties. He had short, grizzled grey hair and the rasp of a heavy smoker. The room he led me into was large and comfortable, with crimson velvet walls, squashy leather sofas and an array of Eastern pictures and ornaments including a huge, mounted, ivory tusk. He was polite and relaxed.

'Denard wasn't in the room when Abdallah was killed,' he said immediately. 'That is the key. Marquès went mad, he did it. Denard tried to cover up. It was a big mistake.'

'Why would he want to do that?'

'For two reasons: firstly, out of loyalty to his men and secondly, because he couldn't bear people to know that he had lost control of a small faction of them. You see, South Africa and France wanted to get rid of the mercenaries. Denard knew about this and he agreed. But there was a group of hardliners who didn't want to leave. They had a row with Abdallah – in an attempt to scare him into changing his mind. It went terribly wrong and the President died.'

'Are you convinced Denard wasn't there?'

'Yes. There were good relations between Denard and Abdallah – although Denard had accused the President of being a thief. But they were still good friends.'

'What do you, as a soldier, think of Denard's professional abilities?' I asked.

'I personally, as an officer, think Denard had a complex stemming from his days as an under-officer in the navy. He always wanted to make up for this by being the perfect officer. He was capable and honourable and very courageous. He was a good soldier and a good commander, but . . . I don't think he ever really had the mercenary mentality. He was very meticulous in his planning and organisation and obsessively neat – that side came from his days in the French forces – his hero was General Bigard, ex-minister of war. But he was not mad, he didn't like killing.'

'So do you think his sole motivation in becoming a great mercenary leader stemmed from his failure to achieve officer status in the French forces?'

'I think that was very important. He could have been an officer, you know. He had great vitality and he was very loyal to his men and his friends. His mentality was that of a bourgeois; happy, kind, perhaps a bit lazy. I tell you though, Denard did not kill Abdallah. The story of the Comoros is the story of a mistake by the French services, who were influenced into action by international opinion. Giscard brought Denard to the islands in the first place.'

Unfortunately, Lartéguy had to cut short our meeting. We walked out on to the street together, where he climbed into a Mini, waved and drove off. I thought about what he had said and decided the theory of a huge cover-up by Denard to save his men was too far-fetched.

*

I organised a meeting with the Abdallah family's flamboyant and controversial lawyer, Maître Jacques Vergès. He was already something of a legend both in France and Africa. Born in Thailand in 1925 (his father was from the island of Reunion, his mother was Vietnamese and his brother is the present leader of the Communist Party in Reunion) Vergès is an avowed anticolonialist with an appetite for championing the cause of the underdog. He spends much of his time in small, troubled, African states, but came to world attention when he defended Klaus Barbie, an action which resulted in his nicknames, 'The Devil's Advocate' and 'the Bright Bastard'. In court, he shocked the audience and jury when he justified his belief in his client: 'My mother didn't have to wear a yellow star,' he told them. 'She was yellow from her head to her toes!'

Vergès was hired by Abdallah's sister several months after the President's death in an obvious attempt to politicise a case that the French judiciary appeared eager to sweep under the carpet.

I found his offices in an old stone building off a private courtyard in the 9th Arrondissement. I climbed the impressive curved staircase to be greeted by Maître Vergès. He was a small man with a round face, gold-rimmed spectacles and a ready smile. His hair was just going grey at the edges, but he looked young for his years. He led me into his vast office.

'I wish I could help you more,' he said. 'But unfortunately the case is still under consideration and thus I am bound by law not to talk about it.'

'When do you think it will come to court?'

He shrugged.

'Do you think you have a chance of convicting the mercenaries?'

'If there is a tribunal, I would be present, I would cross-examine the witnesses and give my version of the chain of events. But it is possible that the authorities would accept Monsieur Denard's version.'

He would not be drawn further, but it was clear that he did not think there was a strong chance of Denard going to jail for the murder of President Abdallah.

'He did not want me to take on this case,' Vergés continued. 'He telephoned Nassuf Abdallah – the President's eldest son – one morning in the summer of 1990. He told him that he was willing to meet with him and Salim – but only if I was not present: "You know, Nassuf, that guy is going to make trouble," he said. "He isn't liked; not by France, nor South Africa, nor the Comoros. If you continue with him, you are only going to wrong yourself and your father – his memory."

'Then Monsieur Denard said that he was prepared to meet when and where Nassuf wanted, if he came with his other lawyer, Maître Puylegarde – and not with me. "He's someone who has pleaded for the FLN [the Algerian liberation movement] and Klaus Barbie," Monsieur Denard told Nassuf.' Vergés chuckled, obviously tickled by Denard's disregard.

'In the same conversation, Monsieur Denard [he always referred to him as "Monsieur Denard"] tried to convince Nassuf of his innocence. "It was an unfortunate accident," he told him. "It should not have happened but afterwards, I wanted to safeguard your goods, nothing was stolen."

'When Nassuf asked Monsieur Denard how Djaffar could have killed his father without a gun, Denard replied: "Who can prove this?" Then he said that: "Ahmed, the Commandant, said that I wanted to kill him too. If I had wanted to, he would already be dead. For what reason would I plot against your father?"

'Nassuf replied: "Because he didn't want you any more." To which Monsieur Denard said: "That's a tall story. I was ready to go. I had even told your father that, during Mitterrand's visit, I would go if he wanted. But he replied that Mitterrand had advised him to retain me, if he trusted me. Don't tarnish your father's memory with Vergès. Think about it." '

Vergès laughed some more. 'The last thing Monsieur Denard said to Nassuf was: "Now, if I was a killer, I wouldn't have left the Comoros with honour. All the Indian Ocean forces came for me. Submarines, boats, helicopters, aeroplanes – a very important deployment of forces." '

Vergés looked at me and shrugged as if to say 'How can you believe a man who lies so blatantly?'

A discreet buzzer sounded from somewhere beneath his desk. He rose and shook my hand. 'If the case comes to court, by all means come to see me again and then, perhaps I will be able to provide more assistance.'

*

Eric the photographer, Max Veillard's friend, had promised to introduce me to Patrick Ollivier. I had been hassling Denard for some months to put me in contact with one of his men, but to no avail. Ollivier had already fought in the Rhodesian civil war when he joined Denard in 1981. He worked for him for a number of years, first as a captain and section commander in the Comoros and later in Paris, but, as a result of the book he wrote about his mercenary experiences, had fallen out with his former leader.

We met in Eric's apartment. I walked in to find a man of medium build, with a shaved head (after a discreet inspection, I decided he had shaved it to disguise premature balding), black eyes under black eyebrows and an intense expression. He was wearing a tweed jacket, a green V-necked jersey over a striped shirt, pressed trousers with turn-ups, and desert boots, a gold wedding ring and digital watch. We sized each other up. I decided that while he looked like a tough and ruthless man, he appeared far too intelligent to fit in with the prototype of a mercenary I had assembled in my mind.

'Are you a typical mercenary?' I asked.

He smiled before replying in an unexpectedly soft voice:

'No. That is because I came into the profession from a regular army – and a fighting army. I was asked to go to the Comoros because Denard was aware that his force wasn't up to standard. All the guys there were holding ranks they had never previously held.'

'What did he think of your book?'

'It didn't please him much. But at the time, there were things I believed had to be said. To a lot of people here – including people in the army – Denard is a myth, France's Lawrence of Arabia. But he's not. Denard used to say that if he had lived under Napoleon, he would have been a field marshal: I say he would have ended up in front of a firing squad.

'He's a pirate. He took over the Comoros and claimed the islands as his bounty. He wanted to live off them for a long time. Whatever he might say, I can tell you that he was heavily involved in making money much of which, incidentally, he keeps at the Banque Piquet in Switzerland. Here's an example of the sort of things he did: Yves LeBret owned the beach where the Galawa Hotel is now; after the coup in 1978 he was sentenced to death and fled the country; Denard just took over the land and later sold it to Sun International to build the hotel on. He was in the Comoros to make money.'

'What kind of man is he?'

Ollivier sighed and raised his eyebrows. 'To people who have been involved with him from the beginning and who know him well, he is . . . intellectually limited. Personally I have nothing against him, he's a nice guy, he reminds me of my father's generation. He has great charisma and he's capable of attracting loyalty – which is a vital characteristic of a mercenary leader. When he's planning something, he is very meticulous. He rehearses and makes quite sure that everything is accounted for. There is always a purpose behind what he does; no room is left for improvisation and he is one hundred per cent in control at all times. He is also capable of taking a lot of hardship and he is very, very, very pragmatic.

'His major problem is the people he surrounds himself with.

The majority of his men were the outcasts of French society. For example, a few of them came out to Rhodesia where I had been working – this was before the Comoros. They behaved so badly that they were kicked out of the army and some were thrown into jail. Marquès was one of this group, he was sentenced to a term of imprisonment. Melis too; he renounced his contract. They both went on to join Denard in the Comoros; they were lucky he would take them. Mercenaries either succeed and do well – or they are complete wipe-outs. That is why I disagree with Bob Denard: you are judged on the people you trust.'

'Why didn't he hire more reliable and better trained men?'

'That's a difficult question. To understand Denard, you have to look at his family. His father was rough on him, he used to lock him up in a kennel with the dog. Denard has always needed recognition and he has always wanted to prove himself, to be someone, not just another dog. In Morocco, he tried desperately to get in with a group of terrorists connected to The Red Hand. His life has been one long quest for recognition and approval.

'He has a very strong class complex. That was another reason he was always keen to have people like Marquès around him. They made him feel superior. Remember, he never made officer class in the French navy. He didn't want good men around because he was afraid they might usurp his position – he was always wary of me. But he did like to have the "gilded youth" working for him – young aristocrats who had served a year in the paratroops and who were looking for adventure. Denard liked having these sort of men looking up to him, he acted like a rock-and-roll star with groupies.

'To a certain degree his attempt to climb the class ladder has been successful. He has friends who are intellectuals and journalists, the kind of people who are fascinated by men of action. It is they who have made Denard what he is now, they helped create the myth. He has had a journalist mistress for a long time, she came to interview him and never left. His downfall started when he began to become big-headed because of his stardom. Look, fifteen days after the 1978 coup, he met with French journalists and completely blew his cover.'

Ollivier's explanation of Denard's character was both lucid and plausible. He had obviously thought hard about his former leader's actions and motivations. Nothing he had told me so far had suggested he had another agenda. As he explained when I asked why he was being so helpful: 'I have nothing to hide. I am just an interested observer and I am not scared of Bob Denard.'

He told me more about the mercenaries, his former colleagues.

'Marquès was a nasty piece of work. I don't know who actually pulled the trigger on Ali Soilih, but Denard couldn't have done something like that. He doesn't have the mentality of an executioner, he thinks like a soldier. The rest of them walked around with their eyes closed. They didn't have a clue what was happening in the world. Marquès knew he was nothing without Denard. After Charles left, Marquès was promoted, legitimised, because he had been there from the beginning. This was very important to him. I told Denard in 1986 to distance himself from the Presidential Guard otherwise, I said, everything would start to go wrong, there would be arrests, torture, shootings. "You are going to lose this country unless you sort out the PG," I told him. Unfortunately for Bob Denard, that is what happened.'

The life the mercenaries led sounded less than rigorous. They lunched each day at the officers' mess – a seaside villa near Itsandra now owned by Salim Abdallah. Tables were arranged along the length of the veranda. The Commandant Charles always ate with the four captains at a separate table – Denard rarely joined them. In the afternoon, some of the officers would head for the beach, where they would scuba dive, sail, water ski or windsurf, or just lie in the sun. Others would return to their women or sleep. The ex-insurance man, Charles, kept a close eye on the movements of the Paris Bourse.

'Contact with the outside, or with the French expatriates was forbidden. We lived in a closed vase, a mistake in my opinion,' Ollivier said. He was involved in training the most promising Comorian soldiers to become officers, but by the end of 1982, he had had enough of the claustrophobic atmosphere in the Comoros – and left.

'Was Denard involved in smuggling arms to Iran?' I asked.

'I am afraid I can't talk about that.'

'What do you think happened on the night of 26th November 1989?'

'I do not know, I wasn't there and I have no theories. All I can lay before you are the facts. Abdallah had contacted Paul Barril. He told him he wanted to replace Denard. After a few meetings Barril agreed to provide a close security force and to help train and equip the armed forces – but only if Denard left first. Abdallah was also under pressure from his cronies – especially the Anjouanais mafia – who wanted to remove the mercenaries in order to get a bigger share of the business cake themselves. They thought the mercenaries were making too much money. Denard, of course, knew about Barril and about this too. He had been feeding the media with inside information. In 1984, when I was working as his "antenne" in Paris, Denard was financing the main opposition newsletter, "La Lettre des Comores". So you see he was not entirely straight, he had his duplicitous ways. But he felt Abdallah was betraying him. He kept telling him: "Don't forget who put you here."

'Abdallah was thus trapped: caught in a trap that would lead to his death. On the Thursday before he died, Abdallah's envoys – Said Kafé and Dr M'tara Maecha, returned from Paris, where they had met with the French government and perhaps told them that the President had decided to get rid of the mercenaries. That evening, I am reliably informed, Denard had a meeting with Marquès. They stayed up until one in the morning which was very unusual, Denard usually went to bed between nine and ten. I think the two of them decided

Abdallah's fate. Maybe they didn't agree to kill him, only to put on the necessary pressure to ensure he changed his mind. The same reliable source suggested the discussion was at times heated – Denard finds it hard to hide his feelings.

'There were five people in the room on the Sunday night. I cannot tell you what happened, but here are some facts:
One: Abdallah was shot five times, four in the chest, and once in the neck. He was sitting and he was shot from above and at close range. All the impacts were close to each other and all were fatal. There was no fire fight.
Two: All the witnesses are dead; Djaffar, Monique Terrasse and Abdallah.
Three: The President's security had been rearranged for that night. No one from his regular close security force was there. Everyone had been removed from the area. All the European officers were on stand-by outside the property.
Four: During the night, the body was wrapped in a blanket, put in the back of a pick-up and taken straight to Anjouan.'

'Are you saying Denard's version of events is full of lies?'

'I am not saying anything. These are just the facts. What I can say is that the meeting with Abdallah on the night of his death was planned.

'The only person who would have known about it was Monique Terrasse and she died the same night. It's crazy, all those crimes and nothing has been done about them. There were at least three murders that night including a French subject and a President. And who has been charged? Where's the justice?'

The implications of the 'three murders' were clear, but I knew Ollivier would not go any further.

'Do you think Denard will ever tell the true story of what happened that night?' I asked.

'Well, he told a prearranged story and he is convinced he is right. He believes his stories. He is a very basic man, he had a dream and he was very lucky and very fortunate. He never really understood what he was doing. He didn't have the foresight to realise that the Comoros' importance for South Africa would wane. It's a complicated game and he was playing checkers when he should have been playing chess. He didn't have enough information and he was surrounded by mental cripples.'

'Do you regret having worked with him?'

'My motive in joining Denard was insane curiosity. I had served for five hard years in Rhodesia and when I finished I wanted to join Denard. At that stage, I would have gone to the North Pole to serve him. You must understand, he had this tremendous reputation. But it was all a myth. I went there to "ride the tiger" but I ended up with a pussycat. For the other men, it was an adventure. They had nothing in common with each other, they were all there for different reasons, federated by Denard for a certain period of time. After my first week in the Comoros, I understood what it was all about: it was about the worst aspects of French mentality. There was no rigour. After Rhodesia, it was like the Club Med for me. As for regrets? No, but I wonder if I could have done something better. There was so much mediocrity there. Abdallah was a tropical dictator – not the worst, no, but he had a complex about coming from slave blood. Denard too had a complex about his origins: he blamed them for his failure to climb the ranks in the navy.

'People are always looking for conspiracies, but in the Comoros there·was no great plot, no conspiracy involving the French Secret Services or any other group. To work out what happened, one has only to look at the individual personalities involved and to demystify them. Look at Denard and at Abdallah and you will understand what happened.'

15

Pieces of a Puzzle

I RETURNED TO SOUTH AFRICA and telephoned Denard to ask him out for lunch.

We met at his favourite restaurant in downtown Pretoria. He was five minutes early, but I was still waiting when he walked into the small French bistro. He wore jeans, a pale blue shirt, navy blazer and the now-familiar sturdy black boots. The Maitre d' followed him closely to the table and greeted him warmly. Denard smiled and turned his full attention to the specials on offer, before ordering a smoked salmon salad and grilled Kingklip.

I liked him more this meeting. He was more relaxed than formerly; less defensive. We talked in general terms. Then, suddenly, he told me he was going back to France at the end of the year.

'Won't you have problems with the Justice Department?' I asked.

He shrugged.

'I have been here for three years and I still don't know what is going on. I can't stay for ever and I feel now as if I am pacing round and round like a lion in a golden cage, so I am going to try to go home.'

'Do you think they'll arrest you?'

Another shrug.

'I am the bad conscience of France in the history of its decolonisation and I fear that they are doing all they can to condemn me, if only to say that they framed Bob Denard. But I am an old man, I have been in prison before and I know I can take it. However, my lawyer and I think we will be able to press for a retrial.'

'This is for the Benin affair? How many years were you sentenced to?'

'Five. But it is wrong. They should punish the head, not the legs.'

'How are you going to go back, I thought you had no passport?'

'Yes I do, here.' He produced a French passport, flicked it open briefly to enable me to see his name and date of birth and returned it to his inside pocket. 'Unfortunately it is not valid, it expired in 1989 and they have refused to renew it. Still, it is an identity document and it is all I have,' he added with a twinkle in his glacier-blue eyes.

'All?'

He smiled.

'When were you last in France?' I asked.

'Officially . . . in 1981 when the socialists came to power.'

'And unofficially?'

He smiled again.

'You know there are rumours which suggest you have been to Paris many times since then.'

'How would I do that?'

'With a false passport.'

He smiled yet again and I thought I caught the twitchings of a wink.

I gave up on that line of questioning.

'So, which of your wives are you going to live with in France?'

This time he laughed. 'That is the million-franc question. They aren't really my wives, just the mothers of my children, I only call them my wives. I was really only married to Philippe's mother, the Moroccan, and once in the Comoros to Amina.'

We talked about *Fire! Le Magazine de l'Homme d'Action*. He had brought me the latest editions, each front cover still displaying a photograph of Denard. He wouldn't tell me how

226

much he had bought the magazine for, just that he was paying the purchase price off monthly and that the circulation had already doubled. He had started, he said, a publishing company called 'Fire Editions', which would produce monthly newsletters about Southern African affairs.

The food arrived. I asked whether he wanted to have more adventures.

'Life is an adventure!' he replied.

'I mean mercenary adventures.'

'No, I think that, for the time being, the mercenary era is over. It was closely tied to decolonisation and that has finished now. You look at the wars nowadays; at Somalia, Liberia, Yugoslavia . . . They are different kinds of wars – bloody civil wars. There is no place there for our kinds of skills – well there is, but no one wants to use us. Look at Yugoslavia, who's there? A bunch of bureaucrats from the United Nations. What good can they do! Civil servants!' He spat out the last two words as if speaking about SCUM! 'If they called me tomorrow,' he continued, 'I would get together a force of two or three thousand men at the drop of a hat and be there next month. No hesitation, no hesitation at all.'

I thought he might find the Yugoslavian conflict a different story from battles with the Simbas in the Congo or bloodless coups in the Comoros. But he seemed sure of himself, convinced of his invincibility. Things have moved on but Denard is still living in a world where the enemy is black and fights with spears, where the soldiers are always the good guys and where he is still a powerful, mythical figure.

We discussed recent events in the Comoros. On 26th September 1992, there had been yet another coup attempt – this time led by President Abdallah's twin sons, Cheik and Abderemane, both of whom had trained at the French military academy at Saint Cyr and the Royal Academy in Morocco, and a former member of the Presidential Guard, Captain Combo. They had led a force of about a hundred members of the new Comorian Defence Force (which had replaced the Presidential Guard and CAF) in an attack on the radio station, where they broadcast a statement saying that President Djohar – at that time in Paris – had been ousted. However, just before 11.00 am the caretaker president broadcast another statement which said that the rebels had surrendered and power was back in the hands of the government.

Former ministers Omar Tamou, Said Ahmed Said Ali and Dr M'tara Maecha had been arrested – as well as other leading opposition figures and members of the attacking force.

Two weeks later – in a repetition of the events of the mid-Eighties – there was an attempt to free the soldiers arrested after the failed coup. The guards posted at the entrance of Kandani military camp were killed and a large supply of weapons was stolen. The jailed men were not, however, set free. Violence erupted in the following week and a total of fifteen people were killed. The opposition leader, Taki, was thought to have played some role in its fermentation.

Denard said he was very concerned by the situation and the fate of Abdallah's sons. 'You go to the Comoros now,' he told me, 'you will hear a different story – they all want me to come back to take control of the situation and stop the fighting.'

I began to wonder whether his story of what had happened on the night of Abdallah's death could, in the end, be the truth. His explanation was so bizarre and implausible, maybe it had to be true. Or perhaps it was just that he, himself, believed it: that he had convinced himself of the sequence of events. He appeared to me suddenly as a kaleidoscope of different personalities – one to suit each of his many pseudonyms. He was sometimes the great military leader, then the assured diplomat, the wronged patriot, and suave ladies' man, and occasionally, inadvertently, the defensive failure. But he was almost too naïve to be truly Machiavellian. I still could not relate the charming, urbane man opposite me to one of the most ruthless mercenaries this century. I wrenched my mind back to reality. This is how he wants me to think, I told myself. Be careful, do not be sucked in.

I had to try again to persuade him to tell me the events of the night of Abdallah's death. This time, he was less obstructive. The story he told me tallied in almost all respects with the version he had given in the second press conference in the Comoros on Tuesday 12th December 1989, sixteen days after the President's death.

'As I told you before, the Comorian army was in a rotten state,' he began. 'There was mounting pressure and numerous desertions. The President had agreed that we would have to disarm them soon. On the night of 26th November, the Presidential Guard was on maximum alert; we were hunting for deserters and smugglers. A bit before midnight, I was going to bed when the telephone rang. It was the duty officer, who informed me that shots had been heard around the presidential palace. I rushed there. Marquès and Siam had already arrived. We found the President in the hall, wearing his pyjamas. Shots were coming from everywhere: none of the President's body-guards were there. He had four, all members of his family, and two were meant to be on duty every night. But the Comorians were very unreliable – they went out the whole time. Djaffar arrived at last, breathless, half-dressed and unarmed. He had been drinking, or with a woman. Marquès sent him to get dressed. We took a decision with the President to disarm the army. This was at midnight. Marquès contacted all our units by radio and gave the order to proceed with our disarming plan.

'We went up to the President's study, where he put the disarming order into writing. Marquès went down with the signed order and asked Djaffar to make photocopies to give to the unit commanders. Marquès returned. It was quiet. The President and I talked peacefully. The telephone rang and Siam answered. "It's a woman," he told the President, who said to relay the message that he would call back later. I think it must have been his friend Monique Terrasse, who according to the log book, had left the President at 10.15 pm.

'At around twenty past twelve, the shooting restarted. It was very violent, and appeared to be coming from below our windows on the coastal side of the palace. Our men, as well as the gendarmes posted fifteen hundred metres to the north, opened fire in all directions. There was automatic gunfire, bazookas, the bay windows shook.

'It was then that the President started to panic. He groaned. I crouched at his feet and took his hands to calm him. He uttered semi-articulate phrases in Anjouannais that I couldn't understand. I think he was praying. The door opened and Djaffar surged through. I got up. I wanted to talk to him. For the rest of my life, I will remember Djaffar's mad, dilated eyes. He put his hand to his gun. I threw myself to the floor at the President's feet. The President caught the rifle fire straight on, in his chest. Siam reacted and attacked Djaffar, who fell to the floor.

'The key to the tragedy is panic. As the President's security adviser, I was responsible. Responsible, yes: culpable, no! It is like if you were crossing the road with a kid and a car hits you and kills the child. It is not your fault, but you are responsible.'

He referred me to an interview he had given to Renaud Girard of *Le Figaro* several months earlier.

Girard had asked Denard how he explained the positioning of the bullets. He replied: 'I don't have an explanation. I didn't take part in the autopsy. I imagine the medical reports are in the hands of the inquiry . . .'

'How do you explain the quasi-simultaneity of the attack on the presidency and the operation to disarm the army?' Girard asked.

'Because of the prevailing climate, we had to be on full alert. Many a manoeuvre had proved that we could take control of all the sensitive points in Moroni in seven minutes. The attacks were not simultaneous, but between five and ten minutes apart.'

'What, according to you, was the origin of the shots?'

'I do not know for sure, but I have several hypotheses:

One: The first shot perhaps came from a member of the PG, who fired after being scared by a dog and who is too afraid to admit it. Afterwards, everyone started shooting at each other. Alerts of this kind are common.

Two: Perhaps uncontrollable elements from within the Comorian Armed Forces fired at the palace. There were enough of them roaming around in the bush fully armed. Why? How do I know? Provocation? A desire to stir the pot?

Three: It was perhaps elements from the French Military Assistance (a small force of French soldiers based at the embassy) who wanted to provoke. Knowing the French services, I can tell you that anything is possible. We noticed a change in the make up of the Assistance at the beginning of 1989. The men, normally pot-bellied administrators, were replaced by young and muscular officers.

Four: It could have been a team of professionals from the 13th Regiment of Parachutists or the 11th "Choc". We had proof that one team had already operated on Comorian territory. Three months earlier, we had uncovered the remains of a French army bivouac. Additionally, for a few months, we had been under regular surveillance by the "Atlantic Brequet" of the national fleet. In September 1989, a French para captain based in Reunion told one of my officers – a friend of his – that he was astounded that in all their exercises, the enemy was designated not the usual "red enemy", but the "mercenaries occupying the Comoros".'

'But what was the story with the Commandant Ahmed Mohammed? Why did you need to send troops to Anjouan?' I asked.

'We had orders to disarm the CAF and two hundred of them were based on Anjouan – all armed. So we sent thirty Presidential Guards to join the twenty based there. They went to try to disarm the Commandant, but he had hidden in the roof with a gun. It was logical to use a rocket to try to get him down. And one other thing, he never had two thousand chickens – that was pure fabrication in an attempt to get more money out of the insurance company.'

Few people were left in the restaurant and the Maitre d' was hovering in a disconcerting manner. Denard's concentration, however, did not falter and his blue eyes continued to stare unflickering at me. I asked my final question:

'Are you an optimist or a pessimist?'

'Oh, I am definitely an optimist. Perhaps sometimes I am a bit too direct, a bit too frank. But I think I am honest and I always speak the truth. I am a natural person, a man of the earth. I feel good in my skin. If I die tomorrow, it will be with a clear conscience. I am honest, although I am not a saint, but a man.'

I paid the bill and we walked outside. Once again, in the clear daylight, the force seemed to leave him and he appeared to shrink. I felt the same as I had on first seeing him limping across the car park to the Japanese restaurant. He can dominate small spaces, but in the big outdoors – his former domain – he now looks lost.

We walked in opposite directions to our separate cars.

*

M'PARENI ALI, ADJUTANT IN THE PRESIDENTIAL GUARD

'On the night of 26th November, between 21.00 and 22.00, second-lieutenants Etienne and Thierry woke me up to take me to see the Camp Commandant, Lt. Fouquet.

'He told me that the PG was going to do a big manoeuvre that night and told me to go and join Captain Hoffman (real name, Dominique Cuny) at Itsoundzou camp.

'I said at the time that I wanted to advise the NCOs and soldiers of my company that I was leaving the base, but they refused to let me announce my departure.'

ALI ZAKARIA, CORPORAL IN THE PRESIDENTIAL GUARD

'On the night of November 26th, 1989, around 21.00, on the orders of Captain Hoffman, all the personnel were assembled at Itsoundzou camp. The team leaders were taken aside and armed with different sorts of grenades.

'We were split into six groups – each with a vehicle. We headed south, through Moroni. Near Club des Amis, we turned into the premises of SOCOMECA.

'It was around 23.45. We were informed of our mission. It was to disarm the Comorian Armed Forces because elements of the corps wanted to attack the Presidency the same night . . .'

IBRAHIM ABDILLAI, SOLDIER IN THE PRESIDENTIAL GUARD

'On Sunday night, between 21.00 and 22.00, sergeant-chef Djaffar telephoned Kandani to find out why the SSR (Close Security Unit who guarded the presidential palace) weren't at the President's residence. The reason given to him was the following: "That group has gone on manoeuvres to Mindzaza-Boini-Bambao."

'Normally, when the President of the Republic was on Grand Comore, a group of the SSR would back-up the Guard section at his residence. Each section would guard the residence for a week at a time in rotation.'

WASHINGTON, DRIVER IN THE PRESIDENTIAL GUARD

'My group was due for leave, but on Friday 24th November, our company commander, Captain Jean-Pierre, notified us to return on 26th November at 20.00.

'It was Jean-Pierre who ordered us to replace the SSR, who were out on manoeuvres.

'Some time later, I was awoken by gunfire. Straightaway, I grabbed my gun (AK47) . . . I can clarify that the shots came from the north. During the whole time, the enemy was never revealed to me.

'I only saw Commandant Marquès run alone into the courtyard of the Presidency, shouting "where is Djaffar?" '

HASSAN AHAMADA, SERGEANT OF THE PRESIDENTIAL GUARD

'I was on gate duty on the day of the President's death. At 14.36, President Abdallah went with Lieutenants Frederick and Favier to the south. They returned between 16.00 and 16.30. The officers left and the President stayed alone on the first floor.

'At 20.21 he was visited by some friends. They left at 21.10. Djaffar told me that the gate should not be locked – more specifically that a woman would come in a red car. He told me not to lock up until she had left.

'I was relieved of Guard and went to sleep.

'I was woken at 23.45 by rifle shots coming from the northeast of the presidency. Coming out of the police post, I saw the sergeant-chef Djaffar running, half-dressed, to his room.

'After the shots, Commandant Marquès came to me and asked what had happened. I told him that two of my men had been lightly wounded. He asked me who the bodyguard of the day was. I replied to him that it was the S-C Djaffar, who had gone to change into military uniform. A few minutes later, we saw Djaffar leave his room with his AK47 and head up to the first floor.

'It was around midnight when Bob Denard entered the compound with his driver, Tony . . .

'Personally, I never saw any enemy. I only saw the officers of the Presidential Guard rush into the compound . . .

'We didn't riposte. Only the relief captain, Zoubier Mahadaly, confirmed that he had fired his weapon . . . We didn't riposte for good reason; we hadn't seen our enemy.

'I can clarify that after the officers arrived, the gunshots stopped for a while. After a second mortar shot, accompanied by many rifle shots from outside, I heard repeated rifle shots coming from the first floor.'

SAID ALI MOUSSA. SOLDIER IN THE PRESIDENTIAL GUARD

'Marquès arrived with Siam and Joel. They left their cars outside the gate and entered on foot. They said that Denard would be arriving. He came five minutes later with his driver, Tony, and parked in the same place.

'I remember that five minutes before Marquès and his companions arrived, there were no gunshots.'

ALI ZAKARIA (cont.)

'Around 00.30, Mmadi Moindze and I went to the Mde crossroads to prevent all vehicles – in particular those of the CAF – from going in the direction of the presidency. At 02.00, we were relieved and transported directly to the airport.

'We took the first flight out to Anjouan. There were sixty soldiers, divided into six groups on the plane. Four groups went to the military camp at Patsy, the others to the gendarmerie. After disarming the soldiers, we knocked on the door of the Commandant Ahmed Mohammed's residence. There was no reply. Jean-Pierre gave the signal to shoot RPG7s (Rocket Propelled Grenade launchers) through the window. After a repeated attack, the Commandant emerged from his house. He was badly wounded. We took him to the airport, bleeding all over. We left Anjouan at 10.00.

'Before, at 09.00, Squadron-Chef Cheik Allaoui said to Commandant Ahmed: "The President is dead." It was the first we had heard of it.'

WASHINGTON (cont.)

'I heard the rumour of the President's death at 10.00.

'Having learnt of his death and followed the unfolding scene, my thoughts turned to Bob Denard and his men.

Effectively, with regards to the murder of the head of state, I rest the responsibility on the European mercenaries.'

HASSAN AHAMADA (cont.)
'After the departure of the President's body to Anjouan, we continued to assure security at the presidency . . . During that period, the French mercenaries didn't cease to come and go all day and all night.

'We saw that lots of material was taken away by the mercenaries. They loaded it on to their vehicles.'

*

I have thought long and hard about what happened on the night of Abdallah's death. I have examined, as Patrick Ollivier suggested, the personalities of the main protagonists. Abdallah was a proud and stubborn old statesman. In 1989, he was approaching his eightieth year. I could see that he would not want to retire, or to die, while his islands were still in the stranglehold of foreign mercenaries. Denard is also a proud man. He was extremely loyal to his men, but he was consumed by a drive to be accepted by the establishment, to prove himself and to show that he wasn't just another dog in the kennel, but a far greater beast – a Dog of War. The Comoros was his last stand and his great love. He was not prepared to give up the islands that easily.

There are many hypotheses, many possible scenarios. As both Ollivier and Maître Jacques Vergès have said, we may never find out the events of 26th November, 1989, unless one of the three witnesses – Bob Denard, Dominique Malacrino (Marquès) or Jean-Paul Guerrier (Siam) – decide to give the full, unadulterated version. What I have tried to do in my mind, and in this book, is to examine – through the testimonies of numerous witnesses – the events and emotions preceding and succeeding the President's death. There are several hard facts and logical inferences that would appear to be inconsistent with Denard's version of events:

1:    President Abdallah wanted the mercenaries to leave. He was being subjected to three-way pressure:. . . From France, who regarded Denard and his men as an embarrassment and had threatened to reduce the Comoros' budgetary assistance if the mercenaries had not left by the end of the year. They still held their carrot: Mayotte. Abdallah's lasting wish was to reunite Mayotte with the rest of the Comoros; he saw the mercenaries' departure as his bargaining chip to realise his goal before he retired . . . From a South Africa which was entering a new political era, one where they could not afford to be associated with mercenaries. They now had the opportunity to forge new and important relationships around the world and no longer wanted the trouble and expense of the Comoros . . . And from the Comorian people, who were fed up with being under the guns and heavy-handed rule of foreign mercenaries and who saw their departure as a way to garner a large slice of the meagre business profits on offer.

2:    Abdallah had approached Paul Barril and asked him if he would be able to form an alternative 'Presidential Guard' of some description. His two envoys, Kafé and Maecha, had just returned from France where they had delivered a personal letter from Abdallah to President Mitterrand. The letter allegedly pertained to the Mayotte question. It is probable it confirmed Abdallah's acceptance of his side of the bargain: that in return for the reunification of the Comoros, he gave his word that the mercenaries would be leaving.

3:    Denard had heard about Abdallah's plans. He was thrown into a panic as he had nowhere else to go. Since he was sentenced *in absentia* for the Benin coup, the French had refused to renew his passport. He was a man without a country. He regarded the Comoros as his home and his family's home. He owned substantial property on the islands and had just invested in a new business.

4:   Denard still felt close to the President. I am sure he didn't plan to kill him. Among his men, however, there were hardline elements, characters like Marquès who had staked their entire life on the Comoros and had neither the inclination nor the requisite experience to start again elsewhere. It is known that Denard and Marquès had a late night heated discussion following the return of the envoys.

5:   The regular members of the President's close security unit were on manoeuvres some distance away from the palace the night the President died. Notice of the night exercise had been submitted to the presidency at 12.05 the previous day. They had been replaced for the evening by European officers of the Presidential Guard.

6:   The disarming of the Comorian Armed Forces had been planned well in advance. It was no spur of the moment response to an alleged attack on the presidency. The higher ranking Comorian soldiers were notified of an 'important manoeuvre' at 21.00 and it commenced at 23.45 – twenty-five minutes before Abdallah signed the order.

7:   There was a firefight around the President's residence that night. Numerous people heard shots during a period spanning at least one hour. Only one member of the PG returned fire and no one from the attacking force was wounded or caught. This would appear to rule out Denard's first – and on the surface most plausible – suspect: 'uncontrollable elements from the CAF'. It is highly unlikely that they would have escaped unseen from a vastly superior force. The suggestion that the shooting was in fact started by one of the Comorian members of the Guard, who had been startled by a dog, is also highly unlikely, as it would not account for the protracted period and intermittent nature of the shots. That leaves the possible explanation that it was started by a faction of the French military – either based on the Comoros, or members of a secret insurgency force. This is narrowly feasible, but on balance unlikely. It will probably never be proved one way or another.

8: The President was shot five times around his heart. The shots came from close range and all were fatal. Are these the shots of a man in a state of panic, presumably aiming at Denard, not at his final victim?

9: Denard never explained or accounted for the fact that Djaffar had been – in the words of a witness who saw his body – 'slit from his neck to his toes like a chicken'.

10: Directly after the President's death, Denard dispatched his men to find the Commandant Ahmed. When he was not in his Moroni home, they commandeered the Air Comores plane to send a task force to Anjouan. For several reasons – including the actions of the gardien Abdou – the plane was delayed. When members of the task force caught up with the Commandant, they fired rockets into his bedroom. He still has fragments of metal in his body. Is this a usual way to arrest a man?

11: Abdallah's body was whisked off to Anjouan only hours after his death, and subjected to a cursory autopsy, the results of which are not consistent with Denard's account of events, in which a panicky Djaffar shot the seated President from the doorway. According to professional opinion, the shots were probably fired from close range and, although it is conceivably a coincidence that they all landed in the area of Abdallah's heart by accident when Djaffar had aimed at Denard, that is far from being the most likely scenario.

12: On the night of the President's death, all communications between Moroni and the other islands were cut off. They were reconnected only on Monday morning.

13: There is hardly a Comorian alive who believes that Djaffar killed their President.

*

In Denard's favour:

1:   I do not believe he would kill the President in cold blood. It would have been like killing the goose that laid the proverbial golden eggs. He admitted that the Comoros were 'the greatest love of my life'.

2:   Since he first gave his version of events to the Comorian ministers three hours after the President's death, his version has not wavered.

3:   His story is so far-fetched, illogical and bizarre, it could almost be true. No sensible and experienced man, surely, would make up a story like that.

4:   No hard evidence has been found that would point to Denard and his men's guilt 'without a shadow of reasonable doubt'.

*

There is a version of events that, in the light of these facts and suppositions, appears plausible:

On Sunday 26th November, Abdallah returned from Anjouan where he had renewed close relations with the head of his army, Commandant Ahmed Mohammed. Since the return of the envoys, Denard had known that his time was running out. That evening, he arranged for the President's close security unit to be assigned to night manoeuvres miles away from the palace and set up two or three of his men – marksmen – in strategic positions around the perimeter of the palace grounds. Between eleven and twelve, they started shooting. A member of the Presidential Guard fired wildly at the unseen enemy and the hoped-for diversion materialised. Denard, Marques and Siam rushed to the President's side.

Everything was going according to the plan, which aimed to shock the President into thinking the mercenaries were the only group he could trust. Denard wanted to create a situation where the President was persuaded to disarm – and thus neutralise – the army, thereby transferring the effective power to, and intensifying his reliance on, the Presidential Guard. The three top-ranking mercenaries moved Abdallah into his study, where the undoubtedly frightened President signed the order to disarm the armed forces. While the PG section commanders carried out the well-rehearsed order (Denard said he knew it could be done in seven minutes), Djaffar was sent to photocopy it for later legitimisation. The mercenaries stayed with the President and, with the background of more shooting, tried to persuade him to renew their contracts. Abdallah, however, was stubborn. He had taken a decision and he was going to stick to it. At one point his girlfriend rang and he said he would call her back. The mercenaries resorted to threats. Marquès was becoming particularly over-excited. Eventually – perhaps by mistake or perhaps because they realised that by dint of their threats, Abdallah's death was by now inevitable – he shot the President with the gun he was using to frighten him: once in the thorax. Djaffar burst into the room from his post outside the door in a state of panic, his eyes mad and dilated. Siam knifed him. They then took his gun and shot the dead President in the chest.

It had all gone wrong. Denard was thrown into a panic, he was the most affected by the death of his close friend. However, according to the code he had learnt from his revered officers in the French armed forces, he had always placed loyalty to his men above all else. He was unusually loyal, in an attempt to be the perfect officer. He knew he had to *porte le chapeau*. A contingency plan was rapidly conceived. Marquès or Siam used Djaffar's gun (which they had already taken off him) to shoot the President a further three times around the heart. A scapegoat had been prepared.

However, the Commandant would have been a more plausible culprit. The whole country knew he had resigned from his post after being accused of smuggling. What they did not know was that the two old friends had been reconciled the day before. A lorryload of soldiers was sent to the Commandant's Moroni home, only to hear that he was in Anjouan. Denard sent them to find the pilot to take them there. By the time the plane had been delayed, he had returned to Plan One and told the hastily assembled ministers that Djaffar had killed the President and had in turn been killed.

*

I do not know whether this version of events is the true one and I have no way of finding out. It just seems to fit the facts better than Denard's story. But when did logic play any role in Africa? And is it, in the end, important how the President died?

The death of Ahmed Abdallah Abderemane, President of the Comoro Islands, looks destined to remain one of the many unsolved mysteries in a continent which attracts disaster as surely as honey attracts bees. For a president to die – or even to be murdered – is certainly not unusual in Africa. That some of the suspects are white men, is. That is why the case has attracted even the attention it has. It is not right that white men, or mercenaries, should be able to move around the continent, ruling and killing as they wish. But it is also not right that we should impose our morals and codes of conduct on a place and a people to whom they bear no relevance.

Was Denard good or bad for the Comoros? It is impossible to say, just as it is impossible to predict the future of the tiny, forgotten perfume islands. Recent events indicate that they have not yet seen the last or the worst of the violence. But does that exonerate Denard from blame? Surely not, but it does, still, throw a less harsh light on his doings and misdoings. I realised that I no longer wanted incontrovertible evidence of the guilt of Denard, his men, or anyone else. It would not help to know. It was enough to have studied the events and in doing so, to have gained some insight into the workings of the strange 'dark continent'.

In the end, it was first Ali Soilih and then Abdallah who brought Denard to their country and it is they – and Denard himself – who suffered.

Postscript: A Hero's Welcome?

E ARLY IN THE MORNING of 1st February 1993, Bob
Denard stepped from the first-class cabin of an Air France
jumbo jet. He was greeted on the runway by a group of
policemen brandishing a warrant for his arrest. Without
handcuffs, they bore him straight off to a jail cell. He did not
pass through customs or immigration and thus missed his son,
Philippe; wife, Amina; and their two children, Hamza and
Kaina, waiting to greet him.

He had known, of course, the kind of reception he was going
to receive, when *Le Figaro* newspaper offered to pay his fare
back to his native land. The French authorities had warned
him when he notified them of his intended return. What might
have come as a surprise, however, was that he was arrested not
only in connection with the Benin affair, but also for
questioning about his role in the murder of President Abdallah
and the disappearance of state documents from the Comoros.
The charges of 'accessory to murder' and 'aggravated theft'
were levelled against him.

A week later, according to proper French judicial pro-
cedure, he appeared before the 'Tribunal de Bobigny' – the
nearest court to Charles de Gaulle airport. A date for his
appeal against the Benin sentence was set and his request for
bail, most ably put across by his new lawyer, Maître Soulez-
Larivière, was denied – on the grounds that he represented 'a
threat to national and international peace'. He was transferred
to the more comfortable Prison de la Santé in the Quartier
Latin, where he had his own cell and a television set and

counted among his neighbours Dr Garetta (accused of injecting haemophiliacs with AIDS-contaminated blood) and a former minister of co-operation and development.

At this stage, perhaps he was beginning to think that his gamble was not going to pay off? Or maybe he had something up his sleeve? For why else would a man like Denard leave a comfortable exile in South Africa for the dubious pleasure of a jail cell, even one in his beloved France?

But as he sat in his cell, reading the numerous press articles that had been written about him since his return – leaving only occasionally for gruelling four-hour interrogation sessions with the instructing judge on the Comoros case, Judge Chantal Perdrix – his spirits started to lift. Glowing testimonials had started flowing into the offices of Maître Soulez-Larivière. They came from the pens of such eminent men as Jacques Foccart, De Gaulle's 'Mr Africa' and closest adviser; the former head of French espionage, General Janou Lacaze; and the former commander-in-chief of the French army, General Paul Aussaresses.

On Wednesday, 10th March, he entered the dock of the Fourteenth Tribunal Chamber at the Palais de Justice. He wore a dark blazer and his old regimental tie from his days in the navy, and appeared composed as he sat down, glancing briefly at his diminutive lawyer.

In his opening address, the president of the tribunal, Judge Jean-Claude Antonetti, told the court that the process would allow them to review 'the last thirty years of contemporary Africa'. He explained that it would be impossible to consider the case in isolation, without examining Denard's role in the wider theatre of African decolonisation.

The court was led through the events that had unfolded in Benin sixteen years previously. Maître Soulez-Larivière was preceded by Maître Norman, acting for the complainants – the families of the four Beninois who had died in the botched coup attempt.

Then it was the turn of Soulez. The stocky lawyer was no

stranger to the big political trial. A close friend of President Mitterrand's, he had defended the couple accused of blowing up the *Rainbow Warrior*. This time, he used a similar defence: Denard should not be convicted of this charge of 'criminal association', he said, because during the course of his long career, he had always acted with the knowledge of western governments. With a flourish, he produced his sheaf of signed testimonials. Judge Antonetti read aloud from three of them:

'I knew Bob Denard, in the governmental sense, from 1975,' General Lacaze had written. 'I established a relationship of trust with him. I was not involved in the Benin operation, but I cannot imagine that it took place without the endorsement of the French authorities.'

The testimony of Jacques Foccart followed:

'I willingly send my testimony. At the Elysée, between 1968 and 1974, I never had personal relations with Bob Denard, but I was informed of his actions. I believe that his only ambition was to serve his country.'

And lastly, the Judge read extracts of a three-page letter sent by General Aussaresses:

'We never used amateurs in our team. Robert Denard was always an honest operative and an unconditional patriot,' the General had written.

A former French ambassador to Gabon, Maurice Delauney, appeared in person to confirm those opinions. Then Colonel Maurice Robert, a member of SDECE (Service de la Documentation Exterieur et du Contre-Espionage – the French MI6) from 1954 to 1975, for the latter period head of the Africa division, took the stand. He stipulated that he had been 'authorised' to appear as a witness, before going on to say that he had recruited Denard in 1968, to whom he 'subcontracted' covert actions, in accordance with the accepted 'methods used by the French government'. In an interview after the hearing, Robert claimed that Denard's activities in the Comoros – up until his last day on the islands – were monitored, or even directed, by the present-day French secret services.

Denard followed him into the box. 'Robert Denard, born on 7th April 1929 in Bordeaux. Son of Léonce, warrant-officer in the colonial service . . .' He recited the bare facts of his career; quartermaster in Indo-China, until he stepped on a mine and returned to France, before setting off the next year to the United States for a two-year training course. This was followed by Morocco and the attempt on Pierre Mendes-France's life – and from there to Katanga.

'You had a courageous attitude and saved the lives of European hostages,' Antonetti interrupted Denard's account to comment.

The next day, the opposing counsels summed up. The deputy public prosecutor recommended to Judge Antonetti that Denard should receive 'a symbolic sentence' of three to five years – suspended indefinitely. Denard permitted himself a small smile, Soulez-Larivière looked happy and even the complainant's counsel, Maître Norman, didn't look too displeased or surprised at the unfolding events.

Judgement on Bob Denard's case was heard on 5th April 1993. The courtroom was packed with journalists and members of Denard's family. Denard walked in and sat down. His face betrayed no emotion as Antonetti read his long judgement. His family listened. Soulez looked quietly confident. Maître Norman failed to appear.

'It should not be tolerated . . . that an individual can put himself at the service of a foreign state to commit exactions in a third world country,' the judge concluded. 'To admit the contrary would be equivalent to legitimising all attempts to destabilise states or régimes by mercenaries.'

He went on to impose a five-year suspended sentence.

Denard looked up and smiled. His family's side of the courtroom erupted into excited chatter. Denard left the room quietly to return to prison to pack his bags – Judge Chantal Perdrix had announced two days previously that he could be released on bail in connection with the Comoros case.

To all intents and purposes, Denard was a free man. Free, accepted and at home.

*

He limped across the lobby of a hotel near the Bastille to meet me the next day. He looked well, his girth if anything a little expanded from when I had last seen him seven months previously. He was in fine spirits.

'Well, who could have predicted this?' he asked with a chortle.

We went to sit in the bar and ordered cups of tea.

'The testimonies of General Lacaze and Foccart were an immense moral satisfaction. They announced my rehabilitation,' he declared. 'To hear what General Aussaresses said was like receiving the Légion d'honneur.' He beamed.

I asked him about his relationship with the French secret services – something he had refused to speak about on our previous meetings.

'In 1961, I went to Katanga as a freelance soldier. There I had my first contact with SDECE. In those times, maybe, my group was infiltrated by agents of the French government. But from 1968, I always had direct personal contact with the officer-in-charge, Colonel Maurice Robert.'

Denard fed Robert information and in return, he was told whether or nor he had the 'green light' to proceed.

'Every time I had an operation that was within the political framework, I had first to get the green light from the French services,' he said. 'Well, sometimes it was more like an amber light, but I never did – nor ever would – act against France. They never paid me a cent, but I got to keep my autonomy. In that sense I was not a mercenary, but a pirate. France's pirate.

'In the case of very important operations, like Benin, the orders would come directly from Journiac (Rene Journiac, head of African Affairs under Giscard d'Estaing), who would telephone to arrange a discreet rendezvous. I never went to his office [in the Elysée], nor was anything put into writing.'

'Did you receive France's benediction for the Benin coup?' I asked.'

'France would have been pleased had Benin been a success,' he replied.

'Were you still in contact with the French services during your time in the Comoros?'

'No, my relationship with them ended in 1981 when the socialists came to power.'

'Did you work with any other western countries?'

'In Angola, I was in close contact with the CIA – as well as with the French services – and in Yemen with the British MI6. I knew Colonel David Stirling [founder of the SAS] and Billy McLean [British agent in Albania who later became an MP] well.' Denard looked satisfied with himself and pleased to be able to recount the names of the influential, establishment figures he had dealt with.

'Was patriotism therefore your main motivation?'

He gave another deep laugh.

'No, it was adventure of course.'

I asked whether he had come to some kind of agreement with the French before his return. He dismissed this speculation very rapidly.

'No, that is why I chose to return before the elections – because I didn't want it said that "the Rightists let him go". It was a risk and I took it, as I have always taken risks. I could have stayed, my visa had been extended until the end of the year, but I chose to return to face justice. Everyone was surprised when I was released. I was surprised. But I still have a five-year sentence hanging over my head. It is only suspended. If I make the slightest error, I will be sent back to jail.'

At this, still smiling, he bade me goodbye, saying that he had a lot of catching up to do and he planned to go to Bordeaux to celebrate his sixty-fourth birthday the following day with his sister, Georgette.

*

He was interviewed by a local paper a few days later.

'Everybody loves me,' he told the reporter from *France Soir*. 'When I was released from prison on Monday after two months, I was expecting to be treated as an outcast in my own country. But in fact I have discovered an astonishing popularity, and I can't walk one step on the street without somebody greeting me . . .

'I took a taxi from the prison and the driver was a woman. She said she recognised me from pictures in the newspapers but could not remember my name. When I told her, she gushed with pleasure. On arriving at my destination she rushed out and opened the door for me, asked for a kiss and told me not to bother paying as it was such a great honour.'

When asked if he was surprised by this sort of treatment, Denard said: 'Maybe I have not always been a nice guy and maybe I have done some things I should not have done. But I have never deviated from the path of honour or from serving my country.'

*

Denard the patriot. Denard the hero. Denard France's pirate. Denard the establishment's new darling. Is this possible? Or is the smell of roses a little too synthetic?

No one is prepared to go on the record and say it straight out, but many people are thinking the same thing. How is it that a man who has been an outcast for twelve years – since the socialists' accession to power in 1981 – can suddenly be so completely rehabilitated by the same socialists just as they handed over power to the Right?

That Denard has served his country is indisputable. That he has many secrets still up his blazer sleeves, is probable. But were the secrets potent enough to merit a deal whereby he bought his freedom with his silence?

Certainly, everyone has come out of the affair well. The French have been seen to see justice done. The lawyer of the families of the dead Beninois can say with pride that he won the case – that Denard was convicted. The families themselves received no official compensation – but they are not kicking up a fuss. Denard is certainly very happy with the recognition he has always craved.

It is only the appetites of the Abdallah family and their 'devil's advocate', Jacques Vergès, that have not yet been assuaged. It does not now look very likely that they will ever have the satisfaction of seeing anyone put behind bars for the murder of the President.

And they have graver worries at the moment. On 24th April 1993, Abdallah's twin sons, Cheik and Abderemane, were condemned to death – along with seven others – for their role in the attempted coup of October 1992. When their lawyer, Igor Domensik, returned from a visit to Moroni earlier in the year, he said that the prisoners were being detained in terrible conditions in the military camp of Kandani. They were allowed only one outside visit a day, no family visits and no medical treatment. In a formal report, Domensik said that he had seen 'French soldiers living in Kandani . . . and that the medical officer in charge and other soldiers living in camps . . . consider these problems are none of their business.'

'Ask the people of the Comoros what they think of me now,' Denard told me on the telephone, just days after the prisoners' sentences had been commuted to life following alleged personal interventions by Mitterrand and the King of Morocco.

'Don't you think they would like the Colonel back now?'

Bibliography

Very little has been written about the Comoros; 'The Perfume Isles' should almost be renamed 'The Forgotten Isles', but the few books that have been published have been a great help to me. I owe their authors gratitude, especially Professor Malyn Newitt whose well researched and scholarly work was invaluable. As were two other books: Anthony Mockler's *The New Mercenaries* and Pierre Lunel's biography of Denard, *Le Roi de Fortune*.

This is a short bibliography – thank you to all the authors for their knowledge and insight.

Hoare, Mike, *The Seychelles Affair* (Bantam Press, 1986)

Klotchkoff, Jean-Claude, *Les Comores Aujourd'hui* (Editions J. A.)

Lamb, David, *The Africans* (Bodley Head, 1984; pbk ed: Methuen, 1985)

Lunel, Pierre, *Le Roi de Fortune* (Editions 1, 1991)

Mockler, Anthony, *The New Mercenaries* (Sidgwick & Jackson, 1985)

Newitt, Malyn, *The Comoro Islands; Struggle Against Dependency in the Indian Ocean* (Gower, 1984)

Ollivier, Patrick, *Soldat de Fortune* (Editions Gerard de Villiers, 1990)

Smith, Stephen and Glaser, Antoine, *Ces Messieurs Afrique* (Calmann Levy, 1992)

Bibliography

Toihiri, Mohammed Ali, *La Republique des Imberbes* (Editions L'Harmattan, 1985)

Two seminal novels about mercenaries:

Carney, Daniel, *The Wild Geese* (Heinemann, 1977; pbk ed. Corgi, 1987)
Forsyth, Frederick, *The Dogs of War* (Hutchinson, 1974; pbk ed. Corgi, 1975)

There are many journalists whose articles about Denard and the Comoros have been immensely helpful. At risk of appearing over-selective, I would like to mention just a few:

Renaud Girard of *Le Figaro*; Didier François of *Liberation*; Jean Lartéguy of *Paris Match*; Gavin Bell of *The Times* and the anonymous contributors to the *Indian Ocean Newsletter* and *Africa Confidential*.

Acknowledgments

It is a sad inevitability that the people to whom I owe the most, may never have the opportunity to read this book. I truly would have got nowhere without the patience, kindness, and – occasionally misleading – help of all the Comorians whose time I took up. Thank you.

Thank you especially to my good friends, Ali Toihir and Papa Claude. Thank you also to the management and staff of the very comfortable Galawa Beach Hotel in Mitsamiouli. And to Angela Wheeler, Mouzawar Abdallah and Prince Naçr-Ed-Dine, Mahamoud Djambaé and Abdou Mbaé, and Cecile and Michel Buscail, as well as all the other people I talked to, some of whom asked me to conceal their real identities.

Thank you to Adrian Harley, Tigger Luard and Ed Bayntun-Coward, who came so many miles to visit. To Marco Boni in South Africa, Gavin Bell and Aidan Hartley – all of whom were in the Comoros in 1989 and gave me the benefit of their experiences.

In France: thank you especially to Renaud and Eric Girard, Patrick Ollivier, Maître Jacques Vergès and Maurice Botbol of the *Indian Ocean Newsletter*. And to Iona and the Fergusson family; Charlotte and Bertrand Aguirre, whose warm hospitality I fear I took grateful advantage of.

In London: thank you to my agent, Gillon Aitken, and to David Godwin, for their initial faith, willingness to take the plunge and great patience. Thank you to Jenny Cottom, Dan Franklin, Cathie Arrington and Rachel Cugnoni at Cape. And especially to my wonderfully tactful friends, Sally Garland and Charles Spicer, who read the first draft and offered much invaluable advice and input.

My father and sisters, Joanna and Kate, have been immensely supportive, as have all my friends, who have put up with a year and a half of complete self-absorption and frequent absences – and still welcomed me back at the end.

To my oldest friend, Imo Lycett Green, who wrote her first book in tandem and shared my ups and angsts: I couldn't have done it without you 'Mo. Thank you and good luck.

Most of all, the one person without whom I would never have had the courage to even start this book; Giles Andreae, who carried me on his shoulders throughout the low times and egged me on in the good ones. Thank you, thank you, thank you, for all your help, patience, support and love.

Acknowledgments

PICTURE CREDITS

Thanks are due to the following sources for permission to reproduce photographs:

Camera Press, pl. 3 (photo. Latimer Rangers); Gamma/Frank Spooner Pictures, pls. 5, 9, 10 (photo. Eric Girard), 16 (photo. B. Sidler/*Figaro*); Tigger Luard, pls. 7, 8; SIPA/Rex Features, pl. 14; Sygma, pls. 2 (photo. Robert Caputo), 17 (photo. Patrick Durand).

Pls. 1, 6, 13 and 15 were taken by the author.